YOU DON'T PLAY WITH REVOLUTION

REVOLUTION

THE MONTREAL LECTURES OF C.L.R. JAMES

Edited and Introduced by David Austin

Preface by Robert A. Hill

AK PRESS
EDINBURGH · OAKLAND · BALTIMORE

ISBN-13: 978-1-904859-93-2

Library of Congress Control Number: 2009922426

AK Press   AK Press
674-A 23rd Street   PO Box 12766
Oakland, CA 94612   Edinburgh, EH8 9YE
USA   Scotland
www.akpress.org   www.akuk.com
akpress@akpress.org   ak@akedin.demon.co.uk

The above addresses would be delighted to provide you with the latest AK Press distribution catalog, which features the several thousand books, pamphlets, zines, audio
and video products, and stylish apparel published and/or distributed by AK Press.
Alternatively, visit our web site for the complete catalog, latest news, and secure
ordering. Visit us at www.akpress.org *and* www.revolutionbythebook.akpress.org.

Printed in Canada on acid free, recycled paper with union labor.

Cover by Chris Wright (seldomwright.com)

In memory of

Alfie Roberts
Patricia Roberts
Martin Glaberman
Tim Hector
Rosie Douglas

TABLE OF CONTENTS

PART IV: CORRESPONDENCE

APPENDIX I

APPENDIX II

APPENDIX III

Acknowledgements

A number of people helped to make this book possible. I would like to thank Ruth Joseph who transcribed some of the lectures from their initial recordings. I would also like to thank Gwen Schulman who read an early draft of several of the lectures and gave valuable feedback. Over the years I have discussed C.L.R. James and this book with a number of friends and colleagues, all of whom listened patiently or offered encouragement: Mariame Kaba, Adrian Harewood, Ahmer Qadeer, Aaron Kamugisha, Peter Hudson, Gail Belvett, Rosalind Hampton, Kyo Maclear, Isaac Saney, Tom Keefer, Astrid Jacques, Sobukwe Odinga, Fanon Che Wilkins, Patricia Harewood, Richard Iton, Amarkai Laryea, Femi Austin, and Hillina Seife are the names that come to mind, but I know there are others....

I have also had the benefit of being associated with, both personally and professionally, several individuals whose history is reflected in this book. Some time before the summer of 1995, Alfie Roberts, a core member of the Caribbean Conference Committee (CCC), the group that was responsible for bringing James to Canada in 1966, handed me several reels containing recordings of James's Montreal lectures. At the time, neither he nor I were fully aware of their exact contents. I borrowed an old reel-to-reel machine and as I began listening to James's lectures, I found myself transposed in time and space, almost as if I was sitting in Alfie Roberts's living room where several of the lectures were delivered in the form of classes. Along with Franklyn Harvey and Tim Hector, the two other CCC members who were present for James's lectures, I too became one of James's students in that room. That Roberts trusted me, who at the time was in my early twenties, with these recordings meant a great deal to me. Our intention was to edit the lectures together, but Roberts passed away in July 1996 and the burden fell on me. Alfie Roberts was a friend and brother from whom I learned a great deal, and this book is possible because he had the foresight to hold on to this valuable material for almost thirty years, despite several moves within Montreal area. *You Don't Play with Revolution* is dedicated to Alfie Roberts.

I would also like to thank Franklyn Harvey for participating in endless hours of discussion about James, the work of the CCC, and the Caribbean left with me over the years in Montreal and Ottawa. Franklyn is without a doubt one of the most knowledgeable people about James and the Caribbean Left; the late Tim Hector, whom I interviewed for a radio documentary on James in 1999 and then subsequently met in Cuba in 2000; Celia Daniel for sharing her vivid memories of C.L.R. James's presence in Montreal and its impact on her; Viola Daniel, Bridget Joseph, Gloria Simmons, and Jean Depradine all of whom were actively involved in the CCC's work in various ways, for sharing their stories with me; Martin Glaberman, James's longtime associate who, from the first time I visited him in Detroit in 1994, was an encouraging voice. Marty, as he was affectionately known, also sent me an original recording of one of James's 1968 presentations at the Montreal Congress of Black Writers which is reproduced in this book. I would also like to thank Marty's partner, Diane Voss, for the time we spent discussing Marty and philosophy in Detroit in the summer of 2004; and Nettie Kravitz, another longstanding colleague of James, who was generous with her time when I visited Detroit and who was very helpful in clarifying details related to James and his U.S. colleagues during the final stages of editing this book. (I also want to thank her for getting me across the border from Detroit to Windsor in one piece, despite the harrowing car ride.) Discussions with Carolyn Fick have also been very rewarding. Not only was she part of Facing Reality, but she was a student and close friend of C.L.R. James and I have benefited from our conversations about his work and person over the years.

In the case of Robert A. Hill, not only did this manuscript reap the benefit of his keen and very experienced editorial eye in his capacity as C.L.R. James's Literary Executor, but as a former member of the CCC, the C.L.R. James Study Circle, and Facing Reality, and as arguably the leading authority on the vast corpus of James's life and work, I was able to call upon him to clarify information and verify facts related to James, Facing Reality, and West Indians associated with the CCC's work in Canada. I would also like to thank Selma James whom I met and interviewed in her home in London in 2004. Selma was not simply C.L.R.'s wife, but his comrade, and yet, much to my shock, I discovered that, despite all the books that have been published on C.L.R. James since his death in 1989, Selma had not been interviewed about him.

There are several people whom I interviewed in Trinidad in 2003 who informed my understanding of James's life in London and the Caribbean in the 1960s. I would like to thank Norman Girvan, Walton Look Lai, and the late Lloyd Best for sharing their reflections and honest, heartfelt appraisals of James with me. James influence on a whole generation of Caribbean figures who played pivotal roles in a range of political developments in the Caribbean has yet to be fully appreciated. I would also like to thank Kari Polanyi Levitt who was closely associated with the Centre for Developing-Area Studies at McGill University in the 1960s and 1970s when it was a meeting place for many of the Caribbean's foremost intellectuals. Rosalind Boyd, former director of the Centre, has also been generous with her time and has shared part of her personal diary which, dating back to the 1960s, contains valuable details on the Montreal-Caribbean scene in the mid-1960s.

Over the years I have revisited the lectures and carried out the tedious but rewarding process of transcribing and editing them, frequently being interrupted by life circumstances. Along the way, my family—Hirut Eyob, and our children, Méshama and Alama Eyob-Austin—bore the weight of my frequent distractions, though Méshama, now six years old, has become quite familiar with C.L.R. James voice and persona, almost as if he were a distant or long lost uncle. I have to thank them all for their patience and understanding.

This book, which also contains correspondence and interviews, would not have been possible without the cooperation of several institutions. I would like to thank the personnel and Trustees of The Alfie Roberts Institute in Montreal and the George Padmore Institute in London. The Walter P. Reuther Library at Wayne State University for granting me access to Martin and Jessie Glaberman's Papers. I would also like to thank François Furstenberg of Université de Montréal whose research grant made a visit to the Glaberman Papers possible. And The Main Library of The University of the West Indies, St. Augustine Campus, West Indiana and Special Collections Division for granting me access to C.L.R. James's papers.

The personnel at AK Press were enthusiastic about this book from the outset and weathered several missed deadlines and lapses on my part without losing (at least not openly) faith that this book would come to fruition. I would especially like to thank Ramsey Kanaan who, when I proposed to him during a 2005 discussion in Montreal that they publish this book, immediately understood the book's importance; and Charles Weigl for patiently seeing it through the publication process.

Having said that, I not only take full responsibility for any errors that keen students of James's work may uncover in this book, but do so with the knowledge that editing is an under-recognized and much underestimated art form which requires skills that are acquired with time and experience—and that there are many individuals who possess a great deal more experience in this area than I do. I also acknowledge that *You Don't Play with Revolution* represents a tiny part of the work that remains to be done in relation, not only to James's ideas, but the work of individuals and groups that were influenced by him in various parts of the world, and especially those that hail from the Caribbean.

D.A.

an act of the creative imagination as much as a reflection of the intensifying postcolonial crisis throughout the whole Caribbean. Between 1965
and 1970, the movement slowly unfolded, gathered steam, and reached its
political climax. In those five crucial years, Caribbean students in Canada
would contribute to the formation and growth of a new pan-Caribbean
ideal of freedom that was the gift of an awakened Caribbean community in
Canada. In the process, the movement would eventually help reshape the
postcolonial political landscape in the Caribbean in ways that would have
been impossible for us to foresee at the time.

Telling the history of this movement is what provides the impetus for
this book. It does so by documenting the range of remarkable lectures presented by C. L. R. James, the individual whose thought helped inspire the
1960s movement of the Caribbean community in Canada. It was C. L. R.
James to whom we turned to discover the latent power that resided in the
people of the Caribbean, both at home and abroad. We did not merely read
James. We *organized* the study of the ideas of this remarkable thinker, even
as we set about trying to apply them to what we were doing.

To take part was the special insight of James, who saw this, in all its
myriad forms, as the great motor-force in history and literature. It was precisely what we were also attempting to do from our own position as students
in Canada. Before he arrived, in 1966, a group of us, calling ourselves "The
C. L. R. James Study Circle," set out to systematically study and discuss the
body of James's writings that was available to us at the time. We read and
we studied, we debated and we discussed, as many of James's classic works
as we could lay our hands on at the time—*The Black Jacobins: Toussaint
L'Ouverture and the San Domingo Revolution* (1938); *State Capitalism and
World Revolution* (1950); *Mariners, Renegades, and Castaways: The Story of
Herman Melville and The World We Live In* (1952); *Modern Politics* (1960);
Party Politics in the West Indies (1962); and *Beyond A Boundary* (1963).

In addition, we obtained and circulated obscure political tracts by James
as well as transcripts of lectures that he had given to small groups, very
much in the style of the lectures that make up this volume. (Some of these
scripts I made myself from tapes of the lectures). Indeed, one of the
achievements of the study group was the preparation and publication of a
mimeographed edition in 1966 of James's remarkable 1948 work,
Dialectics, a study of the Hegelian dialectic and its application to

the crisis of Stalinism that foretold in many uncanny ways the revolt of the Hungarian people in 1956. All of this work we did while we were students. It was invaluable preparation and training for what was soon to come.

There was a powerful sense of recognition in our encounter with James's work, liberating our sense of what was possible when history moved. Moreover, embodied in James's work was not only an extraordinary vision of the creative power of ordinary people as the shapers of history, but also a *method* of getting at it, of where to look for it, and how to go about documenting it. It was this combination of political concept and pedagogy or method that provided a language with which to express what we were about as West Indians seeking to fashion a relationship with our Canadian community as well as our home communities in the Caribbean. The fusion of intellectual seriousness and political purpose was what defined this new burst of energy that propelled us through the exciting, if perilous, decade of the 1960s.

The key to James's political vision and his intellectual identity was the idea of emancipation. In fact, James was always fond of reminding audiences that the West Indian people have been the most rebellious people in history. The idea comes through strong and clear in these lectures and letters assembled by David Austin in the present collection. As a West Indian abroad, David Austin emerges out of the same political bloodline, by way of the late Alfie Roberts, his close friend and mentor, whose life-story appears in an earlier edited volume (*A View for Freedom: Alfie Roberts Speaks on the Caribbean, Cricket, Montreal, and C.L.R. James* [Montreal: Alfie Roberts Institute, 2005]).

What difference does this collection make to our understanding and estimation of James? At the time that we invited James to Canada, he was at a particularly low point in his career. The Workers' and Farmers' Party (WFP), the vehicle which James had spearheaded and helped to organize in Trinidad as a means of challenging the political stranglehold of Eric Williams and the People's National Movement (PNM), had collapsed. Between 1965 and 1968, James seemed to be marking time. Then came the epic political confrontations of 1968 which, one could argue, had been anticipated by James's theory of self-organization and mobilization from below. Throughout the world, East and West, North and South, the established political order was confronted by new movements and new social subjects that existing political theory had no way of accounting for but which James had been pointing to for years.

The conjunction of the turbulent events of 1968 and the renewal of James's legacy is what makes this collection so valuable and timely. The reader will discover here not only the excitements accompanying the early days of the West Indian awakening in Canada, but also a clear exposition of the political ideas of James that guided and engaged our thinking. There is no more valuable resource for grounding the solidarities and spontaneities of those times, both for West Indians as well as others, than the lectures now made available in this book.

To understand that the ideas of C. L. R. James are a still vital and important legacy, as he himself demonstrated in these lectures on the legacy of the great thinkers that he discusses, is the challenge of the current generation of Caribbean activists. James's exemplary attentiveness to the rich and diverse traditions of revolutionary thought traced throughout these lectures represents a gold-mine from which today's students and activists can draw. As they feel their way towards the future, even as we who helped to inaugurate the Caribbean movement in Canada in the 1960s did before them, they will contest the reigning system and its ideas. With these texts, they can avail themselves of the intellectual legacy of James and be confident that they are not acting alone.

To take part was C. L. R. James's fundamental conviction concerning the cultural imperative of the West Indian people. It is what gave him the confidence and the clarity with which he addresses the gathering of young West Indian intellectuals in these lectures. To take part is also the condition of making change. To my mind, there is no better way to reflect on the making of history than through these lectures and the prism of that extraordinary moment when young West Indians who came to Canada in the 1960s, inspired by the ideas of C. L. R. James, forged a new Caribbean political identity and, in doing so, helped to reshape the Canada and the Caribbean of today.

Robert A. Hill

Literary Executor of The C. L. R. James Estate

INTRODUCTION
In Search of a National Identity:
C.L.R. James and the Promise of the Caribbean

The history that we studied in the Caribbean was the history of our colonial masters giving us what they wanted us to know about ourselves…and to learn about them. So when someone like C.L.R. James wrote *The Black Jacobins*… it was a source of pride so when… C.L.R. came [to Montreal]… most young people would flock around him to hear what he had to say. It was in that kind of climate that in 1968 he came here for the Black Writers Conference and a few of us had sort of a private audience with him. And it was here that I saw…the kind of more human side of him because we all heard of him as the revolutionary, the historian, the socialist or Marxist, or communist… one person who spoke out for human rights and lived it, preached it, and wrote about it. So when I met him I was sort of hoping that he would be speaking that way.

But instead I found a more gentle, elderly gentleman, white hair. And the setting just stuck in my head because he was sitting up in bed in his sort of maroon frock coat like a gentleman. We were sitting all around the room and he had his pipe, sort of a clay pipe that he was smoking. And he was very gentle and affable. He laughed and joked, and in many ways he reminded me of my grandmother and of many our grandmothers and, I suppose, grandfathers, who, as Caribbean people, would smoke a pipe before turning in at night. And as he was sitting there on the bed, that's what came to me, what I remembered, as though he was telling us a fairy tale or something because he was talking about *Moby Dick*… that American classic about the big white whale and the story that went with it. But his whole twist on *Moby Dick* is something that changed my thinking as to how I perceive written work. What happened that evening taught me that writers are the chroniclers of the time; they sort of set down for you the way people thought, their attitudes, the way that they perceived life, the way they perceived other people, and whatever was happening at the time that they were alive and living—all of that is reflected in what they write.

Celia Daniel, 1999

Twenty years ago C.L.R. James passed away in his modest flat in Brixton, the heart of London's Black community. At the time of his death, the 88 year-old polymath was recognized by those most familiar with him as one of the genuine original and creative thinkers of the 20th century. Since his death, it is fair to say that he has attained a kind of legendary status, not only as an intellectual, but as someone who bore witness to or participated in some of the 20th century's most significant events related to African, Caribbean, and socialist politics. Working in London in the 1930s along-side another remarkable Trinidadian, George Padmore, he collaborated with Ras Makonnen, Amy Ashwood Garvey, and several central figures in African independence movements such as I.T.A. Wallace Johnson of Sierra Leone and Kenya's Jomo Kenyatta. Later in the United States, he befriended Kwame Nkrumah whom he introduced to Padmore. Together, Nkrumah and Padmore helped pave the road for the independence move-ment that, beginning with Ghana, swept across the African continent in the 1950s and 1960s.

James also collaborated with the exiled Leon Trotsky in Mexico and played an important part in the international socialist movement that drew inspiration from Trotsky's opposition to Stalin. From this period, 1938 to 1953, he honed his skills as a Marxist theoretician in the United States. Later, between 1958 and 1962 and then in 1965–66, he tried his hand at conventional politics in Trinidad and Tobago, but never forsook his socialist ideals. He was an intellectual in the finest sense of the word, someone who had, in George Lamming's words, chosen the "life of the mind,"[1] but who also wrote, thought, and acted in order to change the world.

C.L.R. James's longtime collaborator and former wife, Selma James, has argued that his lasting legacy resides in his commitment to the ques-tion of how one organizes to change society,[2] to which we might add his preoccupation with how one thinks about the question of how to organize for change. To slightly distort Marx's maxim that the point is to change the world and not simply interpret it, James was a political philosopher who attempted to change the world. He was one of Antonio Gramsci's much-heralded organic intellectuals[3] who, according to Edward Said—whose admiration for Caribbean writers and thinkers such as James, George Lam-ming, Frantz Fanon, Aimé Césaire, and Walter Rodney is evident in his work *Culture and Imperialism*—was a quintessential example of an exiled intellectual. Said describes exile as "being liberated from the usual career, in which 'doing well' and following time-honored footsteps are the main milestones." Exile "means that you are always going to be marginal and that what you do as an intellectual has to be made up because you cannot follow a prescribed path. If you can experience that fate," he continues, "not as a deprivation and as something to be bewailed, but as a sort of freedom, a process of discovery in which you do things according to your own pattern, as various interests seize your attention, and as the particular goal you set for yourself dictates: that is a unique pleasure."[4]

As Said's remarks imply, James sat on the margins of conventional academia most of his adult life and was almost seventy years old before he assumed a teaching position at a university. It might then come as a surprise that he has been compared to two individuals whose ideas are firmly ensconced in academia—Hegel and Plato.[5] Hegel's philosophy was important for James, in so far as his dialectic shaped James's understanding of Marx and Marxism, politics, and history.[6] And like Hegel and Plato, James made unique contributions to the study of a range of fields: history, political theory, literary criticism, drama, philosophy, and sport. Yet, if this kind of comparison has merit, the comparison to Plato as opposed to Aristotle is somewhat curious given that, although Aristotle shares Plato's canonical stature, he is seen as having been somewhat less authoritarian than his predecessor—a fact that James no doubt appreciated.[7] And, of the two philosophers, it was Aristotle's work, not Plato's, that left the deepest impression on James, as is evident in his manuscript *Preface to Criticism*.[8]

James championed Ancient Greece (and to a lesser extent, Europe's medieval city-states) as a model of democracy.[9] He argued that it was Ancient Greece's democratic ideals and system of government—in which "every cook" governed—that allowed most of its great philosophers, dramatists, and artists to flourish.[10] Ancient Greece, and especially Athens, was central to his vision of the form that the New Society might take, though he clearly minimized the role of slavery in Ancient Greek society, not to mention the fact that women were denied citizenship.[11] In line with conventional wisdom, James also attributed the foundation of Western civilization to Ancient Greece, while neglecting the global reach of the African continent, the Near and Middle East, and Asia (he also neglected the presence of North African Moors in medieval Europe). It was precisely these kinds of elusions that later caused Tim Hector, one of James's avid followers, to question the appropriateness of Ancient Greece as a model for the Caribbean.[12]

While James's great admiration of Ancient Greek democracy, drama, and philosophy is well known, what is perhaps less appreciated is the parallels that he drew between the Ancient Greek city-states and the modern Caribbean. As the British West Indies inched its way towards independence following the collapse of the West Indies Federation in 1962, James turned his intellectual energies towards developing a framework for understanding the peculiarities of Caribbean society, and Athens was central to his reflections. Marxism was born out of a tradition of philosophy that extends from Aristotle to Hegel and, according to Hannah Arendt, Marx's notion of a classless society has its roots in the leisure and recreational time that Ancient Greek democracy afforded its citizens. But whereas, for Arendt, Marxism represented a breach with this philosophical tradition that premised reason over action,[13] James, a Marxist, returned to Athens in an attempt to frame a democratic, cultural, and intellectual tradition for the Caribbean.

FROM ATHENS TO TRINIDAD

James placed great stock in the Caribbean's artists and intellectuals whose exceptional talents were, for him, reminiscent of their Athenian antecedents. Like Greece, the Caribbean is comprised of islands with small populations, has a close relationship between town and country, and uses a modern "community of language," all conditions which, in Ancient Greece, permitted its democracy and artists to flourish. Moreover, the Caribbean had the modern advantage of radio and television, which facilitated mass communication and permitted the transmission of information and ideas in ways that could not have been imagined in ancient times.[14] James had deep respect for the Caribbean's native talent[15] which, by the mid-1960s, had developed an international reputation for producing exceptional, and in some cases, ingenious writers, poets, intellectuals, singers, and athletes—V.S. Naipaul and Derek Walcott who are, respectively, among the most important writers of fiction and poetry in the English language today; George Lamming, Wilson Harris, Eric Williams, Aimé Césaire, Frantz Fanon, Edouard Glissant, to which we could add today Patrick Chamoiseau and Maryse Condé; the calypsonian The Mighty Sparrow, and cricketers Gary Sobers and Rohan Kanhai. These and many more were among the gifted artists, intellectuals, and athletes anointed by James, and in the case of Kanhai, his cricket batting prowess evoked for James images of the ebullience of Dionysus and the discipline of Apollo.[16]

In essence, C.L.R. James was attempting to frame the cultural and intellectual experience of the Caribbean people into a tradition or, to put it another way, to articulate and elaborate a notion of a Caribbean civilization that long existed but had yet to be named. James is not the only West Indian to have drawn parallels between Ancient Greece and the Caribbean. As Emily Greenwood has shown, Caribbean intellectuals have had a longstanding engagement with Classical Greece and Rome.[17] According to Robert Hill and Barbara Blair, Marcus Garvey's theory of education, which emphasized "self-mastery and self-culture as precursors to good race leadership," has its roots in the "classical model of education."[18] Moreover, Garvey's notion of "absolute authority" draws on Aristotle's notion of absolute kingship, and his idea that the central function of law is to maintain authority borrowed from both Aristotle and Plato.[19]

In his early days as premier, Eric Williams often interwove Caribbean and world history with references to Ancient Greek philosophers in his speeches and lectures at the "University of Woodford Square" in the heart of Trinidad and Tobago's capital, Port of Spain. And in a 1964 article, one year before James was placed under house arrest by Williams's government during a period of labor unrest in the country, the prime minister wrote about Trinidad and Tobago's contribution to humanity, emphasizing the importance of democratic practice, popular consultation, and public debate in the country. Williams too compared Trinidad's size and small population to Ancient Greece and medieval European city-states, although, curiously, he qualified his observations by stating that he was not suggesting that Trinidad would produce an Aristotle or Socrates.[20] He also cited a British prime minister, possibly Alec Douglas-Home, who, in referring to the high level of political discussion in Trinidad and Tobago, described it as the "Athens of the Caribbean."[21] In closing, Williams cited the funeral oration of Pericles, which affirmed the virtues of Athenian democracy, as an utterance of his own ideal of democracy in Trinidad and Tobago.[22]

Nobel Laureate poet Derek Walcott's magnum opus, *Omeros*, which is set in his native St. Lucia, is perhaps the most obvious literary example of the Ancient Greece-modern Caribbean analogy. In a 1990 interview, Walcott somewhat coarsely described the Ancient Greeks as the "niggers of the Mediterranean," whose aesthetic tastes would have been very familiar to West Indians.[23] In Wilson Harris's novel *The Secret Ladder*, Poseidon, named after the Greek god of the seas, is one of the story's protagonists. Harris also draws on Ancient Greek myth in a 1954 collection of poems, *Eternity to Season*.[24] But while James and other Caribbean writers have been quick to draw parallels between Ancient Athens and the Caribbean—no doubt in large part due to their education in British-modeled schools in the West Indies—the Caribbean's African heritage has often been approached with ambivalence by many of the Caribbean's most accomplished writers.

Once, when asked about Africa's cultural and linguistic contribution to the Caribbean, James curtly replied, "I do not know what are the African roots of the language and culture of Caribbean intellectuals. I am not aware of the African roots of my use of language and culture," James argued, adding that despite their black skin, the people "of the Caribbean have not got an African past," and that "the African civilization is not ours. The basis of our civilization in the Caribbean is an adaptation of Western civilization."[25] Paget Henry has commented on what he describes as "the invisibility of African traditional thought in James's historicism,"[26] as well as the absence of "[African] mythic and religious dimensions"[27] and traditional African philosophy and cosmology in James's writing—all of which Henry attributes to an overdependence on European philosophy and its concepts of modernity.[28] Nicosia Shakes has noted the same phenomenon in James's work and poses the question, "can we ever reconcile the two identities of Europe and Africa [in the Caribbean] without one being negated and delegitimized by the other?"[29]

And yet James made important contributions to African anti-colonial struggles and recognized their importance, both on their own terms and as universal articulations of the dynamics inherent in liberation struggles. He was a pioneering Pan-Africanist whose work within the International African Friends of Ethiopia and the International African Service Bureau in the 1930s inspired his classic study of the Haitian Revolution, *The Black Jacobins*. And, as he was well aware, Africa has been central to the Caribbean's self-discovery and freedom in that, in the process of eschewing notions of African inferiority, many West Indians discovered their own humanity. James reminds us that Marcus Garvey, George Padmore, Aimé Césaire—to which we can add Elma Francois and Claudia Jones—discovered "that the salvation for the West Indies lies in Africa, the original home and ancestry of the West Indian people."[30] James also acknowledged what the Haitian writer Jean Price-Mars described as the "African way of life of the Haitian peasant." Yet, for some reason, he failed to consistently recognize the same phenomenon in the Anglophone Caribbean.[31]

As he attempted to chart a course for the Caribbean in the wake of its failed attempt at federation, in the aftermath of Trinidad and Jamaica's independence, and with the imminent independence of Guyana and Barbados, James turned to his knowledge of Ancient Greece, not Africa, for inspiration. As one commentator has written, James saw "a premonition of the rebirth in the West Indies of the glories of Athenian democracy, philosophy, and art. The Greeks had their Olympic games and their tragic drama. Trinidad has its great Calypso singer, the Mighty Sparrow, and [as] its counterpart to the artistic expression of Sophocle[s] and Euripides, Trinidad has Queen's Park and cricket."[32] James's conception of Athens in particular conjured up images of his boyhood days in the Caribbean, a fact that shows in abundance in his classic study of cricket, *Beyond a Boundary*. As he reminisced, cricket, not simply as sport but, at its best, as an art form, took center stage in Trinidad, an island that not only produced world-class cricketers—including the great Learie Constantine and, more recently, Brian Lara, perhaps the greatest batsman ever—but important intellectual and political figures. The latter included James and George Padmore, their Pan-Africanist predecessor Henry Sylvester Williams, and Eric Williams as historian.[33] Trinidad was one island, but the fact that the cluster of tiny territories in the Caribbean archipelago produced remarkable intellectuals, athletes, artists, writers, and poets—well out of proportion to their size and populations—appeared to justify the comparisons between the two civilizations, despite their separation in time and space.

Towards a New Caribbean

The Caribbean was not only in search of an identity in the 1960s. The governments and parties that had inaugurated the region's independence movements faced mounting opposition from political groups at home and from exiles abroad. As the reality set in that the face of government had changed but the new economic regime strongly resembled its pre-independence form, James Millette summed up the situation as follows on the eve of Guyana and Barbados's independence in 1966. With the ghost of the West Indies Federation still looming large over the region, Millette argued that "independence is a prelude to the total reorganization of the colonial society" which can only be achieved "by a wholesale destruction of attitudes, prejudices and assumptions which, more than the external machinery of colonialism itself, gave the system its character." But in the case of Jamaica and Trinidad, at the time the only independent former British colonies in the Caribbean, the post-colonial period "has become a shameful interlude in the progress to a new and just West Indian society" in which the "Puerto Rican model flourishes; giving new validity and strength to the very forces against which the dialectic of national assertion was once directed. The age of independence has become the age of grosser and grosser inequalities, and of massive unemployment."[34]

In this climate of feigned confidence and growing despair emerged a new wave of West Indian political groups. In St. Vincent, the Kingstown Study Group gave birth to a quarterly journal, *Flambeau*[35] to which Alfie Roberts, one of the key figures in the group that was responsible for bringing James to Canada during this period, contributed articles.[36] In Trinidad and Tobago, the labor movement, and particularly the Oilfield Workers' Trade Union, asserted itself under the leadership of George Weekes, who also joined C.L.R. James in 1965 in the Workers' and Farmers' Party. In Jamaica, The Young Socialist League (YSL) surfaced. The YSL was spawned by the planning committee of the People's National Party (PNP) in Jamaica in 1963 as part its process of rethinking socialism in light of the collapse of the West Indies federation and the PNP's subsequent defeat in Jamaica's general election.[37] The YSL quickly became an active political entity of its own with close ties to Jamaica's workers and underclass. Robert Hill, who helped orchestrate James's sojourn in Canada between December 1966 and March 1967, was encouraged to participate in the YSL by fellow Jamaican Norman Girvan, a member of the YSL's policy-planning group. Soon after, Hill was addressing YSL meetings in Kingston, Jamaica's capital, and the neighboring Spanish Town.[38]

But the YSL's ties to the PNP quickly became a bone of contention within the group, and Hill became the chief critic of the YSL-PNP relationship. During the 1964 YSL national conference he presented a paper, "The Struggle for Freedom and Socialism," in which he argued that the YSL had to decide whether it would remain tied to the PNP or become an independent body. As the YSL's popularity and stature grew among ordinary Jamaicans, Hill argued that Jamaicans yearned for cultural and political expression, but as long as the YSL remained linked to the PNP (the public was generally unaware of the YSL's connection to the party), it could not be a vehicle for a genuine mass movement.[39] By this time Hill was already studying the work of C.L.R. James, whom he had met in London through Norman Girvan. Girvan, along with fellow Jamaicans Joan French, Orlando Patterson, and Richard Small, as well as Walton Look-Lai and Raymond Watts of Trinidad, Stanley French of St. Lucia, and Walter Rodney of Guyana were part of a Marxist study group that regularly met in James's London home. Many of James's keenest followers were West Indians living abroad who formed similar groups, including the Montreal-based Caribbean Conference Committee (CCC) and its sister organization, the C.L.R. James Study Circle (CLRJSC). Hill was instrumental in forming both groups and their core political members read James's books and pamphlets, organized a North American lecture tour for him and, inspired by his ideas, developed their own analyses of Caribbean and global politics.

KINDRED SOULS

When Robert Hill left Jamaica to pursue an undergraduate degree in Canada in 1964, he brought his experience in the YSL with him. Along with Alfie Roberts of St. Vincent, Franklyn Harvey of Grenada, Anne Cools of Barbados, and Tim Hector of Antigua, he formed the political nucleus of the CCC and CLRJSC. Other key founding members of the CCC included Alvin Johnson of Jamaica and Hugh O'Neile of Grenada and, though based in Montreal, both groups had centers in Toronto, Halifax, Ottawa, and New York. Rosie Douglass, future prime minister of Dominica, was also a CCC co-founder, and Arnhim Eustace, who later became prime minister of St. Vincent and the Grenadines, and his fellow countryman Kerwyn Morris, were closely associated with the CCC. Later Raymond Watts and Walton Look Lai joined the group in Montreal, but Hill, Roberts, Harvey, Cools, and Hector were the closest in terms of political affinity.

They were all students,[40] but to see them simply as students would be a mistake. Before migrating to Canada, some of them had worked as teachers or in customs, or arrived in Canada with concrete political experience. Moreover, they came of age during a time in which radical student politics infused societies across the globe. Like students in Pakistan, Senegal, the

United States, and France, they represented a kind of vanguard of political struggle. They were "kindred souls," according to Alfie Roberts,[41] who coalesced to organize events that would spawn Canada's Black radical tradition and profoundly influence political developments in the Caribbean.[42]

The obvious question here is why Canada? One answer is that, as the British government began to enact policies designed to stem the flow of Caribbean nationals who were once encouraged to migrate to rebuild a war-torn Britain, Caribbean governments successfully pressured the Canadian government to retract its "climate unsuitability" clause and other regulations that restricted immigration on the basis of "nationality, citizenship, ethnic group, occupation, class, or geographical area of origin." The result was that thousands of skilled Black laborers, domestic workers, and students populated cities such as Montreal, Toronto, Ottawa throughout the 1960s and into the 1970s.[43]

But that is only part of the answer. The Garvey movement had been strong in Canada (Louise Langdon, Malcolm X's Grenadian mother was actively involved in Garvey's UNIA in Montreal) and the country had a long history of Caribbean and Black organizations dating back to the turn of the 20th century. And spurred by the heightened sense of French Québecois nationalism and the struggle against Anglo-Canadian and American economic and cultural domination in the 1960s, and inspired by the United State's Black Power movement and the anti-colonial struggles being waged in Africa and other parts of the world, as well as the ideas of Frantz Fanon, Aimé Césaire, Albert Memmi, and Jean-Paul Sartre, among others, Montreal became a city of protest and rebellion.[44] It was in this politically charged atmosphere, coupled with a growing disenchantment with the new order in the Caribbean and the fiery climate of the global 1960s, that the CCC-CLRSC came into being.[45]

Between 1962 and 1966, James moved between the Caribbean and London, writing, delivering lectures and, in 1965–1966, campaigning in Trinidad and Tobago's elections as a candidate for the Workers' and Farmers' Party. It was during this period that the CCC-CLRJSC made contact with him, and when the group organized a speaking tour for him between December 1966 and March 1967, the island of Montreal—which, for all intents and purposes, had become for West Indians a composite island of Caribbean nationalities—became home to a kind of Aristotelian lyceum for James where he tutored his precocious disciples in politics and Marxism. They were exceptionally bright and, equally important, as fellow West Indians they appreciated the full range of his ideas. They shared his wide-ranging interests in history, the arts, and his political-intellectual pursuits, but they also understood the Caribbean socio-cultural context that had shaped and nurtured him because they too were forged in it. And of course they shared his love of cricket, that quintessentially English sport that West Indians had mastered and made their own. (Alfie Roberts had been a kind of cricket boy wonder who was recruited along with Gary Sobers and Rohan Kanhai to play for the West Indies by the legendary Everton Weekes. We are left to imagine the kinds of conversations that he and James would have had about the sport.)

In London, the study group in C.L.R. James's home played an important role in the lives of several young West Indians, including Walter Rodney, then a prodigious student of history at the School of Oriental and African Studies. Rodney later remarked that these regular meetings afforded him "the opportunity… to acquire a knowledge of Marxism, a more precise understanding of the Russian Revolution, and of historical formulation."[46] Commenting on the impact of James's political classes in Montreal, Alfie Roberts makes similar remarks: "James's intervention with us, at that point in time, was very crucial in helping us to clarify… things that we were thinking about. We got hold of a lot of his writings from the 1940s when he was in the United States and we began to read them… They had a tremendous impact on us."[47] Many of the classes took place in Roberts's home: "When James was going to do something with us, even if it was just three, four of us, he took his watch out, put his watch down, and proceeded to say what he had to say as if he was talking to 300 people."[48]

London was also home to the Caribbean Artists' Movement (CAM) in the 1960s,[49] but it was Canada, and particularly Montreal, that became the most active site of exile Anglophone Caribbean *political* activity in this period. The key actors here—principally those associated with the CCC-CLRJSC—would later play central roles in the wave of left-Black Power groups that emerged in the region in the late 1960s and early 1970s. But Montreal also had an active chapter of the influential New World Group and its founder, Lloyd Best, actually lived in Montreal for a period of time and worked alongside economist Kari Polanyi-Levitt, daughter of Karl

Polanyi. New World's emphasis on research and economic analysis of the Caribbean paralleled and complemented the work of the CCC in particular, and some CCC members were also involved in New World.[50] But the CCC's political core were largely oriented towards transforming the Caribbean from the bottom up, and between 1965 and 1967 the group organized a series of annual conferences that brought many of the Caribbean's leading thinkers and artists to the city,[51] although the absence of prominent women intellectuals in this roster—Elsa Goveia or Sylvia Wynter, as examples—is palpable. The negation of women in the historiography of Black, Caribbean, and Pan-African left groups, the absence of gender analyses within these groups, and the failure of their chroniclers to acknowledge this void has increasingly come under fire.[52] In CCC-CLRJSC's case, its most politically active woman, Anne Cools (there were other women who were more on the periphery of the group's political core) was never entirely at ease within the group. She eventually became active in the Canadian and international women's movement and her 1971 critical appraisal of the relationship between Black women and men might be read as critique of her male counterparts in the CCC-CLRSC.[53] This being said, the group's conferences attracted West Indians living in Canada, the United States, Britain, and the West Indies and raised awareness about social, cultural, and political developments in the Caribbean. Nothing like these meetings had ever occurred in Canada and George Lamming believed that the group's inaugural meeting was the first of its kind anywhere.[54]

But it was James's political analysis and his notion of self-organization and liberation from below that struck the highest note within the group, and during this period Robert Hill and Alfie Roberts began corresponding with Martin Glaberman, James's longtime comrade and chairperson of the Detroit-based Marxist group that James co-founded, Facing Reality (FR). Initially they acquired some of James's more obscure writings from FR, but Glaberman was subsequently invited to speak on James at the CCC inaugural conference in October 1965, and soon Hill and Roberts were writing under pseudonyms for FR's political tract, *Speak Out*.[55] Hill and Glaberman attended the inaugural Socialist Scholars conference at Rutgers University in the fall of 1965. By the second CCC conference a year later, Hill had prepared for publication C.L.R. James's *Notes on Dialectics*—a manuscript originally written in Nevada in 1948 in which he read the history of and prospects for international socialism through Hegel's dialectic—as part of a joint CLRJSC and FR effort.

As he confided in Alfie Roberts, preparing the manuscript for publication was an arduous task but he had little doubt that the book would be critical to the group's work.[56] He was right. The dialectical framework and notion of self-activity espoused in *Notes on Dialectics* not only framed the group's political analysis of the Caribbean, but also their discussions and writing on the Cuban Revolution, the France 1968 uprising, the struggle of the Vietnamese against U.S. imperialism, a critique of Louis Althusser's scientism, and a polemic on James's *The Black Jacobins*.[57] Considering the importance that James attached to *Notes on Dialectics*, which he once described as his most significant work,[58] its publication by a small group of West Indians in Canada was, without a doubt, one of their crowing achievements.

Reading Glaberman and Hill's correspondence, we are left with the distinct impression that the relationship between these young West Indians and FR injected a renewed sense of urgency and purpose into FR's work—which it did.[59] Despite the differences in age and political experience, the relationship was mutually beneficial. But for Facing Reality, a small, struggling organization that had suffered several major splits, including the departure of Raya Dunayevskaya and Grace and Jimmy Boggs, collaborating with the CCC-CLRJSC infused the group with much-needed intellectual energy and together they conspired to bring James to Canada and the U.S.[60]

A Necessary Reprieve

C.L.R. James's visit to Montreal in October 1966 to deliver the keynote address during the Caribbean Conference Committee's second annual conference provided him with welcome relief from a heated election campaign in Trinidad and Tobago. In February 1965, James left London for Trinidad to cover the Australian cricket team's tour of the West Indies. His visit coincided with worker unrest in the country's oil belt and fearing that his presence might fuel the restive mood in the country, his former friend, prime Minister Eric Williams, used the recently adopted Industrial Stabilization Act (ISA) to place James under house arrest and to suppress the striking workers.

Some feared that James's detention reflected a step towards dictatorial tendencies by Williams and the rescinding civil liberties throughout the Anglophone Caribbean. There were demonstrations and denunciations in support of James in England, Canada and the United States (according to Derek Walcott, the incident sparked his first and only physical political protest).[61] James's arrest lasted over a week, but he returned to Trinidad in May 1965 and shortly thereafter co-founded the Workers' and Farmers' Party (WFP). The WFP's platform was simple. It called for the redistribution of farmland, tighter control over foreign investment in the country, and more emphasis on local industry. Perhaps the enthusiasm that initially greeted the WFP is best summarized in the words of Robert Hill and Tim Hector. Writing to Martin Glaberman on August 30, 1965, Hill reported news from his uncle Ken Hill in Trinidad that James had co-founded the WFP and that "it seems that Williams might be in serious political trouble." Perhaps anticipating Glaberman's ambivalence to James's renewed political involvement in Caribbean politics, he reminded him that James "is first and last a Trinidadian, and the political decadence there must have been truly enormous for him to jeopardize his very health."

Tim Hector's enthusiasm for James and the WFP were obvious in his March 29, 1966 letter to Hill, written from Wolfville, Nova Scotia:

> At Christmas in Montreal I continued my efforts to get Trinidadians interested in the significance of the WFP. To me, this is the most significant event in the West Indies and Caribbean history since the uprisings in the Fyzabad,[62] and comparable only (but only comparable) to Fidel Castro's struggle and Cuba's struggle with the ever-grasping tentacles of colonialism and its bed-fellow, neo-colonialism. Now, with the WFP, *a Caribbean* is a distinct possibility.

For Hill and Hector, the WFP augured a new day for the entire Caribbean. But the euphoria was short-lived and, in hindsight, James's foray into Trinidad politics was destined to end in disappointment. Reflecting three decades later, Alfie Roberts suggests that James was "stung" into action and forced to react to Williams after being detained,[63] inferring that James acted more out of pride than political necessity. Likewise, George Lamming suggests that James's involvement in the WFP was motivated by his need to demonstrate that he could contest and beat Williams at his own game.[64] Selma James and members of Facing Reality in the U.S. were discouraged by his descent into parliamentary politics,[65] and as Glaberman wrote to C.L.R. James, "the involvement in West Indian politics seems to me to be an entirely unwarranted drain on your resources," and asked, "what business have we there?" "How does it fit into the building of a Marxist group? What perspectives can I say we have in Trinidad? What organization, what theory are we building there?"[66]

Glaberman apparently failed to heed Hill's caution about James's "Trinidadianess." But in fairness to him, in London and the Caribbean, many of James's West Indian admirers also questioned his entry into Trinidad politics[67] and subsequently described it as one of the low points in his life.[68] And yet, given the growing opposition to Eric Williams's government at the time, coupled with James's vision of the Caribbean as a place of immense creative potential, it is conceivable that he saw his involvement in the WFP as his last opportunity to make a direct political contribution to the kind of Caribbean envisioned in his writing and lectures. As he over-optimistically wrote about the WFP to Selma James, "If we manage it here, it is certain that the whole Caribbean will follow."[69] And although she was highly critical of his return to the Caribbean, Selma argued that her husband's involvement in the WFP was, in part, an attempt to save Trinidad and Tobago from bloodshed and possible dictatorship.[70]

From the outset, the WFP was plagued with disorganization and financial difficulties. James was forced to depend on funds from his supporters in Canada and the U.S. and, despite the party's potential, he was painfully aware of the unreliability of his WFP colleagues and their inattentiveness to his precarious finances and poor health.[71] In this sense, the results of the November 1966 election were predictable. Despite James's optimistic forecasts, the WFP did not win a single electoral seat. In his correspondence with Martin Glaberman and Robert Hill immediately after the election, James argued that the government rigged the voting machines in its favor,[72] but he left for Canada shortly after, apparently with the intention of returning to Trinidad, but he instead returned to England when the lecture tour ended.

THE MONTREAL LECTURES

James's presence in Canada, first in October 1966, just prior to the Trinidad and Tobago election, and then in December 1966 through to March 1967, provided him with welcome relief. Not only did the election campaign put his frail frame under undue stress, but there was at least one attempt on his life as well as what James believed to be an imminent one, all of which required that he travel with a bodyguard.[73] In many ways, the CCC-CLR-JSC handed him a lifeline, which he enthusiastically grabbed. They provided him with a platform for his ideas and found in him a ready and willing teacher. Reading the private lectures he delivered to the group in Montreal, it is obvious that he was consciously tutoring his Caribbean pupils in preparation for the political roles he anticipated that they would play in the Caribbean and, recognizing their precocity, he tailored his classes to their specific needs. Paul Buhle describes the relationship between the CCC-CLRJSC and James in his biography on Tim Hector. He writes: "These ardent young intellectuals and activists met formally and informally, naturally more often at close range as friends, to discuss and argue over texts, to become intimates that only fellow exile-revolutionaries are likely ever to be. They also hosted James in visits that would change their collective lives."[74] As they read James, Hegel, Marx, and Lenin alongside Caribbean history and fiction, he nurtured their political ideas in an "extended non-academic tutorial" during which they would present their views and James "would listen and then ask questions that prompted the speakers to see the error of their own thinking."[75] Buhle captures the spirit of the group's relationship with James, but overstates his case. There is no question that, in their eyes, James's was a master of revolutionary theory with years of experience in socialist, Caribbean, and African politics. But they had their own agenda. They were bright, focused, and determined and, having adopted him as their mentor, they respectfully engaged, pushed, and prodded him to provide them with the answers they sought. James was so struck by their sense of purpose that on one occasion he is said to have turned to them and asked, "Who are you people?" In essence, this was James's way of saying that he had never seen their likes before.

Between 7 December 1966 and 8 March 1967, James delivered a series of public and private lectures on a range of subjects. Three of the public lectures—on the evolution of the people of the Caribbean, Shakespeare's *King Lear*, and the Haitian Revolution, originally titled "The Haitian Revolution and the History of Slave Revolt," which was delivered at the 1968 Montreal Congress of Black Writers—are reproduced in *You Don't Play with Revolution*. Five others, including two that were also delivered at the Congress of Black Writers (one was titled "The History and Economics of Slavery in the New World," and the other, "Les Origines et la Signification de la Négritude," delivered in French, was a substitute lecture for the Haitian poet René Depestre who was unable to participate in the Congress); one on policies and programs for developing countries; the man-woman relationship; and a report on the Trinidad and Tobago 1966 election have been excluded from this book because of the poor quality and fragmentary nature of the recordings. The other four lectures—on Rousseau, Marx's *Eighteenth Brumaire of Louis Bonaparte* and *Capital*, and Lenin and the historic Russian Trade Union Debate—were actually private classes for Alfie Roberts, Franklyn Harvey, and Tim Hector and a few others (Robert Hill was not present and Anne Cools was living in England at the time).[76] The other private lecture on Heidegger, existentialism, and Marxism was delivered to members of Facing Reality, including Robert Hill who by this time was an active member of the group. In many ways, these lectures—which, with the exception of "The Making of the Caribbean People," have never been published before—represent James at the height of his political maturity. In addition to his theoretical and historical understanding of politics, he also brought more than three decades of personal experience to bear on his talks as he sought to impart to his students some of the vicissitudes and exigencies of political struggle. And although the classes explored themes whose roots lie in European history and thought, his constant allusions to Caribbean politics and personalities grounded the presentations in the contemporary political context of the region.

In this sense, *You Don't Play with Revolution* has a lot in common with James's 1960 Trinidad lectures published in *Modern Politics*. Kent Worcester suggests that the Trinidad lectures draw both on classical Greece as a model of active mass democratic participation in the Caribbean, and the Marxist tradition, emphasizing "the capacity of ordinary workers effectively to [sic] intervene in revolutionary situations."[77] While it might be more accurate to say that *Modern Politics* provides a history of Western politics that is animated and informed by the Marxist approach, James was obviously still buoyed by the nationalist and Pan-Caribbean fervor that was penetrating the Caribbean when he delivered the Trinidad lectures. But in 1966, in the aftermath of the failed West Indies Federation and his break with Eric Williams, and amidst the disturbing signs that Caribbean independence

promised continued dependence on foreign capital and neo-colonial interests, James was less concerned with Ancient Athens as a model and Classical Greece goes unmentioned in the lectures. Instead, he sought to make
explicit those aspects of Marxism, Western revolutionary history, and the
history of the Caribbean that could inform the current stage of political
struggle in which the Caribbean's new leadership, seen as representatives of
old interests, would be challenged.

Yet James still demonstrates his abiding preoccupation with the plight
of workers and the underclass and his belief in the capacity of "ordinary
people" to do the extraordinary. This is evident in "The Making of the
Caribbean People," his presentation at the second annual gathering of
the CCC. After citing several passages from *The Black Jacobins* describing
the remarkable feats of Haitian slaves during their war of independence
against Napoleon's army, James declares in an uncharacteristically personal
tone, "These are my ancestors, these are my people. They are yours too,
if you want them. We are descendants from the same stock and the same
kind of life on the sugar plantations which made them what they were.
Faced with certain difficulties, we would respond in the same way," James
adds, hinting that the contemporary Caribbean warrants the same kind of
creative-intellectual energy and revolutionary verve that the ex-slaves of
Haiti displayed.

James's public lectures appealed to students, academics, and members
of the general public, but his private classes were specifically catered to his
young disciples whose ultimate objective was to return to the Caribbean
and transform the region that, in James's words, was drifting "towards reaction internally and neo-colonialist relations with a Great Power" within a
system of national independence that was "only the old colonial system writ
large."[78] Again, James emphasized that power rests, or should, in the hands
of society's marginalized and the working class. In his talk on Jean-Jacques
Rousseau, for example, James draws on a passage from *The Social Contract*
to argue that power should lie in the hands of the general populace because,
as Fanon also argued, once politicians are elected they inevitably represent
their own class interests. His belief in the latent capacities of the workers
and the poor and underprivileged—that they held the key to genuine social
transformation—was further demonstrated in his class on Marx's *Capital*. As James informs us, "somewhere about 1848, the extension of labor-

power had reached such a stage that the civilization, the level of physical and intellectual development of the working-class, was falling to pieces.... [T]hese circumstances, and by the struggles of the working-class, not for an eight-hour day, but to defend its very habits of life, resulted in people passing laws" to limit the working-day. It was under these circumstances that capital began developing machinery to intensify the working-day in order to increase the rate of profit. According to James, "the development of profit by means of machinery was the direct result... of the battles that the working-class fought in order to save the civilization, health, and general intellectual and moral development of the working-class." In other words, the defiance of workers not only contributed to improved work conditions for them, but also pushed the capitalist class to develop and improve industrial technology.

James's belief in workers and the underclass is not without qualification. As his class on Marx's *Eighteenth Brumaire* attests, his notion of self-organization is tempered by his reading of history and by personal experience. Here James emphasizes that politics is not an exact science and that revolution has no magic mathematical formula or calculus. Paraphrasing Marx, he argues that there are situations in which neither class struggle nor economics determine a political outcome, and he cautions his students that "Marxism does not give you a blueprint in which you know what to do every time." "It creates a situation where you observe the classes based upon the economic relations and you face the decisions." For James politics is a complex and multifaceted process and its actors have to be acutely attuned to the interplay of forces that contribute to, or hinder, social and political change. To quote his declaration in *Party Politics in the West Indies*, "I am a Marxist, I have studied revolution for many years, and among other things you learn not to play with it."[79] And as he explains in the 1968 interview in the *McGill Reporter* reproduced in this book, this quote referred to the anti-communist paranoia associated with left politics in the Caribbean.[80] But the mantra can be equally applied to his view that politics is a timely, sensitive, measured process in which human and often unanticipated objective social factors combine to present unique political circumstances—unpredictable breaches or openings that can create possibilities for change.

Perhaps the best example in *You Don't Play with Revolution* of the unscientific nature of Marxism and revolutionary politics is found in his treat-

ment of the 1920-1921 trade union debate in Russia. This class was deliv
ered in three separate sessions, an indication of his admiration for Lenin's
thought as well as the relevance he attached to this debate for his young
protégés. In James's eyes, this debate, along with Lenin's reflections on the
Russian Revolution during the last years of his life, is crucial to understanding not only the Russian Revolution but also the challenges confronting
newly-independent or arising nations. (Surprisingly, a recent anthology on
Lenin's life and work designed to resurrect his ideas completely ignores this
debate, although reference is made to James and *Notes on Dialectics*.[81]) For
James, the trade union debate illustrated Lenin's "magnificent honesty—the
absolute plainness, the regard for truth." James's Lenin is a seasoned politician whose ability to cut through the miasma and, when necessary, boldly
assess and dissect social and political problems, he admired. After years of
reflection and political agitation—and as a veteran of the Russian Revolution whose party survived the ravages of civil war—Lenin was confronted
with the challenge of transforming a war-torn and besieged society into
a workers' state. Faced with this mammoth task, he attempted to develop
policies and programs that would engage the entire population, without
which, he believed, the Revolution was doomed. This became Lenin's great
preoccupation towards the end of his life and is the main reason why James
states at the beginning of his class that this debate "is one of the finest political discussions that I know anywhere." Lenin's critical analysis provides "an
education not only in politics, but in the moral approach to a political situation" and James recommended reading Lenin alongside Shakespeare, Rousseau, and Marx, after which his students could begin "to master and tackle the
West Indian problem."

For James politics is, in part, a process of trial and error and without the
deliberate involvement of the mass of the population, the process is destined
to fail. This is the sentiment that Lenin attempted to convey to Trotsky
and other Bolsheviks who advocated a more bureaucratic approach to politics which, in the case of the Russia's trade unions, meant administering
them from above. (Ironically, Hannah Arendt accuses Lenin, not Trotsky,
of mistaking the bureaucratic and administrative approach for "radical and
universal equality."[82]) James insisted that a similar situation confronted the
Caribbean, Africa, and the Third World as a whole. After winning the Civil
War, the Bolsheviks were faced with the daunting task of rebuilding Russia.

Lenin was adamant that the only way to build socialism in Russia was "by practical experience and involving the mass of the population," and a failure to appreciate this "in Africa, in the Caribbean and all these places—is bound to end in disaster" according to James.

C.L.R. James is known for the depth of his intellectual contributions in many spheres. Given this reputation, the range of interests represented in this book, supplemented by correspondence and interviews, should come as no surprise. But what is perhaps surprising is James's fascination with the work of Martin Heidegger and existentialist philosophy. Sylvia Wynter has argued that the uniqueness of James's theoretical contributions rests in his ability to stretch and bend the boundaries of Marxism. According to Wynter, James understood that exploitation, oppression, and resistance to capital occurred in multiple forms that can not be explained by the simple labor/capital binary; that the creative power of the marginalized, dispossessed, and alienated can not be reduced to a "labor conceptual framework" which fails to account for popular arts, the transgression of conventional gender roles, and the emergence of popular social and cultural movements such as Rastafari and calypso.[83] In this sense, read alongside his analysis of Guyanese novelist Wilson Harris, James's lecture on "Existentialism and Marxism" might be considered part of his quest to keep Marxism relevant by stretching its categories in keeping with his lived experience as a Trinidadian. The lecture, which appears to have been drawn from an unpublished article written by James,[84] was delivered to a few members of Facing Reality in 1966, including Martin Glaberman, William Gorman, and Robert Hill. The bulk of the presentation focuses on Martin Heidegger, and James's enthusiasm for Heidegger's *Being and Time* and its relevance for Marxism is evident in the following remark:

> Marxism has to develop, and this is one of the reasons that I bring Heidegger's work to you. Lenin insists that idealism can become very important and follow important lines of human thought. And everywhere citizens are concerned with precisely this because the ordinary canons of logic can no longer be applied with any effectiveness and real satisfaction to what is happening in society or to what is happening to him. Heidegger and existentialism is an attempt to be able to say: "Well, this is a method that you can use." We shall have to see.

This is perhaps the closest James ever came to openly questioning the fundamental tenets of Marxism. Yet his study of Heidegger's "idealism" clearly remained rooted in an appreciation of Marxist thought and his refrain, "We shall have to see" suggests that he was a reticent convert to existentialism. That being said, his embrace of Heidegger represents an attempt by a Marxist to grapple with the place of the individual *qua* individual in society and to go beyond the substructure/superstructure debate that has preoccupied Marxists. And although he is primarily concerned with the relationship between Marxism and existentialism, the Caribbean remained in direct sight. In his presentation, James refers to the existentialist fiction of Guyanese writer Wilson Harris, in essence tying it to a lecture that he delivered on Harris the year before in Trinidad, shortly after he was released from house arrest.[85] James also penned an introduction to a Harris lecture published the same year in which he wrote, "you can see and feel" the West Indian's "past, latent in their contemporary personality—others besides myself call it a search for national identity. That identity conceals or rather constricts an enormous potential. We have a history, we don't know it, our present, our past and our future. On this interrelation, Harris is very strong and very clear."[86] The introduction's Heideggerian overtones are obvious when read in relation to the Montreal lecture in which he explains Heidegger's conception of time: "The futural, time for the individual—we have known that also for the social group—is never at a particular historical time. It is only when you have a future in mind, and when you are conscious of what has been in the past, that you can take over and find out what is your own, what time is at the particular moment."

In both instances, James insists that the present is conditioned by past experience and our vision of the future; that it is only when we come to terms with the past and envision a future that we become conscious of what is possible in the present. This is one of the overall lessons that James attempted to impart to his students in Montreal by drawing on Marx, Lenin, and Caribbean history. But the similarities between James, Harris, and Heidegger do not simply suggest the obvious—that Heidegger gave James insight into Harris and the Caribbean's social reality; rather they suggest that Harris's writing and James's experience as a West Indian helped to make Heidegger's existentialism concrete for James and relevant for Marxism, just as his Trinidadianess illuminated his understanding of Marx, the modern world, and the history, philosophy, art, and theater of Ancient Greece. Notwithstanding his brilliance, James's Caribbean vantage point—emanating from a place viewed as being outside of history and time—is largely responsible for the unique perspective he brought to Marxism and the range of subjects to which he contributed.

Lasting Legacy

The CCC-CLRJSC adopted James as its mentor because they recognized that he could help prepare them for their return to the Caribbean, and the fact that they went on to play pivotal roles in the emergence of the region's New Left is in part a testament to James's influence on them.[87] In a letter to Franklyn Harvey in January 1970, Robert Hill reflected on the CCC-CLRJSC's accomplishments. At the time Harvey was living in Trinidad as the coalescence of Black Power, the trade union movement, and disaffected military officers threatened to topple the government of Eric Williams. Some, most notably Deryck R. Brown, have tried to link these events directly to James who, it is argued, lurked behind the scene, encouraging a small cadre of Marxist-Leninists, including military personnel, to overthrow the government.[88] This is perhaps, at best, an exaggerated truth that, nonetheless, provides a hint of James's influence on the Caribbean New Left. Hill, who was living in Jamaica at the time and one of the central figures in the popular group Abeng, reminded Harvey of the CCC-CLRJC's accomplishments in Canada. The publication of James's *Notes on Dialectics* was one of the group's milestones, but there were others: "We have done exhaustive work on James' work. We have... assisted in the publication of the *Perspectives and Proposals*.[89] We have made [James's] books and pamphlets available on a scale never before achieved, and this was done in conjunction with the work of FR organization." Hill also noted that they did what they could to maintain James financially in his work and that, "Today we are looking to our own publication and the publication of James in a *Selected Works* edition."[90] These were significant achievements for a small group with limited resources.

But the group's relationship with James went even further, touching him at a crucial point in his personal and political life by providing the frail and aging revolutionary with a North American audience. James's entry into the U.S. in 1967 was his first sustained visit there since his forced departure in 1953 in the midst of Senator Joseph McCarthy's anti-communist purges.[91] The tour organized by the CCC-CLRJSC put James into contact with members of the Black Power movement in the United States such as Stokely Carmichael whom James first met in Windsor, Ontario during his lecture tour and then subsequently in Montreal in 1967, when Carmichael spoke at Sir George Williams University. James and Carmichael also shared the stage during the 1968 Congress of Black Writers in Montreal, where James Forman, Harry Edwards, Michael Thelwell, Jimmy Garrett and other advocates of Black Power and Black Studies were present.[92] Garrett later invited James to teach at Federal City College in Washington D.C., paving the way for James to spend the next ten years teaching in the United States, where he became a prized public speaker and an important influence on the American Black left.

James was also a kind of iconic mentor to members of the New Left, and especially the circle of Students for a Democratic Society associated with Paul Buhle and the journal *Radical America*. While part of his appeal rested on his Marxist critique of Marxist orthodoxies and Stalinism, and on the flexibility of his thought, his ties to the New Left were in large part due to the work of the Caribbean Conference Committee and the C.L.R. James Study Circle. If today James is acknowledged as one of the great minds of the 20th century, some of this recognition is owed to members of the CCC-CLRJSC, which disseminated his work and provided him with a platform for his ideas in Canada and the United States.

Reading them some forty years after they were first delivered, as the cracks in the edifice of the world's superpower widen, and at a time when the global economic crisis has even arch conservatives pondering economic solutions that, only a year ago, would have been the butt of anti-communist invective, James's lectures assume an added significance. Barbadian political theorist Aaron Kamugisha has joined the chorus of Caribbean thinkers decrying the acute social and economic crisis that plagues the region. Kamugisha is primarily concerned with what he calls the "coloniality of citizenship," a "complex amalgam of elite domination, neoliberalism and the legacy of colonial authoritarianism, which continue to frustrate and deny the aspirations of many Caribbean people."[93] This "absurdity," he writes, "reinscribes the tropes of coloniality that have for so long presented the Caribbean people as deficient, backward, and incapable of the considered reflection that could lead to genuine transformation of their societies."[94] Given its Naipaulian undertones, Kamugisha acknowledges that absurdity is perhaps a harsh word, but he nonetheless poses the question, "what if absurdity was instead a reflective position, a momentary sigh, before a cry of ethical revolt against the present?"[95] This is a specter that haunts the Caribbean, and the entire globe.

In revisiting C.L.R. James's Montreal lectures which were delivered at a time in which there was widespread hope that genuine and positive social transformation could occur in the Caribbean and throughout the world, we are soberly reminded of both the challenges and rewards that social change—that revolution—engender. In 1804, the former slaves of Saint Domingue defeated the superpowers of their time—Spain, England, and ultimately France—and established the independent state of Haiti. Recent research suggests that the triumph of these former slaves inspired Hegel's notion of the master-slave dialectic,[96] one of the cornerstones of his system of thought which laid the theoretical foundation for Marx's notion of class struggle and the primacy of labor. We are left to ponder if and how knowledge of this Haiti-Hegel relationship would have influenced James's analysis of both the Haitian Revolution and his reading of Hegel. The victory of the former slaves struck a blow for Black freedom and was a triumph for humankind as a whole. The Haitian Revolution embodied what were, up until that point, the hallowed but hollow ideals of European Enlightenment. It was and remains one of the Caribbean's many gifts to the world, and C.L.R. James was chiefly responsible for bringing its significance to our attention in his magisterial history, *The Black Jacobins*.

Were James lecturing in the 21st century, he would have an entire body of radical Caribbean literature to draw on—much of which has been built upon his work—and he would no doubt have to abandon some of his most cherished beliefs about the Western canon. The Caribbean continues to grapple with the legacy of slavery and colonialism in a world contending with the deep sense of uncertainty and hushed optimism that the crass reality of an ailing empire and a faulty economic system brings. In this climate of despair and tempered hope, James's lectures remind us that ideas, theory, and the lessons of history are potent weapons in the struggle to build the New Society that the Haitian Revolution, the ideals of socialism, the anti-colonial struggles of the post-Second World War period, and the global 1960s movements promised. He not only reminds us that the chant "another world is possible" is real, but also helps us chart a course toward creating this new world in the present.

David Austin

January 2009

PART I

PUBLIC LECTURES

The Making of the Caribbean People

Thank you, Mr. Chairman, for your kind words. I often receive words kind and unkind. I know how to distinguish between them.

This evening I am to speak on "The Making of the Caribbean People," a people, in my opinion, unique in the modern world. That is the theme which I will develop. I know nobody like them, nobody like us, both positively and negatively. I'll tell you how I will treat such a tremendous subject. I will begin by stating the kind of opinions that educated people, and well-meaning, progressive people, have of us, the Caribbean people. Naturally on such a wide subject, in such a limited time, I will have to be quite precise in the quotations that I give. They are chosen because they have more than passing value.

When I have stated what is the general opinion, I shall then proceed to state my own, which is utterly and completely opposed to the opinions held by most educated people, West Indians and non-West Indians alike. I will do that by going into the history and sociology of the West Indian at the beginning of their entry into modern Western society.

I shall concentrate to a large degree on what took place between 1600 and 1800. When I have established that, I will then move more rapidly through our history and what has been happening since. But I will depend on what has been established in the early part to be able to move quickly and easily into matters which are more familiar to us.

First of all then, what is the general opinion held about us by people who are West Indians or who are interested in the West Indies? I will begin with a quotation from the Moyne Report. A number of excellent English gentlemen and ladies, of broad views, sympathetic to the West Indies, who were sent there by King George V in 1938 on a Royal Commission. They wrote a report which is one of the foremost reports that has ever been made about the West Indies. They were not hostile to the West Indies. They were merely profoundly ignorant of what they were dealing with. Here is a quotation from that report: "Negroes were taken from lands where they lived no doubt in a primitive state."[1]

I don't know where they got that from, because the early Portuguese and the rest who "discovered" Africa did not find very much difference between the Negro civilizations they met and the great masses of the peasantry they had left at home. In many respects, many Africans were more advanced. These commissioners writing the report took for granted that all Africans lived in Africa in a primitive state—but Africans lived in social conditions and were subject to customs and usages which, anthropology increasingly shows, had definite social, economic and cultural value. Well, at any rate, that is much better than what they used to teach twenty or thirty years ago.

The Moyne report goes on to say that "their transfer to the West Indies unlike most other large-scale movements of population, did not involve the transfer of any important traces of their traditions and customs, but rather their most complete destruction." Now, it is impossible to produce a sentence that contains more mistakes and more gross misunderstandings and misrepresentations. The Negroes who came from Africa brought themselves. The Amerindians could not stand the impact of slavery. Chinese came afterwards and couldn't make it: they couldn't do the work. The Europeans tried Portuguese laborers: they were not successful.

People of African descent, the African from Africa, made the perpetuation of Western Civilization possible in the West Indies. The report says that they left everything behind. But the Africans themselves are the most important and most valuable representatives of their civilization, and of course when they came here they brought themselves—something of such primary importance never seems to come to the mind of all these people who write reports.

Now they go on to say that "the negroes had one function only, the provision of cheap labor on the estates owned and managed by Europeans for the production of their valuable export crops. They lost their language, customs and religions, and no systematic attempt was made to substitute any other." They lost their language, yes. But they rapidly mastered the English, the French, and the Spanish languages. So, if they lost their language, it is necessary to say they had to learn new ones and they learned them very well. They could do that being the people that they were.

Now, this Moyne report is the opinion of a whole body of British MPs of various disciplines and various other persons. These things left their mark— we had been inhumanly treated, as the "primitives" we were. We continued to be. The coming of Emancipation gave a strong, if temporary, impetus to such forces as were working for the betterment of the Negro population: churches and their attempt to teach Negroes Christianity, to read and to write, and to improve their morals, so that they shouldn't have so many illegitimate children. That was a primary conception for the betterment of the Negro. I hope before I have concluded to show you how superficial, how entirely false, was this estimate of Negro morals and capability.

Now I want to add to that a statement by no less a person than Professor W. Arthur Lewis. You will find it in a pamphlet I have published in Trinidad. It is a statement made to an economic conference,[2] which he addressed as follows: the professors of economics, the economist—so said Professor Lewis—do not know much more about development than the ordinary person does. Economic development depends on saving some of what you have now, in order to improve yourself later. He says that is all there is to it; that there is no special economic theory or economic knowledge required. He says that what is required is the effort and readiness to sacrifice by a great part of the population. And, he concludes, people don't know whether the population, the West Indian population, will make that effort or not. He more than implies that it is a matter of doubt as to whether the West Indian population has got that necessary feeling, that impetus to make the sacrifices necessary, for the development of the West Indian economy.

I want to dissociate myself completely from Professor Lewis's view. I have never found that West Indians, when called upon in a critical situation, do not respond. That is their life: I believe that they can't help but to respond. Beginning as we do in a new civilization and leaving such elements that they might have brought with them behind, they have always responded to a fundamental and serious challenge. That has been our way of life. That is why we are still alive. What has happened to us is that economic and social forces are sitting upon our backs and preventing us from developing ourselves in vital spheres. Where we have had an opportunity to work freely, there we have shown great distinction. Where we have not shown it is because we have been prevented. It is not the lack of capacity.

I want you to understand that. I strongly remove myself from the view expressed by Professor Lewis that it depends on us whether we shall rise to the occasion. If those on our backs get off our backs, we shall be able to rise: we have done pretty well with the burdens that we have always carried and are still carrying.

This whole business consists of criticism and doubts of a "primitive" people. We began with nothing, and have learned a great deal, but we still have a lot to learn! That is not my view of the West Indian. I think that we have learned all that it was possible for us to have learned. We have learned far more than other people in similar situations have learned. The difficulties that we have met, that stood in our way, were difficulties of a breadth and weight which would have crushed a people of lesser power and less understanding of the fact that we had to do all we got to get somewhere.

Now I want to begin with Richard Ligon's *History of Barbados*.[3] It was written in 1653. You can't begin much earlier. He had been in Barbados up to 1647. The island was populated by Englishmen in the 1620s, and Ligon says that at the beginning, or very soon after, there were eleven-thousand white peasant farmers in Barbados. They were on their way to becoming what New England in the United States became later. But then came the sugar plantations and the Negroes were brought in in order to work on the sugar plantations. That was somewhere between 1640 or thereabouts, and Ligon gives this account of what happened to the Negroes, who at that time had not been in Barbados for more than about ten years. I will give a full account of what he says. Don't think it's a little long: it is very important and means a great deal for our future understanding of the whole 300 years of *West Indian history* that follows it.

I want to interpolate here that I fully agree with Gilberto Freyre that the African who made the Middle Passage and came to live in the West Indies was an entirely new historical and social category.[4] He was not even an African, he was a West Indian Black who was a slave. And there had never been people like that before and there haven't been any since. And what I shall make clear is the uniqueness of our history and the unique developments which have resulted.

Back now to Ligon:

A little before I came thence, there was such a combination amongst them, as the like was never seen there before. Their sufferings being grown to a great height, and their daily complainings to one another (of the intolerable burdens they labor'd under) being spread throughout the Iland: at the last, some amongst them, whose spirits were not able to endure such slavery, resolved to break through it, or die in the act; and so conspired with some others of their acquaintance, whose sufferings were equall, if not above theirs; and their spirits no way inferiour, resolved to draw as many of the discontented party into this plot, as possible they could; and those of this perswasion, were the greatest number of servants in the Iland. So that a day was appointed to fall upon their Masters, and cut all their throats, and by that means, to make themselves not only freemen, but Masters of the Iland.

Now that is the very beginning (and the continuation) of West Indian history. They wanted not only their freedom but to remove their masters and make themselves masters of the island. That is what happened essentially in San Domingo about 150 years afterwards and that is what happened in Cuba in 1958. They got rid of their masters and made themselves masters of the island. Masters isn't exactly the same as Ligon's statement but if I may quote a resilient lawyer: "The principle is the same."

I believe the above to be characteristic of the West Indies and our history. When West Indians reach a certain stage, they wish to make a complete change, and that is because all of us come from abroad. Liberty means something to us that is very unusual. There were many generations of slaves in Africa, of that we are quite sure. And in Africa they took it and no doubt fought against it at certain times. But when we made the Middle Passage and came to the Caribbean, we went straight into a modern industry—and sugar plantation—and there we saw that to be a slave was the result of our being black. A white man was not a slave. The West Indian slave was not accustomed to that kind of slavery in Africa; and, therefore, in the history of the West Indies, there is one dominant fact, and that is the desire—sometimes expressed, sometimes unexpressed, but always there—the desire for liberty; the ridding oneself of the particular burden which is the special inheritance of the black skin.

If you don't know that about West Indian people, you know nothing about them. They have been the most rebellious people in history and that is the reason. It is because being a Black man, he was made a slave, and the White man, whatever his limitations, was a free subject, a man able to do what he could in the community. That is the history of the West Indies. No hint of that appears in the report of Lord Moyne and if we read any number, not only of government reports, but works of economists and historians, some of them by West Indians, they have no conception whatever of the people that they are dealing with, where we have come from, whom they are dealing with and where we are headed.

To go on with Ligon:

> And so closely was this plot carried, as no discovery was made, till the day before they were to put it in act: And then one of them, either by the failing of his courage, or some obligation from the love of his Master, revealed this long plotted conspiracy; and so by this timely advertisement, the Masters were saved. Justice Hethersall (whose servant this was) sending letters to all his friends, and they to theirs, and so to one another, till they were all secured; and, by examination, found out the greatest part of them.

Now it is interesting to note that this fellow who betrayed the plot was working with a Justice, Justice Hethersall. Whether he loved his master or had some other reason (that is a matter for the psychologists), I don't know. What I think, what I suspect, is that working in the house of a Justice of the Peace, he had acquired a certain respect, a subservience to the conceptions of law and order of the masters of the society which he had just entered. And I say that because we shall see this type constantly reappearing; it is most prominent in West Indian society today: the house-slave. A man is a part of the mass of the population; the mass of the population moves in a certain direction, and for some reason or other, he betrays the cause. We have that West Indian pattern of betrayal from the very beginning.

Ligon continues:

> [W]hereof eighteen of the principall men in the conspiracy, and they were the first leaders and contrivers of the plot, were put to death, for example to the rest. And the reason why they made examples of so many, was, they found these so haughty in their resolutions, and so incorrigible, as they were like enough to become actors in a second plot; and so they thought good, to secure them; and for the rest, to have a speciall eye over them.

Now, there in sharp outline at the very beginning is the history of the West Indies. After barely ten years they, all of them, are knit together, not merely by the common bond of color, but far more by a common oppression. They have the majority of people in the island. (I feel fairly certain that it was the sugar plantation and working in it that gave them this possibility. I don't believe they would have been able to organize themselves so well and so clearly in Africa. *That is not important.*) Anyway, this thing is planned. Then this person working with Justice Hethersall betrays. He tells his master what amounts to: "I am with you, not with them, that is what they are plotting to do."

That is permanent in the history of the West Indies and we shall see that as we go on. Note how the leaders who are caught are incorrigible and absolutely determined not to give way in the slightest respect; they have to be executed, all of them, because that is the only way in which their masters could feel safe in the future. That is the history we ought to teach in our schools. That is *our* history, *West Indian history*.

Now, I've chosen that because I believe that it is symbolic of the whole of West Indian history, and as I go on, especially when I come to my special study, *The Black Jacobins*,[5] I shall go into that in some detail. Some of you may believe that you have read the book. I did more than that, I wrote it. But it is only in late years that I am able to understand and to appreciate the full significance of what I wrote in that book. We shall go into that in time.

Now I want to move to another feature which is not understood by numerous West Indian economists, sociologists, historians, and writers. This which I hold up before you is a work called *Merchants and Planters*, by Richard Pares. He is one of the greatest West Indian scholars, a scholar in that he has done a lot of studies and is a man of great learning. (He has not written one book and gone about claiming to be a scholar.) *Merchants and Planters* is a study of the Caribbean and was published for the Economic History Society, Cambridge University Press. Pares notes that

> [I]n all the inventories which are to be found among the West Indian archives, it is very usual for the mill, the cauldron, the still, and the buildings to count for more than one-sixth of the total capital; in most plantations one-tenth would be nearer the mark. By far the greatest capital items were the value of the slaves and the acreage planted in canes by their previous labour.[6]

The greatest capital value (this is about 1760) of the sugar plantation, was the labor of the slaves and the acreages they had planted. All sorts of economists do all sorts of studies about the West Indies but they don't know that. They write little studies about how this was worth that and that was worth this, and this was worth the other. But that the real value of those economic units was the slaves and the land they had developed by their labor, this escapes nearly all, except this English scholar. Pares goes on to say:

> Yet, when we look closely, we find that the industrial capital required was much larger than a sixth of the total value. With the mill, the boiling house, and the still went an army of specialists—almost all of them slaves, but nonetheless specialists for that.

If you take little away from this meeting and you take that, you will have done well. There was an army of slaves, but he says they were specialists; they were slaves, it was true, but nevertheless they were specialists. That is very hard to grasp. Try hard. This tremendous economy that made so much wealth, particularly for British society—it was the slaves who ran those plantations. Note that, so you get what Pares is saying: the statisticians never write down the real value of the important industrial capital of the plantations. And Pares says (this is terrific):

> They were not only numerous, but because of their skill, they had a high value. If we add their cost to that of the instruments and machinery which they used, we find that the industrial capital of the plantations, without which it could not be a plantation at all, was probably not much less than half its total capital.

I hope that there are some economists here who have done research in this field who will stand up and take part in the discussion, telling us what they have written, or to be more precise, what they have not written. It takes an Englishman to write this. And here let me, in advance, correct a misunderstanding that is very prevalent today. I denounce European colonialist scholarship. But I respect the learning and the profound discoveries of Western civilization. It is by means of the work of the great men of Ancient Greece; of Michelet, the French historian; of Hegel, Marx, and Lenin; of Du Bois; of contemporary Europeans and Englishmen like Pares and E.P. Thompson; of an African like the late Chisiza, that my eyes and ears have been opened and I can today see and hear what we were, what we are, and what we can be, in other words, the Making of the Caribbean People.

Pares goes on to say,

> When we examine specifications of the negro, we find so many boilers, masons, carters, boatswains of the mill, etc., that we cannot feel much confidence in our categories especially when we find individuals described as "an excellent boiler and field negro" ...

So that in about 1766 Negroes ran the plantations. That is what this scholar is saying. A man is described as an excellent boiler and field Negro, this prevents us from putting such persons on either side of the line. He not only worked in the fields, but he also did the necessary technical work. Further complications arise from the fact that specialist jobs were awarded to the sickly and the ruptured. The sickly or the ruptured were given the technical jobs to do—note the spread of technical skill. That gave me, and I had read it elsewhere, an entirely different picture of the kind of civilization that existed in the West Indies well before the French Revolution of 1789.

I have found other evidence elsewhere and it seems to me that they, the slaves, ran that society; they were the persons responsible. If they had been removed, the society would have collapsed. That is perfectly clear in certain writings about Trinidad and Tobago. But the West Indian economists, the West Indian sociologists, the West Indian historians—they write, but I have never met any one of them who understood that, and I would be very glad if either here, or if you feel ashamed about it, in private, you would let me know, one or two of you, why this had to be done by an Englishman, an English scholar.

I want to put it as sharply as possible. Slaves ran the plantations; those tremendous plantations, the great source of wealth for so many English aristocrats and merchants, the merchant princes who cut such a figure in English society (and French, too, but we are speaking here of English society). Those plantations were run by the slaves. That is what Pares is saying. Slave labor was not an advanced stage of labor, but those plantations created millions and slaves ran them from top to bottom.

Now we are able to understand one of the greatest events in the history of the West Indian people, which I will now spend some time upon in the light of what we have said of the earlier part. It will deal with the

San Domingo Revolution. I wrote the book, *The Black Jacobins*. I studied that society very closely, but it is only in later years, with my acquaintance with the West Indian people and actual contact with them, political and to some degree sociological, that I have learned to understand what I wrote in this book. And I have learned to understand it because as I read educated persons' writings about the West Indies, it becomes clear that they have no understanding whatever of the West Indian people.

I will take an excerpt here and there and spend a word or two on each, but I prefer to deal with the extracts themselves. The first one is from Sir John Fortescue, the historian of the British Army.[7] Fortescue writes about what happened to the British expedition to San Domingo in 1792. This is the sentence I want you to bear in mind. That was the war in which England was fighting for its life against revolutionary France. Fortescue says, "The secret of England's impotence for the first six years of the war may be said to lie in two fatal words—San Domingo." Fortescue puts the blame on Pitt and Dundas,

> who had full warning that on this occasion they would have to fight not only the poor, sickly Frenchmen, but the Negro population of the West Indies. Yet they poured their troops into these pestilent islands, in the expectation that thereby they would destroy the power of France, only to discover, when it was too late, that they had practically destroyed the British Army.

Now I have done some teaching, a great deal of teaching: I was a member of that noble army of martyrs for twelve years and I have met many students who knew all about the Battle of Hastings, the Battle of Waterloo, the Battle of the Great Armada. Some of them were pretty bright on Blank in the Battle of Blank, but that the British Army was destroyed by slaves in San Domingo, and England was impotent for the first six years of the greatest war in history up to 1914; they simply don't know anything about that. I wonder how many of you know that. I wouldn't press it any further.

Now an important thing is that the slaves worked collectively on the sugar plantation, and I am going to read a statement now which shows what that had made of them. A few years after the revolution began (it began in 1791 and this is about 1796), a French official, Roume, notes the change in the people:

In the North [*James: "that is where the great sugar plantations were, in the great North plain."*] they came out to sustain royalty, nobility and religion against the poor whites and the Patriots. But they were soon formed into regiments and were hardened by fighting. They organized themselves into armed sections and into popular bodies, and even while fighting for royalty they adopted instinctively and rigidly observed all the forms of republican organization.

This is in 1796, only five years after the revolt began.

Slogans and rallying cries were established between the chiefs of the sections and divisions and gave them points of contact from one extremity of the plains and towns of the North to the other.

Over one-third of the island of San Domingo. This was not a few, but the mass:

This guaranteed the leaders a means of calling out the laborers and sending them back at will. These forms were extended to the districts in the West Province, and were faithfully observed by the black laborers, whether fighting for Spain and royalty or for the republic, Roume assured Bonaparte that he recognized these slogans, even during the insurrection which forced him to authorize the taking of Spanish San Domingo.

This was written some years afterwards.

Now, I wonder what conclusions you draw from this self-mobilization and self-discipline of a West Indian population. The conclusion I draw is the absolute impertinence and stupidity of a Colonial Office which, as late as 1950, was wondering whether the people of Trinidad and Tobago should have freedom or not, or whether they should have five members or more in the Legislature or in the Executive; playing a game of checkers, they put one member and they see how it goes; then they put two and wait a bit; and they put another one, but he did not do so well, so they take him away. And that is the kind of business, that is what they were doing, they said, to train the people for democracy.

But look at our people in 1796. They were illiterate: Toussaint used to say that two-thirds of them had made the Middle Passage and could not speak a word of French. They knew a few words of patois. But they worked on sugar plantations. They were masters of the technical necessities of the plantation, and when the time came they were able to organize themselves over the whole of the North Plain, and their leaders could call them out and send them back home merely by the use of political slogans.

Obviously, any population which could act in this way, while only a few years from slavery, was fitted for full parliamentary democracy 150 years afterward.

British colonial officials have understood nothing about the development of colonial peoples. They have stood in the way of their forward movement from colonial status to freedom. The people who understand this had to go to jail. Gandhi and Nehru went to jail for any number of years. Nkrumah went to jail. Dr. Hastings Banda went to jail. Nyerere went to jail. All of them, and that priest in Cyprus, he went to jail also. So you notice that they didn't learn about democracy in British schools, they learned it in the jails into which the British had put them; and from those jails they taught the population and taught the Colonial Office about the realities of political independence.

I don't mind the nonsense the British historians and economists write. But our writers, our West Indian writer, he is the man I am concerned with. He does not seem to understand anything of what I am saying to you here.

Toussaint, in about 1801 or 1802, came to a conception for which the only word is genius. He wrote a constitution for San Domingo and he didn't submit it to the French government. He declared in the constitution that San Domingo would be governed by the ex-slaves. French officials asked him: what is the place of the French Government in the Constitution? He replied, "They will send commissioners to talk with me"— and that was all he would say. His plan was absolute local independence on the one hand, but, on the other hand, French capital and French commissioners to establish the relation. He begged them to help him develop and educate the country, and to *send a high official from France as a link between both governments. The local power was too well safeguarded for us to call it a protectorate.*

All the evidence shows that Toussaint, working alone, had reached forward to that form of political relation which we know today as dominion status. This was forty years before the famous report on Canada, forty years before the Durham Report.[8]

Toussaint said, we must have absolute independence, but we admit the sovereignty of France; France must send educators, officials, and a commissioner who will speak with me. In this political proposal, he was far beyond the politicians and officials of the time. This point they were only to reach in 1932 at Ottawa, when they accepted the complete independence of the colonies, with a High Commissioner to speak with the local governments of Canada, Australia, and so forth.

Over and over again I am aware, in these early days of struggles by these early West Indians, that they laid down lines which could be followed without too much difficulty by their descendents, but for the obstacle of their political education by the Colonial Office. (Toussaint knew and introduced a literacy campaign.)

You may think that Toussaint L'Ouverture was an exceptional person. So he was. But you will see the same tremendous spirit, energy, and political creativeness in Marcus Garvey, George Padmore, Frantz Fanon, and other West Indians, shall we say, "too numerous to mention" or "too near to home?" That is the breed. Until the Colonial Office gets hold of us to educate us.

But listen to this typically West Indian passage. It is about Toussaint again. I quote from *The Black Jacobins*:

Firm as was his grasp of reality, old Toussaint looked beyond San Domingo with a boldness of imagination surpassed by no contemporary. In the Constitution he authorized the slave-trade because the island needed people to cultivate it. When the Africans landed, however, they would be free men. But while loaded with the cares of government, he cherished a project of sailing to Africa with arms, ammunition, and a thousand of his best soldiers, and there conquering vast tracts of country, putting an end to the slave-trade, and making millions of blacks "free and French," as his constitution had made the blacks of San Domingo. It was no dream. He had sent millions of francs to America to wait for the day when he would be ready. He was already 55. What spirit was it that moved him? Ideas do not fall from heaven. The great revolution had propelled him out of his humble joys and obscure destiny, and the trumpets of its heroic period rang ever in his ears. In him, born a slave and the leader of slaves, the concrete realization of liberty, equality and fraternity was the womb of ideas and the springs of power, which overflowed their narrow environment and embraced the whole of the world. But for the revolution, this extraordinary man and his band of gifted associates would have lived their lives as slaves, serving the commonplace creatures who owned them, standing barefooted and in rags to watch inflated little governors and mediocre officials from Europe pass by, as many a talented African stands in Africa today.

That was Toussaint, the West Indian, who having established a base at home showed himself the ancestor of Garvey, Padmore, and Fanon. They had to go abroad to develop their West Indian characteristics. One West Indian who did not have to go abroad to carry out his West Indian ideas was the one who has built himself a base at home—Fidel Castro.

Let me repeat the end of that quotation:

> But for the revolution, this extraordinary man and his band of gifted associates who had lived their lives as slaves, serving the commonplace creatures who owned them, standing barefooted and in rags to watch inflated little governors and mediocre officials from Europe pass by as many a talented African stands in Africa today.

I wrote that in 1938. I am very proud of it. There were not may people thinking in those terms as far back as 1938. There are not enough who are thinking in those terms today.

Let us go on with these extraordinary people, these West Indians. They won their freedom in 1803. Up to 1791, they had been slaves. All this was done within 12 years. They defeated a Spanish army of some 50,000 soldiers, a British army of 60,000 soldiers, and another 60,000 Frenchmen sent by Bonaparte to re-establish slavery. They fought Bonaparte's great army and drove it off their land.

Now, for the making of our people since these glorious and creative days. Some of you, I have no doubt, are profoundly aware of the savage ferocity of some of the West Indian rulers today toward the populations who have put them in power. In 1966, this is appearing in island after island in the Caribbean. What we have to do is to see the origin of this, its early appearance at the very moment when freedom was won. That will give us the historic fact and the historic origins of the fact. I shall confine myself to the period after Toussaint had been captured and sent away, and General Leclerc had been compelled to employ the Negro generals as members of his staff to help keep "order." Then the news came that the old colonial regime, slavery and Mulatto discrimination, had been restored in Guadeloupe. The insurrection among the mass of the population in San Domingo became general.

What we have to do now is to see, first, the behavior of the mass of the population, the rank and file, the man in the street, the ordinary peasant, the agricultural laborer. And on the other hand, we must examine the behavior of those who, formerly slaves, had now become generals, high officials, and members of the governing body. This is how the masses behave, the masses from whom the masses of today (and some of us here) are descended.

Back to *The Black Jacobins*:

> With a skill and tenacity which astonished their seasoned opponents, the little local leaders not only beat off attacks but maintained a ceaseless harrying of the French posts, giving them no peace, so that the soldiers were worn out and nerve-wracked, and fell in thousands to the yellow fever. When the French sent large expeditions against them they disappeared in the mountains, leaving a trail of flames behind them, returning when the weary French retreated, to destroy still more plantations and carry their attacks into the French lines. Running short of ammunition, the laborers in the mountains around Port-de-Paix attacked this important town, drove out the garrison, killed the whites, burned the houses that had been rebuilt, and took possession of the fort with 25,000 pounds of powder. Who comes to capture it? Maurepas, who had commanded in the district and had so valiantly driven off the attacks of Humbert, Debelle, and Hardy. He and the French, with a vigorous counterattack, recaptured the fort, "but the insurgents with incredible activity... men, women and children, all had got back to the mountains more or less heavily laden." The masses of the North plain ran to put themselves under the guidance of these new leaders.

Now, we leave these heroic people and will go straight on to what I call the old gang, those who had become generals, administrators, and part of the new government. They would not join the new revolution, but joined with the French government to suppress the revolutionaries. They had become house-slaves of the most subservient kind. Here is what I had to write immediately after that last passage describing the heroism of the mass:

> All that old gang would do was to threaten Leclerc. Some of the blacks who had been slaves attempted to purchase their freedom from their masters. These refused and singled out as their private property high officials and officers, men who had shed their blood on the battlefield and served with distinction in the administration. Christophe told General Ramel

that if he thought slavery was to be restored, he would burn the whole of San Domingo to the ground. A black general dining with Lacroix pointed to his two daughters and asked him, "Are these to go back to slavery?" It was as if they could not believe it.

The whole house-slave character of these new masters of the sweets of government is summed up in the observation of a French historian who was part of the French expedition:

> But no one observed that in the new insurrection of San Domingo, as in all insurrections which attack constitutional authority, it was not the avowed chiefs who gave the signal for revolt, but obscure creatures for the greater part personal enemies of the colored generals.

This subservience to a ruling class by new rulers is rampant all over the Caribbean today, and I understand it much better when I read and get it into my head that after just ten years of freedom and becoming masters of San Domingo, that was the way they behaved to the emissary sent by Bonaparte. They were totally and completely subservient and it took a man like Dessalines, an absolute barbarian, to lead the people finally to their freedom. Dessalines could not write: the name of many a Haitian general had to be traced for him in pencil for him to trace it over in ink. But he, Dessalines, was the one who could lead the rebellious mass of the population. All the educated ones, all those who were not so educated but who had sat for a while in the seats of power, they were prepared to submit to any indignity in order to remain, not with power, but merely the symbols and to enjoy the profits of power.

I have two more quotations, one written fifty years later by a soldier who had fought against them, and one written at the time by general Leclerc, the brother-in-law of Napoleon, who was in command of the expedition. General Lemmonier-Delafosse (who believed in slavery), wrote in his memoirs:

> But what men these blacks are! How they fight and how they die! One has to make war against them to know their reckless courage in braving danger when they can no longer have recourse to stratagem. I have seen a solid column, torn by grape-shot from four pieces of cannon, advance without making a retrograde step. The more they fell, the greater seemed to be the courage of the rest. They advanced singing, for the Negro sings

everywhere, makes songs on everything. Their song was a song of brave men and went as follows:

> To the attack, grenadier,
> Who gets killed, that's his affair.
> Forget your ma,
> Forget your pa,
> To the attack, grenadier,
> Who gets killed, that's his affair.

This song was worth all of our republican songs. Three times these brave men, arms in hand, advanced without firing a shot, and each time repulsed, only retired after leaving the ground strewed with three-quarters of their troop. One must have seen this bravery to have any conception of it. Those songs shouted into the sky in unison by 2,000 voices, to which the cannon formed a base, produced a thrilling effect. French courage alone could resist it. Indeed large ditches, an excellent artillery, perfect soldiers gave us a great advantage. But for many a day that massed square which marched singing to its death, lighted by a magnificent sun, remained in my thoughts, and even to-day after more than forty years, this majestic and glorious spectacle still lives as vividly in my imagination as the moment when I saw it.

Finally, General Leclerc wrote to his brother-in-law Napoleon Bonaparte: "We have in Europe a false idea of the country and the men whom we fight against." That was written by a defeated general over 150 years ago. Today, 150 years after, not only in Europe and the United states, but in the very West Indies itself, there is a false idea of the country in which our people live and the quality of the people who live in it.

These are my ancestors, these are my people. They are yours, too, if you want them. We are descendants from the same stock and the same kind of life on the sugar plantations which made them what they were. Faced with certain difficulties, we would respond in the same way. That seems to be inherent in people who have made the Middle Passage and had to learn all that they can and build a new life with what they gathered from the standards, the ideas, and the ideologies of the people and the new civilization in which they live. But I repeat: we had brought ourselves. We had not come with nothing.

I do not think it was at all accidental that, after a dozen years of fighting, these men showed themselves equal to the soldiers of Napoleon, the finest army Europe had then known. They are our people. They are our ancestors. If we want to know what the ordinary population can do, let us know what they have done in the past. It is the way of life, not blood, that matters.

The Negro people in the Caribbean are of the same stock as the men who played such a role in the history of their time. We are the product of the same historical past and the same type of life, and as long as we are not being educated by the Colonial Office (or the stooges of financial interests), we shall be able to do whatever we have to do. We have to remember that where slavery was abolished by law, the great mass of the Negro slaves had shown that they were ready to take any steps that were necessary to free themselves. That was a very important step in the making of the Caribbean people.

We now have to move on to more modern times, and we shall be able to do that more confidently and easily because what we are, both positively and negatively, is the result of what we have been. I shall use two examples, the example of Trinidad and the example of Barbados. Trinidad first. I shall use this to explain the particularity of the insular history of the different islands. We know that Trinidad produced the most remarkable politician of the British West Indies during the twentieth century, Arthur Andrew Cipriani.[9] Now, where did he come from? In Trinidad, we had a number of Frenchmen who came to the island in the last years of the 18th century. First of all, they were able to find a source of economic progress independent of the sugar estates, and therefore were independent of the sugar magnates and of the colonial officials. They were, some of them, men of great culture, and fully able to stand up against the domination of sugar planters and colonial officials. They had a language of their own, in addition to their economic independence. They had a religion of their own, they were Roman Catholic and therefore were able to feel a differentiation between their religion and the Protestant religion of British domination. Therefore, while they shared to some degree the superior status and opportunities that all local Whites had, they were constantly aware of themselves as a body of people distinct from, and even opposed to at times, the British colonial caste.

That was the origin of the independent political attitude that Cipriani took from the beginning of the First World War toward the opportunities for West Indian self-assertion that the War of 1914–1918 presented to the West Indian people, at least in the general opinion of the times. So we get it clearly, Cipriani was able to take the stand that he did because the French Creoles had a long tradition of independent economic life and social differentiation.

That's to begin with. But there was more to Cipriani. I remember seeing the soldiers who went to the war of 1914–1918. Many of them wore shoes consistently for the first time. To the astonishment of everybody (I believe not excluding the men themselves and Captain Cipriani), they became soldiers who were able to hold their own in the complicated techniques of modern warfare and the social relations that accompany it; to hold their own with soldiers not only from Britain, but from some of the most advanced countries in the Commonwealth.

Cipriani never forgot that, never. From that time, he advocated independence, self-government, and federation on the basis that the West Indian rank and file, "the bare-footed man," as he called him, was able to hold his own with any sort of people anywhere. He had seen it in war, a stern test. That was the basis of his ceaseless agitation from island to island in the British Caribbean, mobilizing labor against capital for the independence and federation of the West Indies.

So, you see that Cipriani was no historical accident. He was able to discover that the tremendous qualities of the Caribbean population (I began with this) were due to the fact that history had presented him with political opportunities unfolding the capacities of a highly developed people. These West Indian soldiers were the descendants of Toussaint's army.

Now another example, Barbados. Barbados is one of the most highly developed, most highly civilized territories in the extra-European world. You will have noticed that, of the middle-class people in the early years of political activity, there was only one member of the Black middle class who took a prominent and, in fact, very important part. That was Sir Grantley Adams. And while I do not wish to make Grantley and the fine work he did merely a product of historical circumstances, I have to say that, of the Caribbean territories, Barbados alone has had an unbroken tradition of political activity and actually had a House of Assembly.

In Barbados, therefore, there was something for Grantley Adams to join. He had to sacrifice a great deal. At times, his life was in danger. But we have to know that in those revolutionary days, nowhere else did any member of the Black middle class enter into politics. Today a whole lot of them are very noisy politicos, the way is very easy; you get a good salary, you can become a minister, and you can go to England and be entertained by English royalty! But Cipriani and Grantley Adams started before World War II. In those days, there was nothing but work and danger.

Now, I come to my final contention. As late as 1945, the number of people in the Caribbean who had the vote was less than 5 percent. I say that if we look properly at who and what we were, we were long ready for self-government and independence, most certainly by 1920. I go further, and I say that by delaying the achievement of self-government, having to appoint a Royal Commission after the upheavals of 1937–1938, and by the mean and grudging granting to so many the vote, so many to become ministers, and all the palaver and so-called education by which the British government claimed that it trained the West Indian population for self-government, a terrible damage was inflicted upon us.

In reality, our people were mis-educated, our political consciousness was twisted and broken. Far from being guided to independence by the 1960s, from the 1920 onwards, for forty years, the imperialist governments poisoned and corrupted that sense of self-confidence and political dynamic needed for any people about to embark on the uncharted seas of independence and nationhood. We are still without that self-confidence and that dynamic today. We lack them because for the last half-century we were deprived of making the Caribbean people what our history and achievements had made possible, and for which we were ready. That, then is my conclusion. They have not educated, they have mis-educated us, stood in our way, piled burdens on our backs.

Let me quote one of our most profound analysts: "Free is how you is from the start, an' when it look different you got to move, just move, an' when you movin' say that it is a natural freedom that make you move."[106] That is George Lamming, than whom no one has a clearer view of words like independence, freedom, and liberty.

Still, we have made history. As evidence of what we can make of ourselves, I need only add some of the names our people from the Caribbean have inscribed on the pages of history.

Here I shall give a list of names, a list without which it is impossible to write of the history and literature of Western Civilization. No account of Western civilization could leave out the names of Toussaint L'Ouverture, Alexander Hamilton, Alexander Dumas (the father), Leconte Delisle, Jose Maria de Heredia, Marcus Garvey, Rene Maran, Saint-John Perse, Aimé Césaire, George Padmore, Frantz Fanon, and allow me to include one contemporary, a Cuban writer, Alejo Carpentier. I do not mention the remarkable novelists whom we of the British Caribbean have produced during the last twenty years. I end this list by a name acknowledged by critics all over the world as an unprecedented, unimaginable practitioner of his particular art—I refer, of course, to Garfield Sobers.

The Haitian Revolution in the Making of the Modern World

Thank you Mr. Chairman. Now, I like to know for myself, and I mention it to you in passing, the time now I take to be five-minutes to four o'clock. I will be finished at twenty-five or twenty to five, when the questions begin. I don't want to speak longer than about forty to forty-five minutes.

The history of the Haitian Revolution is not a difficult subject for me to do within a certain time. But, on this occasion, we have to take the Haitian Revolution as symbolic of the whole series of revolts of Black people in the New World. That's what I'm going to do. I'm going to begin with the Haitian Revolution and after that I'm going to spend some time on the Civil War in the United States. There, again, we have Black people, Black slaves, moving into a great historical situation.

But before I do that, I want to say a few words about the Cuban Revolution, because the Haitian slave revolt was a revolt in a West Indian island of a certain social structure. Cuba is of the same kind and the Haitian Revolution has many affiliations with the Cuban Revolution. So, I will begin within Cuban Revolution, then I will go to the Haitian Revolution; then I will go to the Civil War in the United States, and then I'll go somewhere which you will know when I tell you. I'm going to keep that a secret and I hope you will be pleasantly titillated. [*Laughter*]

Now, the Cuban Revolution takes place in the 20th century. It is the twentieth-century representative of what had taken place previously in French San Domingo at the end of the 18th century. The two revolutions are very closely allied. It is not so much a question of race or of color. That is what I want to emphasize. There will be, perhaps, a third of the population of Cuba which is Colored. The point is they are both West Indian communities; both are sugar plantation communities; both are, to some degree, communities which, while not advanced, nevertheless are built on the structure of Western civilization. Although many of them, much of the population in those parts of the world, are living at a level scarcely above slavery, in social structure and, above all, in the language that they use, they have a European cast of mind. That is why the Cuban Revolution has taken place in the way that it has. That is another reason why it has not yet taken place in many of the other West Indian islands; because, among other reasons, if and when it does take place, it will take place along the structure of the Haitian Revolution and of the Cuban Revolution.

So what is there about the Cuban Revolution that I want you to know? There are a few things. Number one: after ten years, it is today stronger than ever it was before [*Applause*]. Now, that is not merely something inspiring and something that I say to lift us up. After the English Revolution, they cut off Charles the I's head in 1649, and that was a decisive point—decisive for his head and decisive for the revolution [*Laughter*]. Ten years afterwards, Charles I came back, 1659–1660. It is quite true and, as Hilaire Belloc has said, royalty came back, monarchy did not.[1] Cromwell had settled that for good and all. But in ten years, that revolution was done. In the French Revolution of 1789, they accomplished miracles by 1794. By 1799 they had descended into the grip of Napoleon Bonaparte, the First Consul—ten years. In the Russian Revolution of 1917, by 1927 everything that was Leninist was wiped away. The Cuban Revolution is the first of the great revolutions which, after ten years, is stronger than it was at the beginning. [*Applause*]

Now, it is very interesting to watch how that revolution has gone. When the English Revolution took place and Charles's head was rolling in the basket or whatever it was, Cromwell and company then had to sit down to decide what they were going to do with this society that they had taken over. Whatever the program and policy, whatever the kind of party, when the revolutionary body actually seizes power, it then is faced, for the first time, with what it is going to do with it. Cromwell was in a lot of trouble. First, he tried to continue with the Parliament, then he tried to become the Major-General. Then he tried himself as Protector, and that ended it. When he died, the whole thing was over.

Likewise, the French Revolution was in a lot of trouble until 1793, and between 1793 and 1794 it found itself with the Committee of Public Safety and the Committee of General Security. The Russian Revolution in October 1917 didn't know exactly where it was. The workers were saying one thing. Lenin was saying, "Well, nationalize, but don't nationalize too much. Let's have workers' power, but not workers' power but workers' control," etc. That went on until the Tenth Party Congress in 1921. Having defeated the counter-revolution, the Russian Communist Party settled down to find out what they were going do with this country that they now had hold of. Every revolution tells you the same thing.

The Cuban Revolution is no different. When Castro had gone a certain distance with the Cuban Revolution, had taken power, he was talking about the need to help the peasant proprietor and the agricultural laborer, and the need to overthrow Batista. But when that was done, what were they going to do with the revolution? They didn't know. Then came the Bay of Pigs, and immediately after the Bay of Pigs Castro announced, "Well, we are now Marxist-Leninists." They asked him, "How long?" He said, "I don't know. When I was younger, I was a Marxist-Leninist by instinct, but I didn't know it. But now we are Marxist-Leninists." [*Applause*]

I am not in any way disturbed that they found their way to it in that way because, in the history of revolutions, that is how they find their way. In the San Domingo Revolution, they found their way in the same manner, but it is very noticeable that, ultimately, in the San Domingo Revolution there was a clean sweep of everything and everybody who was connected with the old regime. In the Cuban Revolution of today, there is a clean sweep of everything and everybody concerned with the old regime. That is not due to the fact that they are Black people; that is due to the fact that they are a West Indian community, closely allied, using a modern language, jammed together, and able to develop themselves with tremendous force. If they were in some parts Africa, they wouldn't be able to do it that way. I want you to watch the social structure and the geographical structure of the community to understand the Cuban Revolution and also to understand the Haitian Revolution.

I can now go back to the Haitian Revolution. This revolution took place in close association with the French Revolution. The French Revolution began in 1789, but they didn't bother with the slaves. Later, when the Girondins came into power and the bourgeoisie was in power, then they began to think, well, they should help the Haitian mulattoes and give them power, but they left the slaves alone. Then, by 1791, the slaves said, "Well, we are going deal with it." They felt that they were following the French Revolution. But in France, they thought the Black slaves had killed their masters and taken over the property. They weren't exactly correct but, more or less, they had the thing in general—the slaves had swept away the plantation owners and took over the sugar estates.

Now, to understand the course of that revolution, you have to understand that the sugar estates were one of the most advanced forms of economic structure in the world at the time. Although they are a very backward element in the 20th century, in the 18th century they were very advanced and were making a great deal of money. There were large plantations in the northern part San Domingo—500 slaves here, a 1000 slaves there, 200, 300—a vast number of slaves concentrated in large sugar plantations. So, altogether, they were nearer to the modern proletariat than any other social structure of plebeians or revolutionaries of the time. You must think of that as a highly organized social structure with the great mass of the slaves living around the plantation. That was the basic geographical structure. They had at their disposal the French language in which to express themselves and, still more important, they had the ideas of the French Revolution by which to develop themselves. In other words, that was a perfect situation and they developed it perfectly.

These people were backward, but as we learned this morning,[2] they had a certain integrity, a certain social consciousness of their own, which was developed apart from their masters. That was shown, not only in general and by observers who watched them closely, but also by what took place in the revolution. The revolution took place and, before long, they had made a clean sweep and were completely in charge of San Domingo.

Now I want to show the influence that this revolution had on the French Revolution. This morning I made it clear that the French Revolution, which was the political counterpart, one might say, of the industrial revolution, marked a tremendous stage in the development of human society. What I want you to know, and what historians don't usually pay attention to—none of the great French historians, a body of people whom I respect profoundly—none of them have ever been able to treat this question of the immense value that the San Domingo Revolution had for the French Revolution. For six years the British army was trying to capture the French colony of San Domingo and they were defeated, hook, line, and sinker, by the ex-slave army.

Fortescue, the historian of the British Army, says that England's impotence for the first six years of the war, up to that time, the greatest war in history,[3] was to be explained by two words—San Domingo. Fortescue says that Pitt and Dundas believed that they only had to fight some backward Negro slaves, but after six years they found that they had destroyed the British army. It is the greatest defeat ever suffered by any expedition from Great Britain. It is established by the official historian of the British Army that they endured that defeat and were paralyzed in their attempts to deal with the French Revolution by what happened with the slaves fighting under the French colors in San Domingo. That, I think, is a great historical event.

The second thing I want to refer to, as a historical development, is the abolition of slavery. Now, all of you here know a lot about Pitt and you know about Wilberforce, and you know also that the queen abolished slavery—which she did not. When the Bill was passed, she was not even on the throne of England. It was passed 1834, and she came to the throne in 1837. But these are absurdities and falsities which the West Indian people still have. The time will come when they will clear that away. [*Applause*]

What I want you to note is this: slavery was abolished by a European parliamentary body in 1794, and the way it was abolished was this: French San Domingo sent three representatives to the French parliament. One was a White man, one was a Colored man, a mulatto, and one was a Black man. The name of the Black man was Bellay. They were welcomed by the president of the assembly and, the day following, Bellay made a tremendous speech in the Chamber, calling upon the French parliament to abolish slavery. After the speech, Levasseur (of Sarthe) got up and told the president, "We have not done properly by the Negroes and I move that this assembly abolish slavery without a debate." Slavery was abolished without a debate after the speech by Bellay, who was himself a slave who had bought his own freedom. I believe that when we are studying the Negro past, that is a piece of history that we should know as well as we know Pitt and Wilberforce and the rest of them. [*Applause*]

So, they did this work and they fought until 1798. The British army was destroyed and they had to form a new army, and so on; the French kept on; the Negro slaves made progress; Toussaint L'Ouverture was made the

Governor and then he became Commander-in-Chief. There were many Negro generals, some of whom could not sign their name. Their names had to be written in pencil and then they traced it over in ink (I have read the reports). Nevertheless, they dictated first class reports. To dictate a first class report, you need not know how to write, you need not know how to read. I am sure that it is so today as it was a hundred and fifty years ago [*Laughter*]. To dictate a first class report, you have to do something, and those men were doing something, and to see their reports and signatures in the French national archives is very extraordinary.

Well, in 1799 or thereabouts, Napoleon sent an army to fight against them. The slaves had fought against the Spaniards, they had fought against the local plantation owners, they had fought against the British and defeated a British army of nearly 100,000 men. Then Napoleon sent this expedition to fight against them. When he sent them, Toussaint was already the Governor and I want to read you one or two passages on Toussaint as Governor of San Domingo. (Bobby has been talking about Marcus Garvey and putting him in historical framework.[4] I'm very glad to hear this, because that is the way you understand, and are able to take part in, great events, in a concrete manner but, nevertheless, aware of what is taking place.) This concern with the international movement has been a characteristic of Negro slaves in the New World. This is a passage I wrote about Toussaint:

> Firm as was his grasp of reality, old Toussaint looked beyond San Domingo with a boldness of imagination surpassed by no contemporary. In the Constitution, he authorized the slave-trade because the island needed people to cultivate it. When the Africans landed, however, they would be free men. But while loaded with the cares of government, he cherished a project *[James: Take note of this please when you think of Garvey]* of sailing to Africa with arms, ammunition and a thousand of his best soldiers, and there conquering vast tracts of country, putting an end to the slave-trade, and making millions of blacks "free and French," as his Constitution had made the blacks of San Domingo.[5]

There is something in the African who is in the New World that gives him this tremendous scope in any action. The originator of the movement that we know today as Pan-Africanism is nobody else than that American scholar, William Edward Burghart Du Bois.[6] He is the person who did it; started it in every way, did the historical writings, organized to suit, and organized Pan-African conference after Pan-African conference. When I see Toussaint doing these things, something strikes me and I wonder a great deal at what is happening—I get a little clearer as to what is to happen, too.

> It was no dream. He had sent millions of francs to America to wait for the day when he would be ready. He was already 55. What spirit was it that moved him? Ideas do not fall from heaven. The great revolution had propelled him out of his humble joys and obscure destiny, and the trumpets of its heroic period run ever in his ears. In him, born a slave and the leader of slaves, the concrete realization of liberty, equality and fraternity was the womb of ideas and the springs of power, which overflowed their narrow environment and embraced the whole of the world.[7]

Now take note of this:

> But for the revolution, this extraordinary man and his band of gifted associates would have lived their lives as slaves, serving the commonplace creatures who owned them, standing barefooted and in rags to watch inflated little governors and mediocre officials from Europe pass by, as many a talented African stands in Africa to-day.[8]

That I wrote in 1938. I am very proud of it. I was not afraid that things were going to take place. [*Applause*]

Then came the great War of Independence. If you want to know who are the African people in the Caribbean today and what they are capable of, we have to know what our ancestors were, what they did, because we are the same type of people. We must not forget that. It's in the history of San Domingo and the history of these revolts that you will see the potential of these people in the New World. Before we are finished, I will give a glimpse of what has taken place in Africa under very different circumstances.

Now, here is General Leclerc and his army in San Domingo. Bonaparte has sent him (Leclerc is married to Bonaparte's sister) and Leclerc is writing letters home. He says, "The first attacks have driven the rebels from the positions they occupied [*James: You know, if you are fighting for freedom, you're a rebel (Applause and laughter)*]; but they fell back to other cantons and in the insurrection there is a veritable fanaticism. These men get themselves killed, but they refuse to surrender."[9] Those are my ancestors and I am very proud of them [*Applause*]. Here is some more. Leclerc is writing again to his brother-in-law, the great Napoleon: "It is not enough to have taken away Toussaint, there are 2,000 leaders to be taken away."[10]

You know, you go about and listen to some of these people today asking, "Where are the leaders? We have no leaders. This one is not good, that one is only there because so and so, that other one ...." I am positive that in Jamaica, in Trinidad, in Barbados today, there are 20,000 leaders ready to take whatever ... [words drowned out by applause]. I'm getting near to the end of this. Leclerc finally writes: "Unfortunately the condition of the colonies is not known in France. We have there a false idea of the Negro"[11] "We have in Europe a false idea of the country in which we fight and the men whom we fight against."[12] It was bad enough for Leclerc, a stranger, to have a false idea of the country in which he fought and of the men whom he fought against. In 1968, there are West Indians in the West Indies who have a false idea of the country in which they live and the men who live around them. [*Applause*]

Now let me give you a final statement about the San Domingo Revolution. Lemmonier-Delafosse was a soldier who fought in the War of Independence. Many years afterwards he wrote his memoirs of the last stage of the war in which they were defeated. Here is what he says. It is a notable passage. They (the slaves) sang their songs and he says:

> "This song was worth all of our republican songs. Three times these brave men, arms in hand, advanced without firing a shot, and each time repulsed, only retired after leaving the ground strewed with three-quarters of their troops. One must have seen this bravery to have any conception of it. Those songs shouted into the sky in unison by 2,000 voices, to which the cannon formed the bass, produced a thrilling effect. French courage alone could resist it. Indeed, large ditches, an excellent artillery, perfect soldiers gave us a great advantage. But for many a day, that massed square which marched singing to its death, lighted by a magnificent sun, remained in my thoughts, and even to-day after more than 40 years, this majestic and glorious spectacle still lives as vividly in my imagination as in the moments when I saw it."[13]

A dozen years before these people had been slaves. Then they were able to fight the army of Napoleon which, up to that day, was the finest army that Europe had yet seen. But in 1920 they (the colonialists) say, "Well, we don't know if you are fit for self-government. We will have five more men in the Legislature; and then, in 1930, we'll put one in the Executive Council; and then in 1935 we'll put two more in the Executive Council. But in 1937, it isn't doing so well, we will take away all of those. So we are training you up all the time."

Now, I want you to understand my point of view. What has been happening is this: for the last fifty years the British government, the French government, and the rest of them have been corrupting the political consciousness of the mass of the population in the Caribbean territories [*Applause*] by constantly arguing about whether they are fit enough to govern or whether they could have two men more in the Legislature and one man more in the Executive; to what extent the Governor would have powers; whether he should be in charge of the police and the army; whether they could take the police but not the army [*Laughter*] and all this kind of business. They have been a source of corruption of the political development of the people in the Caribbean.

The history of San Domingo shows that after a few years of civil war, they were perfectly able to do anything that the Europeans were able to do, both as an army and in terms of government. Many of the governors of San Domingo were slaves, unable to write. Yet people who examined them said that they showed a capacity to govern which was better than the capacity that would have been shown by French peasants and other persons of a low order in France. That was because they had nothing in their minds but freedom, and they saw freedom in the terms of the French Revolution, which had helped them to liberate themselves. We need not be afraid of what the Caribbean people are likely to do. The stage of revolution that has been reached in the world at the time, and the ideas which have been developed, will be taken over by any revolution of the great mass of the population, as those ideas were taken over by the French revolutionaries in the French colony of San Domingo.

Now, I want to stop there for a minute and go over to the United States. We have a tremendous movement in the Civil War in the United States. First of all, we had revolts—Nat Turner, Denmark Vesey, and these other revolts. Then, around 1830, they decide that the plain, straightforward revolt against the oppressors would not do, and they worked out another system. I don't think we thoroughly understand what was taking place in the United States between 1830 and, say, 1878. The American Negro slaves or Afro-

Americans, whatever the phrase is (I don't want to give any offence, I'll call him whatever it is [Laughter]), decided that they were not going to make a plain, straightforward revolt. They were going to use the Underground Railroad and, by the thousands, escape from slavery into freedom. That helped to break up the system, the fact that in their numbers, by tens, by dozens—day after day—they were escaping.

Not only did those who left give the slave owners trouble, but they [the slave-masters] never knew whom they had, who would escape, or who would not escape. That was the situation in the country. When Garrison began in the North, there was hostility to the idea of the abolitionists' end of slavery. But later, the South wanted to make an arrangement whereby they would be compelled, in the North, to capture any slaves who had escaped, and the North revolted. They said, "To hell with you. You come for your slaves. We are not going to be any catcher of slaves for you." The result was that the arrangement which the North wanted to work out with the South could not be worked out—they could not manage it—and the abolitionist movement began in the wake of this and the constant escaping of Negro slaves.

The abolitionist movement—that is one of the great political movements of the United States. The people of the United States do not know that. As the years go by, they will begin to find out that the real beginnings of independent revolutionary politics in the Untied States have to be sought in the abolitionist movement. That movement was predominantly a movement of Negro slaves and free Negroes in the North. The abolitionist papers were supported by and subscribed to by a majority of Negro people. The great leaders of the abolitionist movement were not only Garrison and Wendell Phillips, but one of the greatest political leaders America has ever had, Fredrick Douglass.

Working out policies, Garrison and Phillips stated, "We have our movement and the Constitution of the United States is a slave constitution and, therefore, the southern part of the United States must be split off from the north and, therefore, we will have freedom in the north when the Constitution allows us to split away because the Constitution is a slave constitution." Wendell Phillips, a most remarkable man, said further: "If that takes place and we split off from them and they are free, inevitably there will be a Negro revolt and the Negroes will take power and we'll be able to join again." Garrison didn't go so far. Douglass broke with them on that issue and founded his own paper. This split was serious because fundamental issues were involved.

Douglass said, "You are saying that the Constitution of the United States is a pro-slavery constitution. It is nothing of the kind. Both in its origin, and in the details of the Constitution, it is not a pro-slavery document." He says (I remember certain parts), "'We the people.' That's what it says. It doesn't say we the horses, we the dogs, we the cows. It says, 'we the people,' and if Black people are people it means we the Black people too." He fought tremendously with Garrison and these fellows on that issue, and that caused the split in the movement. It was a split, you can understand, on a highly political issue. When the Civil War came, it was proved that Douglass was the man along whose lines the battle was fought.

Now, there is something which I am very sorry I do not hear more about. I want to read to you passage from a very great historian. It is from one of the greatest history books ever written, *Black Reconstruction*, by W.E. Burghart Du Bois. Du Bois quotes a passage from Lincoln where Lincoln says,

ABANDON ALL THE POSTS NOW GARRISONED BY BLACK MEN; TAKE TWO HUNDRED THOUSAND MEN FROM OUR SIDE AND PUT THEM IN BATTLEFIELD OR CORNFIELD AGAINST US, AND WE WOULD BE COMPELLED TO ABANDON THE WAR IN THREE WEEKS.[14]

Lincoln said it repeatedly. The fact is that the Civil War and the victory of the North, which made the United States a modern country and what it is today, could not have been won without the active participation of Black people, in labor and in the army, whom it was supposed to free at the time [*Applause*]. That is the reality. I know one reason why that has taken place. Lincoln had said, "I would abolish slavery if it would help to cement the Union; and to maintain the Union, I would free half the slaves and keep half of them slaves. And if needed be, to maintain the Union, I would maintain all as slaves." That, undoubtedly, Lincoln said. But that is not the main thing. I want to go into some statements about Lincoln. Do you remember what he said at the Second Inaugural? It was a tremendous statement:

One-eighth of the whole population were colored slaves, not distributed generally over the Union, but localized in the southern part of it. These slaves constituted a peculiar and powerful interest. All knew that this interest was somehow the cause of the war. To strengthen, perpetuate, and extend this interest was the object for which the insurgents would rend the Union even by war, while the Government claimed no right to do more than to restrict the territorial enlargement of it. Neither party expected for the war the magnitude or the duration which it has already attained. Neither anticipated that the *cause* of the conflict might cease with, or even before, the conflict itself should cease. Each looked for an easier triumph, and a result less fundamental and astounding. Both read the same Bible, and pray to the same God; and each invokes His aid against the other. It may seem strange that any men should dare to ask a just God's assistance in wringing their bread from the sweat of other men's faces [*James: It isn't so strange today (Laughter from the crowd).*] but let us judge not, that we be not judged. The prayers of both could not be answered. That of neither has been answered fully. The Almighty has His own purposes. "Woe unto the world because of offenses; for it must needs be that offenses come, but woe to that man by whom the offense cometh." If we shall suppose that American slavery is one of those offenses which, in the providence of God, must needs come, but which, having continued through His appointed time, He now wills to remove, and that He gives to both North and South this terrible war as the woe due to those by whom the offense came, shall we discern therein any departure from those divine attributes which the believers in a living God always ascribe to Him? Fondly do we hope, fervently do we pray, that this mighty scourge of war may speedily pass away. Yet, if God wills that it continue until all the wealth piled by the bondsman's two hundred and fifty years of unrequited toil shall be sunk, and until every drop of blood drawn with the lash shall be paid by another drawn with the sword, as was said three thousand years ago, so still it must be said "the judgments of the Lord are true and righteous altogether."

Now, that is a tremendous thing that Lincoln said. I'll read it again. [*Laughter*]

Yet, if God wills that it continue until all the wealth piled by the bondsman's two hundred and fifty years of unrequited toil shall be sunk, and until every drop of blood drawn with the lash shall be paid by another drawn with the sword, as was said three thousand years ago, so still it must be said "the judgments of the Lord are true and righteous altogether."

Now, people were wondering if America was going to destroy itself because of the slaves who were persecuted. Lincoln did not begin that way. There is a letter that he wrote to a friend some time in 1841. He said he was traveling on the boat and there was a family of Negro slaves there. He says they were being driven away from their friends, being sold to the South, and they were the funniest people you could think of. They were laughing and making jokes all the time, and he couldn't understand how people in that situation could have behaved in that way. That is a very striking thing for Lincoln to have said because, later, Lincoln was to say, "We who made the revolution in 1776 formed a particular generation. Our children still have that tradition in them." He says, "People from abroad may come from different parts of Europe and learn this revolutionary tradition that makes the nation what it is." He didn't say, but he believed, that Negroes could not make it; that they could not take part in what he felt that the American nation was. Lincoln believed that right up to 1862.

In 1862, the people, the colonizationists, the people who were saying that the Negroes should be deported to some parts of Africa or something, had a sympathetic ear from Lincoln. He said, "Well, let us discuss it." But later he began to see that to win the war he had to bring the Negroes in. He finally brought them in, uncertain whether they would stand to that high pitch which he felt had been established in America by those who had fought the revolution of 1776, and which had been descended to them through the years. He got to know that Negroes were able to stand it; that they were enabled by the war to stand up to all the pressures and necessities.

We have that tremendous statement which so many Americans don't understand, "that government of the people, by the people, for the people shall not perish from the earth." What does that mean? Lincoln says, "Four score and seven years ago we founded a new society. And if now we have to see that government of the people, by the people, for the people, should not perish, it means government of the people"—including the Black people— "for the people"—including the Black people—"by the people"—including the Black people.[15]

Those later speeches by Lincoln, the Second Inaugural and the Gettysburg speech, were speeches that incorporated the mass of the Negro people, the ex-slaves, into the American community. Lincoln now had a very advanced conception of what the American community was. Following the Civil War, Lincoln thought, "Well, we must bring them in because they are perfectly able to take part in it." I would like to hear their propagandists and others of the American community make the situation of Lincoln and these others quite clear. The war was not fought for the abolition of slavery, but the war came to an end because the slaves had proved themselves fully able to stand by anybody in the American community and carry out the great principles that had been established in 1776.

That is the American Civil War. Now, I go to what I have been keeping secret. I want to speak about what happened in an African state, what happened in Kenya, in 1953. The Kenyan people had not been under the domination of the British for many years. They, unfortunately for them, had a high plateau with a nice piece of land and good climate, and some Europeans settled themselves there and established some agricultural plantations and said, "Kenya is ours and we are going to live here. We are going to help the poor Africans, but this is ours and we are going to remain here." In 1953, a Kenyan minister landed at the airport in London and they asked him, "What is the situation in Kenya?" and he said, "It has never been so good. Everything is going fine and the people are quite satisfied and we are carrying on the colony as it ought to be carried on." It wasn't a few weeks afterwards that the revolt broke out.

We have not been able, as yet, to get a proper account of what took place in Kenya. We are in the habit of talking about Mau Mau. Now it is clearly proved today that Mau Mau was a creation of British colonialism. It was nothing native to the people of Kenya. It was the result of their attempt to try to get something with which they could fight against the Christian missionaries and the "democracy" and "advanced morals" which the British had been giving to them, and of which they were tired. The people of Kenya were not able to fight as the West Indians have been able to fight, as the American slaves were able to fight—to join an army in a modern society. They had to take to the woods and form their armies in the woods. They would hit and run in Nairobi and round about, but, essentially, their basis was what they could do in the woods, fighting with a native army, made up, how they could, with troops acquired cheaply from the people they were fighting against.

Then there was General Kimathi, who unfortunately was killed, and General China, who is alive today. They organized themselves and they fought the British to a standstill. At one time, the British had two divisions there, a great number of airplanes, walkie-talkies (radios)—every blessed thing that they could have to defeat the people. At one time, the British not only defeated the Mau Mau army in the field, they also had 50,000 Kenyan people in detention camps, and had won the war. They had Kenyatta in prison, but they now had to settle and they couldn't do anything with the people in the detention camps whom they told, "If you say you will change and will not do any old thing, etc., we'll let you go." And they [the Kenyans] told them, "You go to hell, we are not going to say anything. We are going to stay right here."

The British were absolutely paralyzed by it. You must remember that they had won the war in Kenya. They had defeated the army and the Mau Mau were hiding in the forest. And they found that they couldn't govern the people at all. So, they had to send for Kenyatta and allow him to move around and govern in Kenya. Today they are giving up the land on the plateau.

I mention this to say that we talked about the Haitian slave revolt, and I have talked about the Civil War in the United States and the tremendous role played there by the slaves, but let us not forget Africa, Kenya in particular. On the one side, there was Nkrumah organizing them in the modern democratic way and demanding democratic rights from the British government; on the other side of Africa, there was an absolutely independent revolutionary struggle which had tremendous odds to compete against, which was actually defeated in the field, but such was the power of the people that the British government finally had to give way.

I don't think we can understand the Haitian Revolution and the revolts in the New World by the slaves unless we understand what was taking place in Africa many years afterwards, and link the two of them together, as Bobby has tried to do with Garvey.

Thank you very much, Mr. Chairman. [*Long applause*]

MODERATOR: Thank you Mr. James. Ladies and gentlemen, I'm sure you have heard more than the usual point of controversial statements in the last speech and I'm sure that you will have plenty of questions.

QUESTION: Mr. James has made a very brilliant analysis of the Haitian Revolution and, as a Black man, I am very proud that my ancestors were so great. But for the benefit of my Black American and Black West Indian brothers, I want to speak about the situation in Haiti now.

After the revolution, the White imperialists have tried their best to isolate us because they thought it could help the slave system by which they live. In 1915, American imperialism sent their troops down there. They were trying to make some plantations so they would have sugar cane. They killed thousands of Haitians by mating with decent Haitians because of the lady factor. When they finally left, because they could not really have the whole country like a whole American plantation— the resistance was too hard—they left a social crisis behind them. This is called neo-colonialism.

Now, right now in Haiti, we have a man, he's a Black man, he's the ruler of Haiti. He did not just come. He's representative of the social crisis called neo-colonialism in which a certain class of the society exploits or serves as the servants of American imperialism. Excuse me. I know I was supposed to ask a question [*Laughter*]. You will excuse me. I find it is very vital, you know, because [*Applause*] I have spent three months in the United States and I find that many Black Americans tell me that they love Papa Doc because he's a Black man. I'm telling you, I'm going to identify with no Black man because he's a Black man [*Applause*]. I will identify with a Black American because he struggles, because he is fighting against White American capitalism. That means, when the Black Panthers, or whatever you have down there, start breaking down or blowing up Wall Street [*Sporadic applause*], the citizens of America will, at the same time, have to send troops to Haiti because we have revolutionary parties working down there [in] guerrilla warfare. It is very low right now, but it's going. [*Applause*]

We are very aware of the fact that Americans will have to send troops down there to protect the Black puppets, to protect the interests of their servants. These servants are Black, culturally speaking—a lot of shit about the cultural aspect of Black Power, you see. Now this is Black Power, you know—Black men running the country. Now the question is a statement to you. Once you want to use the capitalist system, I tell you, you are going to work hand-in-hand with the same men that are killing children in Vietnam now [*Applause*]. So, I will repeat that [*Laughter*]. I mean that, I will repeat, I myself, when I go in a demonstration, or do something that contests the system, the capitalist system, I know I am working for the liberation of my people. I know that I am working for the bringing up of that new world. So that it is not just an idealistic thing because, in Haiti, ninety-three percent of the population, they don't know how to read, you know. They don't know about human dignity. They need help, whereas you can go into town and find those Black bourgeois with 1968 American cars and tall buildings.

So, therefore, I will stress again that I identify with the struggle of Black Americans and I would do anything to help this struggle as long as the Black American is fighting, not just against a substance called racism which is the cause of that system; but as long as the Black American is fighting racism, is fighting in my interest, and I am fighting in his interest too. I thank you. [*Long Applause*]

JAMES: I am very glad that that comrade had the determination to interpret the word "question" in a very revolutionary way [*Laughter and applause*]. Secondly, I would like to tell you a few facts and one or two things that we think. I have been invited to Haiti. I was invited by the head of the military mission when they had read my book, *The Black Jacobans*, translated into French.[16] And I was able to tell them, very politely (I'm a polite person), that I am afraid that I couldn't possibly come there under any circumstances. I would have to go and say, "Well, I'm very happy to be here and I think you are doing well enough," or something. I would have to do it. I preferred not to go. That is why I have not been able to go to Haiti. [*Applause*]

Secondly, I hope my friend there knows that the real support of Duvalier is the United States government [*Applause*]. Duvalier's government is the worst and most corrupt government in Latin America. There is no doubt about it [*Applause*]. But he is able to continue because, although he is rude to the United States and he robs tourists who go there, etc., nevertheless, the United States continues to support him, and not to support anybody who wants to overthrow him. And the reason is very simple: they prefer a thousand Duvaliers to another revolution that might produce another Fidel Castro [*Applause*]. They can stand Duvalier, any number of Duvaliers. They have some at home too [*Laughter*], but a revolt, they don't want to have. And we must be aware of this.

I have no doubt whatever that the American State Department and the rest of them are quite aware of what took place in the San Domingo Revolution. They are more than ever aware of what took place in the Cuban Revolution, and they are aware—they ran to the Dominican Republic quick in order to prevent a revolution because any revolution that takes place in the Caribbean is going to do what the other two have done, its going to make a clean sweep [*Applause*]. Maybe a little later I will tell you something about what one expert in Caribbean revolution has said, but the occasion has not appeared for the time being, and maybe it will before we are finished this afternoon.[17]

QUESTION: I think that we should break to attach this thought to what Mr. James just said. I hope that this congress gives the American State Department justifiable reason for being aware of what's going on here this weekend [*Sporadic laughter*]. And for the brother over there, I would like to say that we in America will do our best to keep the American troops as busy as possible [*Applause, laughter, and cheers*]. We're going to do this because we're all pretty much aware of the great significance of the revolution in the West Indies. And if you identify, my brother, with the struggle in Black America, then you automatically identify with the struggle in Africa, which must be our intellectual and revolutionary focal point.

And now to pose my questions [*Laughter*]. This is not directly about Haiti, but we are all indirectly associated with one another so my question is good [*Laughter*]. My question is regarding the ultimate goal of the African liberation struggle in the United States, and it's in four parts. [*Laughter*]

JAMES: One part at a time please. [*Laughter*]

QUESTION: You'll find that each question refines the other until you end up with one question [*Laughter*]. Part one: What should one of the objectives of African Americans be? Part two: Seeing that it is difficult to fight for land, what should the goal be? Part three: How do you envision the lives of Black Americans once the struggle has been waged and won? And part four: What message would this congress send back to Black Americans to give them a better understanding about the kinds of power they see while they live in an ocean of white faces? [*Applause*]

JAMES: Now the last question, what message the congress should send? Naturally, I'll leave that to the congress, so I haven't to answer that one. In regard to the rest of the struggle, I want to make some statements that refer to this struggle in a rather historical and yet concrete manner.

The first point I wish to make is, in 1935–1936, George Padmore began the International African Service Bureau. And Jomo Kenyatta came into it, and later Kwame Nkrumah came, Wallace-Johnson, and one or two others. There were never more than ten of us. Never. And most of the people we dealt with thought that we were perhaps some politically well-meaning, but politically illiterate, West Indians talking and writing about the independence of Africa—"What kind of nonsense is that?" The journalists, the members of parliament, the heads of departments, the writers of books, the propagandists, and all of them, they knew that we were wrong. If even they paid any attention to us, it was in a kindly, paternalist, well-meaning manner: "You boys are trying but, at any rate, that is not serious." But it turned out that we were right and they were wrong. Now don't forget that please. You never can tell what is likely to happen. You get your analysis of the situation and you charge, and then see what takes place. As Napoleon says, "On *s'engage,*" you engage, "*puis s'en voit,*" and then you see. And you cannot really see unless you engage. [*Applause*]

Now the second point is this: We were talking about the independence of Africa. We had many contacts in Africa, but none of them seemed to us to be contacts that would really lead the struggle for independence. But we had to take it as it came. We were determined to go ahead and we went ahead and things came our way. Now I want to tell you something else. In 1957, I was in Ghana with George Padmore talking to Nkrumah, and we discussed the beginning of the movement and how it had got to where it was. And if anybody had told us, or we had heard him say, in 1957 that within ten years there would be thirty new African states and over 100 million African people freed, what we would have done would be to get together and get a pamphlet ready and, in a piece of agitation and propaganda say, "That man is monster, he doesn't know what he is talking about. He's going to lead you in adventurous ways," etc., "and that cannot happen." And nobody believed more in the African revolution than we did. But we hadn't the conception that the movement would have moved with such tremendous rapidity as it has moved. That is something we have to remember today. When the comrade asked me what is the message, etc., I can only say, do what you have to do, the message will come from that. That's all. We didn't know that was going to take place.

Shakespeare's *King Lear*

Thank you, sir, for that brief introduction. The time is now a quarter to one. I have to get through this whole play and I was thinking that forty-five minutes is the most that I can do and, after that, there must be time during which you will ask questions or say what you have to say and what you think about it.

For me, the play is the thing, wherein you will catch the conscience, not of the King, but of the play, particularly of the playwright. And I shall spend the first few minutes—that is, as many as I can—going over the play from the point of view of a play. Shakespeare wrote plays for money. If he lived today he would find his way to Hollywood, I am quite sure.

The second thing is this: People are on both sides today as to whether we must know what is the Elizabethan style, the Elizabethan idea, and so on and so forth. I think that is wrong. I think that if he came back, he would want to know what the people who were going to see the play were thinking and he would adapt the play to suit, because it is the audience that you have to think of all the time. The play was not written (no offense intended) for lecturers to give classes on. Much of the criticism is very clever, very learned, but essentially the criticism of people sitting in studies and writing about plays. Shakespeare did not write like that. It is not illegitimate to do that, but that should be kept within its range. Mr. Maxwell says *King Lear* is a Christian play about a pagan world; that Shakespeare can assume in his audience a different religious standpoint from any of his characters.[1] I don't believe any of that. If anyone chooses to believe it, that's okay with me. But I believe that this kind of thing will lead you to misunderstand the play.

The thing we have to remember about Shakespeare, this play (there are one or two things I will mention as I go on), is that, on the Elizabethan stage, when a man or a woman appeared representing somebody else, the audience accepted that. (I take it that some of you know this play.) When Edgar appears as Poor Tom, the audience accepts him completely as a vagrant. That being so, I think I will go on and do as much of the play as I can because I cannot speak about it unless we are very much aware of the play as a play. I want you to know what we are not going to do.

Let us take the play. Old Gloucester comes on and he says that his son Edmund, who is there, is an illegitimate boy and "there was some good sport at his making." In reality, Gloucester is a very offensive old man and Shakespeare put that right in the first scene. (That is what Shakespeare does quite early in all of his plays.) I don't know what any audience would think about Gloucester and his jokes about "there was some good sport at his making," but an Elizabethan audience would think that, even if he behaved like that, there is no reason to boast about it. Then Gloucester says that he, Edmund, has been away for nine years and he is going to send him away again.

So Gloucester is not only licentious, but he is a very cruel, unfeeling old man. And that is a preparation for Lear. Lear comes and asks his daughters how much they love him. One says she loves him more than words can say; another one says she doesn't say enough. I love you excessively. Lear gives them property and then he turns to Cordelia. Cordelia is a very striking character. She says that she has to speak the truth. (That is a very British statement. Above all, Shakespeare was an English man. The English are very much concerned with what is right and what is wrong—always concerned about that. That leads them into political messes, because when they are carrying out dirty politics, but have to present it as if it is right, they get into a terrible tangle [*Laughter*].)

This Cordelia is a very English character. She says she has to say what is right and cannot say she loves him more than the others. And then Lear misbehaves. I will read what he says:

Lear:	But goes thy heart with this?
Cordelia:	Ay, my good lord.
Lear:	So young, and so untender?
Cordelia:	So young, my lord, and true.

Then the old man shows what a wicked, malicious, cantankerous, old wretch he is:

> Lear: Let it be so, thy truth then be thy dower!
>   For, by the sacred radiance of the sun,
>   The mysteries of the Hecate and the night,
>   By all the operation of the orbs
>   From whom we do exist and cease to be,
>   Here I disclaim all my paternal care,
>   Propinquity and property of blood,
>   And as a stranger to my heart and me
>   Hold thee from this for ever.

Then comes some terrible words:

> Lear: The barbarous Scythian,
>   Or he that makes his generation messes
>   To gorge his appetite, shall to my bosom
>   Be as well neighbored, pitied, and relieved,
>   As thou my sometime daughter.

I take the position that whatever happens to Lear afterwards, he deserves it. As with Gloucester at the beginning, Shakespeare meant that fellow to be seen as a very objectionable man. That is how it is to be played. (I noticed that recently in England there is a man who plays it a little bit like that.) But in reality they take Lear, lay on the storm, and he's cursing against the heaven. He really is a disgusting, cantankerous, cruel, old man. That is the play that we know.

Then comes Edmund, the son of Gloucester. I noticed that Mr. Wilson Knight says that Edmund represents the past.[2] I don't think so at all. Edmund represents the future. The regime that was breaking up was the old feudal regime, with certain standards, certain ideas, certain ways of behavior. Listen to Edmund and see whether he belongs to the succeeding age, essentially the age of individual enterprise, what the Americans call free enterprise—get what you can the best way you can, and, when you get it, then you are established:

Edmund: Thou, Nature, art my goddess; to thy law
               My services are bound. Wherefore should I
               Stand in the plague of custom, and permit
               The curiosity of nations to deprive me,
               For that I am some twelve or fourteen moonshines
               Lag of a brother? Why bastard? Wherefore base,
               When my dimensions are as well compact,
               My mind as generous, and my shape as true,
               As honest madam's issue? Why brand they us
               With base? with baseness? Bastardy base? Base?

You could imagine the Shakespeare audience having a wonderful time. "Why brand they us with baseness? Bastardy base? Base?" That was done purely to get the audience going, and because he meant it.

Edmund: Who, in the lusty stealth of nature, take
               More composition and fierce quality
               Than doth, within a dull, stale, tired bed,
               Go to th' creating a whole tribe of fops?

Edmund is very much like his father, Gloucester. He is illegitimate by law, but he is the son of old Gloucester because he is talking about how when people go to bed and are having a good time, the children are finer than when they are married. Gloucester just told the rest of them that this boy is illegitimate but there was good sport at his making. I can't imagine that Shakespeare was not thinking of these things. If he were not thinking of them, then he either had a very filthy mind, or he was a very bad dramatist. He put those things in there purposefully, and we must bear that in mind. Gloucester, Lear, and even Edmund—there is something about them, although Edmund is a new type. Gloucester is not only licentious, he is not only cruel; he is also very sensitive, in a curious way, to what is taking place in the world around him. Put yourself in the mind of Shakespeare's audience and listen to old Gloucester saying what kind of a world it is. Remember they were very superstitious in those days:

Gloucester: These late eclipses in the sun and moon
               portend no good to us ...
               Love cools, friendship falls off, brothers divide.

> In cities, mutinies; in countries, discord; in palaces, treason; and
> the bond cracked 'twixt son and father ...
> We have seen the best of our time.
> Machinations, hollowness, treachery, and all ruinous disorders
> follow us disquietly to our graves.

I am not concerned with what Shakespeare meant. I am concerned with what he says, and it is clear that Shakespeare is speaking about a time in society in which people are aware that the basic ideas and principles of that society are cracking. Not only does Gloucester say it, but Edmund later repeats it. So we are at once made to feel that something is going on and that the dramatist is dealing with a state of affairs which is not a sound state of affairs.

Every now and then I have to stop and say something. Let us suppose, as we shall see later, that an American dramatist in the thirties had written a play in which the president of the United States went crazy, walked out of the White House, and picked one of the twenty or thirty million unemployed and they both had a discussion together. I don't know whether that play would be allowed at all in the United States, but it would be clear that the dramatist was dealing with some serious problem. This is what is taking place in this play.

Let me say at once: Shakespeare is a very different man from the kind of man we know about. He was asked to write a play for a private performance for King James, not for the Globe Theatre. That's what I understand. And he wrote this one about the crazy king. In other words, there were qualities about him that are not usually talked about, and it is those that I have in mind when I say we must watch this play and see what is going on.

Now, Edmund speaks a little and I want you to think of it as a twentieth-century audience:

Edmund: This is the excellent foppery of the world, that
            when we are sick in fortune, often the surfeits of our own
            behavior, we make guilty of our disaster the sun, the
            moon, and stars; as if we were villains on necessity; fools
            by heavenly compulsion; knaves, thieves, and treachers
            by spherical predominance; drunkards, liars, adulterers
            by an enforced obedience of planetary influence; and all
            that we are evil in, by a divine thrusting on.

I wonder if that means anything to you? Shakespeare is saying, "all of you people believe in your psychology today, that a man is as he is because of certain humors and so forth that he has …."

Now, we can't laugh at them. Today, particularly in the United States, but also everywhere, a man is as he is because of his relation to his father and his mother. All sorts of scientific analysis is given. We call it psycho-analysis, about the behavior of people. Shakespeare is talking about a certain type of would-be scientific analysis of human behavior and he is making it clear that, as far as he is concerned, it is a lot of nonsense. I cannot say what he would say today about psychoanalysis. But he would not, by any means, make people irresponsible for the essentials of human behavior, he never did that at all.

We have another character, Kent, talking to Oswald. Kent is the man whom Lear has thrown away because he told Lear he was not behaving well in sending away his daughter. Lear, the cantankerous, vicious, old man says, "Get out and if I find you are here within ten days you will be killed," which, again, makes very clear what kind of a person Lear is and what kind of a person Shakespeare is putting on there. Now I take Kent who meets Oswald, who is a steward. A steward is a quite important person in the Elizabethan social structure. He ran the big house for the lords and ladies and he was very offensive. He was one of those who helped to build the new capitalist, as opposed the old feudal, society.

Kent meets Oswald and these are Kent's remarks:

> Kent: A knave, a rascal, an eater of broken meats; a base,
>   proud, shallow, beggarly, three-suited, hundred-pound,
>   filthy worsted-stocking knave; a lily-livered, action-
>   taking, whoreson, glass-gazing, superserviceable, finical
>   rogue; one-trunk-inheriting slave; one that wouldst be
>   a very bawd in way of good service, and art nothing but
>   the composition of a knave, beggar, coward, panderer,
>   and the son and heir of a mongrel bitch …

What reason is there that he should abuse the man in this way? There is no basic dramatic reason for it, but I think the Shakespearean audience would understand. Kent is a typical representative of the old feudal age. He pays attention to Lear, as he will say later, because of authority. He says,

"There is something in your face, I like authority." He is a member of the old feudal age. And what he sees in Oswald is that Oswald is a member of the new free-enterprise class of persons, and he cannot stand him. Otherwise, there is no reason—because Oswald met him or bounced against him or something of the kind—for him to be so abusive. (Do you know Burke's famous speech where he spoke about Marie Antoinette? "But the age of chivalry is gone; that of sophisters, economists, and calculators has succeeded, and the glory of Europe has extinguished forever."[3] Marx also refers to the same thing.)

There is a definite distinction between the old feudal age and the new, emergent capitalist society, and Kent's words are to be explained because he saw in Oswald, a steward, one of these kinds of persons, and he didn't like it. Shakespeare would only write that way because the audience would be aware of what he's talking about. They were very much aware of the two different kinds of persons that were in society at the time, and that statement of Kent against Oswald would meet a very strong response of approval in the audience.

Now, the two daughters who have got the property, Goneril and Reagan, they chase Lear out. They say, "old man you are not behaving well." And I am quite certain that from the things that Shakespeare says, and the things that Goneril and Regan say, that that old man was misbehaving himself in Goneril's house. He and his people were behaving badly and Goneril says, "You meddle with maids and carry on in a way that is most improper." Lear says that it is not true, but I don't think it's so because, as he comes into the place, he says, "I want my dinner." The servant says, "Well I've been excused," and he says, "You get my dinner at once." Kent, disguised, looks at Oswald and throws him over and Lear says, that is fine, you will work for me. (Lear is in somebody else's house, by the way). He says, that is fine, you will work for me. In other words, Lear is not only licentious, he is not only cantankerous and cruel; he can't behave himself. And Goneril and Regan, although they are thinking of taking over the kingdom, and although they are not people who are to be looked upon with any satisfaction or pleasure on our part, they are justified in what they begin to do. If Lear gets into trouble, he calls it on himself; otherwise, to me, much of the play is the play that critics are writing about, but not the play that Shakespeare wrote.

Then, Lear finds himself on the open heath. There, the critics go crazy with the things he says. I have been to the Cambridge Theatre with my wife five nights running to watch John Gielgud, whom I admire tremendously, and Peggy Aschcroft, whom I do not admire at all. I watched them in *King Lear*.[4] I wanted to see something. I knew that they had bungled up the play, and I knew where they had bungled it up, and why. I want to spend some time on that.

Now listen to Lear, who has gone crazy:

Lear: Tremble, thou wretch,
That hast within thee undivulgèd crimes
Unwhipped of justice. Hide thee, thou bloody hand,
Thou perjured, and thou simular of virtue
That art incestuous. Caitiff, to pieces shake,
That under covert and convenient seeming
Has practiced on man's life. Close pent-up guilts,
Rive your concealing continents and cry
These dreadful summoners grace …

Lear has been a king. He ruled for about fifty or sixty years and what he is saying is that the kind of people who rule in this society and the people living there are a set of criminals, and the storm ought to destroy them. That is the first thing that Lear says. In other words, it is a merciless indictment of the society which he has ruled over for fifty or sixty years. And if you are playing that, and you are concerned only with what he is doing against the storm (and it is very hard for a big audience to hear any voice at all against that kind of storm), then you miss the play entirely.

Gielgud, I regret to say this, and Peggy Ashcroft, missed it completely. Gielgud was there wailing against the storm when, in reality, Lear is wailing against society. A little later he says what he thinks about what has happened to the poor people of that society. He has already spoken of those who are rich and those who are in control of this society. Now he begins to speak of the poor:

Lear: Poor naked wretches, wheresoe'er you are,
That bide the pelting of this pitiless storm,

How shall your houseless heads and unfed sides,
Your looped and windowed raggedness, defend you
From seasons such as these?

Then comes a confession:

Lear: O, I have ta'en
          Too little are of this! Take physic, pomp;
          Expose thyself to feel what wretches feel,
          That thou mayst shake the superflux to them
          And show the heavens more just.

That was a political statement, if there ever was one. There maybe other things about it, psychological, but that was a political statement and a man playing that part has got to make that what it obviously is, a political statement. I am not interpreting, that's why I am spending so much time reading it. I am saying what is there and I draw some conclusions from what is there.

Now, as soon as he is finished with that, one of the poor appears. Edgar, the son of Gloucester who has been banished, appears in the disguise of Poor Tom. This is the only thing you have to remember of the Shakespearean theater, the Elizabethan theater: When Edgar appears as Poor Tom, the audience accepts him as Poor Tom. Here we have to spend a little time and I would advise you to read Hollingshed's *Chronicles of England, Scotland and Ireland*.

The Poor Toms were a very important part of England. After the dissolution of the monasteries, tens of thousands of them were thrown into the countryside to live how they could and they wandered about the place, becoming vagrants. They were the unemployed and a notable feature of Elizabethan society. You see references to them all over the place. Shakespeare brings one of them onto stage. Just after Lear has said what he has said about the poor, some four or five lines later, one of them actually appears. (If you are playing this play and that is not clear to the audience, which it was not ... Five nights I saw them, and I don't suppose they did it when I wasn't there. That was not clear at all. Gielgud was busy using his magnificent voice against some fake storm and so forth, and this actual social conflict, which is there because Shakespeare put it there, was not brought forward.) Tom says:

> Edgar: Who gives anything to poor Tom? Whom the foul
>   fiend hath led through fire and through flame, through
>   ford an whirlpool, o'er bog and quagmire; that hath
>   laid knives under his pillow and halters in his pew, set
>   ratsbane by his porridge, made him proud of heart, to
>   ride on a bay trotting horse over four-inched bridges, to
>   course his own shadow for a traitor.

Poor Tom says, "that is what is happening to us and do Poor Tom, whom the foul fiend vexes, some charity." Whereas Lear is denouncing society from one side, Poor Tom is also saying his piece. Then they ask him, "How did you become a vagrant?" because any man who was not able to stand in this society became an agricultural vagrant. Edgar speaks of something that I am sure the Elizabethan audience felt:

> Edgar: A servingman, proud in heart and mind; that
>   curled my hair, wore gloves in my cap; served the lust
>   of my mistress' heart, and did the act of darkness with her;
>   swore as many oaths as I spake words, and broke them in
>   the sweet face of heaven. One that slept in the contriving
>   of lust, and waked to do it. Wine loved I deeply, dice
>   dearly; and in woman out-paramoured the Turk. False
>   of heart, light of ear, bloody of hand; hog in sloth, fox in
>   stealth, wolf in greediness, dog in madness, lion in prey.

That, if you will allow me, is a political statement—a description of a type of person whom the Elizabethan audience would understand very well. The agricultural vagrant and the steward. That is the type of person Kent hated so much. (If you read near the end of Clarendon's *The History of Rebellion*, you will see some pages on the role that the stewards played in the break-up of the society under Charles I and Charles II and in the creation of a modern society.⁵) There you will see what Shakespeare is talking about.

Thus, it is clear to me—the way Kent talked about Oswald, and now the way Edgar talks about stewards—that Shakespeare has in mind a certain kind of person whom the audience would understand. I could tell you about certain types of persons in the West Indies, whom, if you wrote about them, everybody would know whom you meant. There would be no problem. That, too, would take place in other plays for other countries. Maybe if a Canadian were to write a play in which he spoke about certain Canadian types, he wouldn't say they came from Vancouver or Toronto, but the audience would understand what they were talking about. I believe that the Shakespearean audience understood that Shakespeare had a certain type in mind.

Now comes, for me, the second most important phrasing in the play. They ask Tom, "Who are you? What are you doing? How can you get on?" And Tom makes an indictment of Elizabethan society from the point of view of the agricultural vagrant. I cannot understand how people can read this and write the things about it that they do. They ask him, "Who are you?" He says,

Edgar: Poor Tom, that eats the swimming frog, the toad,
           the tadpole, the wall-newt and the water; that in the fury
           of his heart, when the foul fiend rages, eats cow-dung
           for sallets, swallows the old rat and the ditch-dog, drinks
           the green mantle of the standing pool; who is whipped
           from tithing to tithing, and stock-punished and
           imprisoned ...

Do you hear that? I know people who have read it and written about it and they haven't heard that. That is an indictment of the society which followed the dissolution of the monarchies; it says, "This is how we live. This is how we are getting on. This is the kind of thing that we suffer from. And, in addition to you up there, there are the stewards, and sometimes there are agricultural vagrants, too." I see all that very clearly in the play and I have to insist upon it because I meet very few people who seem to have seen it.

My eyes are not very good, but I don't think they are seeing what isn't there. I don't think so.

Now comes a tremendous scene. I will only describe it to you. Lear is on the heath. Goneril and Regan are the reigning monarchs of the country, in 17th century England. You must not forget that. Poor Tom is there, and the half crazy boy, the Fool, upon whom critics have spread themselves wonderfully. The two of them are there and Lear is crazy. Lear tells them, "Goneril and Regan, my two daughters, have not behaved well. I am going to appoint you to a commission and you are going to try these two." He puts them up somewhere on some box or something and he says, "You try the two." Now you don't, especially in the 17th century, put a fool and an agricultural laborer to try the king or queen of the country. You don't do that, least of all in England. You don't do that even today. These two people, the agricultural laborer and the fool (he is half crazy), are placed in a situation by Lear where they are trying Goneril and Regan for behavior that is immoral and not suitable to the positions that they hold in the country.

I want to say two things about that scene: First of all, we have two editions of the play today (there may be more, but I know of two), and in the second one, this scene is left out. I can well imagine the Lord Chamberlain of the court saying, "Mr. Shakespeare, it is a very good scene but I think we wouldn't play it for his majesty to see," because that is a very serious thing for them to try monarchs. That is number one. Number two: That was a scene in a play in 1606. You look at the history of the world from 1606 to 1967 and, repeatedly, year after year, people representing the Poor Toms of the country are regularly put to try monarchs for the unsatisfactory way they have behaved. Shakespeare seems to have taken his imagination beyond. I cannot say what he saw, but I say he wrote that and there are people who saw the play who were alive when some Poor Toms and other people tried Charles I and killed him. These two weren't able to do it, but Lear told them, "You sit up there and try these two." Then he lost his head. It is a remarkable scene, and one that is very important for us who are alive today.

Now, I am going on rather quickly. (I hope some of you know the play, and those of you don't can take it as it is, but I won't take more than fifteen minutes.) I want to bring to your notice the role of the peasant in this play. Cornwall gets ahold of Gloucester, who helps Lear to escape, and they blind him. They are very cruel. They are concerned with taking over the kingdom and the two women, Goneril and Regan, are concerned with the man they want. They want him and they are going to get him, whatever the circumstances. But they are about to blind Gloucester and the first servant, who, as will appear later, is a servant in a feudal house, uses some words.

Here I have to ask you to remember Shakespeare's plays in the past. Shakespeare was a great dramatist, but he used poetry and the English language for his best effects. You remember, when Macbeth was in a mess, those superb lines:

> Macbeth: Tomorrow, and tomorrow, and tomorrow,
>   Creeps in this petty pace from day to day
>   To the last syllable of recorded time,

When Lady Macbeth is in trouble, Macbeth says:

> Duncan is in his grave;
> After life's fitful fever he sleeps well.
> Treason has done his worst; nor steel, nor poison,
> Malice domestic, foreign levy, nothing,
> Can touch him further.

Macbeth is saying, "I killed him and have become the king and I am in a terrific mess. That fellow is safe." Over and over again, you hear it in the very ring of the words. This means that Shakespeare is concerned about it.

They are about to blind Gloucester and this servant says (you have to hear the words and know how they will be said):

> Servant: Hold your hand, my lord!
>   I have served you ever since I was a child;
>   But better service have I never done you
>   Than now to bid you hold.

If you know the Shakespearean language properly, you will know that something is going on there. This is not the only place. There are two or three places where the role of the peasant in the crisis of the society is made very strong and very clear by the language that Shakespeare gives to them. They are not characters in the play, but he insisted they play an important role. If he was not doing that, he would not give them those lines. He reserves those for special occasions and it is obvious that the intervention of the peasant in this play is, for him, repeatedly, a very special occasion. (If, when it comes to question time, you ask for some more proof I will give it to you, but I have to go on very rapidly now.)

I go on now to Lear. Lear goes crazy and he begins to talk like a crazy man. (Shakespeare is very clever indeed; he says, "Well, I don't mean it; the man is crazy and that's why he says all these things.") He says, to punish a man for adultery—nonsense when the birds carry on a lot of adultery, the small gilded fly carries on in my sight …it is natural to a man to be adulterous. And he says about women:

> Lear: But to the girdle do the gods inherit,
> Beneath is all the fiend's
> There is hell, there's darkness, there is the sulphurous
> pit; burning, scalding, stench, consumption.

Shakespeare says that the sexual instinct is the driving force of men and women. He would have had some very interesting conversations with Freud.

Now, his conversations with Marx. I want to give you another section which shows how advanced he was. Lear says, "You can't see Gloucester, you are blind?

> Lear: Look with thine ears. See how yond justice
> rails upon yond simple thief. Hark in thine ear: change
> places and, handy-dandy, which is the justice, which is
> the thief?

He says there is a magistrate abusing a poor prisoner. He says, change places, put the prisoner up there and put the magistrate down in the dock "and, handy-dandy," you don't know "which is the justice, which is the thief." That is a very revolutionary thing to say and it is clear that Shakespeare has certain ideas. He goes even further:

> Lear: Plate sin with gold,
> Robes and furred gowns hide all. Plate sin with gold,
> And the strong lance of justice hurtless breaks;
> Arm it in rags, a pygmy's straw does pierce it.

Then comes what I think is the greatest line in Shakespeare that I know:

> Lear· None does offend, none—I say none!

Shakespeare says that a man is in the situation that he is and does the things that he does because of the social position that he holds. The justice talks about this man, the prisoner, because he is a justice. Put this one up there and he will talk like a justice and the justice will have to behave like him. He goes further with it. He says, "You see that policeman there, he is beating that girl for being a whore. What he wants to do really," he says, "is sleep with her, but he is a man of authority, he has got to beat her, he'll continue to beat her." He says, furthermore:

> Lear: Thou hast seen a farmer's dog bark at a beggar?
> Gloucester: Ay, sir.
> Lear: There though mightest behold the great image of
>   authority...

He says that is the image of authority. Put the dog where the man is, and put the man where the dog is, and you will see an absolute change. It is a tremendous passage and I say there he could have had a lot of conversations with Marx as to the situation, the social and economic situation, and the shaping of character by it. And with Freud, he would have been able to talk of the power of the sexual instinct in people. That is what he makes old crazy Lear say.

Lear has been assisted by Edgar, who has been the serving man, and then Shakespeare shows what his play is going to be. Edgar was an educated person, but he had to run away and he became an agricultural vagrant. He spoke on behalf of the agricultural vagrants in that way in the scene on the heath. I am insisting that if you miss that, and if the players are not showing that there are two social systems which Shakespeare has put in violent conflict with each other, then that scene is lost as I saw it lost five times in succession at Cambridge Circus with a very fine player playing.

Now, Gloucester is blind and he asks Edgar, his son who is pretending to be an agricultural vagrant, "Who are you?" Edgar says:

Edgar: A most poor man, made tame to fortune's blows,
                  Who, by the art of known and feeling sorrows,
                  Am pregnant to good pity.

He wouldn't say "good pity" today. The word that is used most often today is compassion. Shakespeare makes Edgar become an agricultural vagrant, fight on behalf of vagrancy, defy Lear and the others, and say that this is the kind of life we live. Then, when they ask him, "Who are you really?" he says, "I am a man, I have suffered in the world and, from being subjected to sorrows and difficulties, I have become pregnant to good people." He is the man destined to rule the state.

I draw the conclusion that Goneril was unsuitable, Regan was unsuitable, Edmund was unsuitable, old Lear had made a fool of himself, but the person who was to take over the state in the mess that it was in, and who leaves you with the idea that he is going to manage the affair, is Edgar. Shakespeare has made Edgar himself say what he is at this stage, after all he has gone through.

At the end of the play, Lear dies and Edgar takes charge. These critics go crazy over Lear. Lear says Cordelia is dying and says wonderful things about Cordelia. But Edgar says:

Edgar: The weight of this sad time we must obey,
                Speak what we feel, not what we ought to say.

If you told a political leader today that he has to say what feels about the situation, and not what he ought to say, he would have you put in prison or try to deport you.

Edgar: The weight of this sad time we must obey,
                Speak what we feel, not what we ought to say.
                The oldest hath borne most; we that are young
                Shall never see so much, nor live so long.

Now, that is the play that I have seen. I am sure I have left out much that I ought to have told you, but if I had told you that, then I would have left out what I have told you. It is a very difficult thing to manage in so brief a time. But it is half past one and I have gone through the whole play in about forty-five minutes. I have made clear what I think about it, how it ought to be approached, and I don't see critics and other people approaching it that way. Some say Shakespeare wasn't unduly disturbed about this society. He made Cordelia and Lear come together and that is very beautiful. They shed tears of beauty at Cordelia and Lear coming together and make the play not a critique of modern society.

The play is a critique of Elizabethan society, of the society that was and of the society that was coming into being. But Shakespeare didn't merely criticize. He put somebody there. He put Edgar, today one of the most important of Shakespeare's characters, and he gave him the training and the discipline, and Edgar himself tells us how fitted he was to take charge of a country that was in ruins and would be in difficulties for some time to come. That is the play, as I want you to think of it, as I have seen it. The rest is now up to you.

Thank you very much. [*Applause*]

PART II
PRIVATE LECTURES

Existentialism and Marxism

Now, I am speaking about existentialism, the existentialist point of view. You will find in the study of dialectics references to Kant, Hegel, and Marx, and since the War, men have had to reject the idea of class structure because the imposition of the ideas of class and its activities destroy the individual completely. This is the existentialist point of view, as I understand it. We are absolutely lost in the massive organizations representing the social differentiations under which we live. Existentialism was a result of recognizing this as emanating from what took place during the war—the cruelties, brutalities, and absolute departures from ordinary standards of civilization that occurred in World War I.[1]

Heidegger and others managed to work out a philosophy that, although it contains many differences, can be summarized in this way: A man does not, as Descartes suggested, examine what is taking place over there. Man is not a single individual, he is part and he is being-in-the-world. So that when a man begins to think, begins to look at what is happening to him— you have to look at him, the kind of food he eats, the kinds of papers he reads, the circumstances that surround him—he lives the kind of life that Heidegger speaks of very bluntly as the life of the "they," what he calls an "inauthentic life." There is no single individual.

You cannot begin to find out anything about a man if you look upon him as Descartes looked upon him and as Kant, and worse still, Hegel suggested; by saying he's part of a certain social force. They argued that he's part of a certain social force, part of the "they"—that he lives an inauthentic life. And Heidegger's existentialism suggests that when a man understands that he's living an inauthentic life and sets his pattern towards something that is peculiar to himself, it is at that time that he is begins to live an authentic life. It is then that the *Dasein*, the *being there*, begins to function.

It is essentially a matter of discussion, of communication; it is not about the isolated individual, although the isolated individual is what emerges when some kind of transcendence takes place. You begin, however, from the individual being part of the "they" that lives an inauthentic life.

The great book that Heidegger has written is *Being and Time*. I must recommend that you get this book. First of all, why has this philosophical system arrived? It has arrived because of the breakdown of European civilization during World War I, and what is happening today is merely the continuation of that.

Secondly, existentialism is not to be considered an essentially false philosophy. I recommend to you an essay by Lenin on dialectics written in 1915. You will find it in volume 38 of *Lenin's Collected Works* where he says that idealism is not necessarily an absurd philosophical doctrine. Idealism represents a certain pattern of thought and, very often, the idealists take hold of an important sequence of thought, which is very valuable, but they carry it to an extreme.[2] Do you know that passage? That is how I see existentialism.

Thirdly, Jean-Paul Sartre made a tremendous attempt (there's a book about him, *Reason and Violence*[3]) to link together Marxism and existentialism—the fact that a man lives a certain type of existence and that you have to take his situation into consideration. Situation is a very important word in Sartre's work. Sartre played about with Marxism for years and it's very important that we do this work. He was totally unable to understand the self-mobilization of the masses. That was entirely absent from Sartre, the result being that he played about with the Communist Party.

Sartre said he supported the Communist Party. But then he said if they came to power in France he would be one of their first victims, but nevertheless, he had to support them because they were opposed to bourgeois society.[4] He played about with this and, though I'm determined to deal with him, I have no need to, just as I have no need to deal with those people who were telling me that Khrushchev instituted a new order. I don't have to argue with them anymore. I look at them and they look elsewhere because the Khrushchev episode has proven that, essentially, the regime in Russia, although there are modifications, is what it always was.

Sartre has finished the matter. He has written a book called *Mots—Words*. It is an autobiography. Did I send you the quotation in which Sartre confesses about a year or two ago that, over the last ten years, he has gradually begun to recognize that what he has been doing is a lot of nonsense and that what he has to do in the future is write? [*Marty Glaberman: Yes.*] But he doesn't know why, except that some people will read him, but he sees his whole future existence as an existence of nonsense; it has been nonsense and he goes on because there is nothing else to do.[5] That is the result of his total incomprehension of what Marxism is and his attempt to unite Marxism and existentialism must fail, has failed, because he doesn't know what Marxism is.

Now, with that introduction, I will now read certain extracts from Heidegger, and from there we will go on. Have no doubt whatever that this will ultimately be very effective in our work. I hadn't the faintest idea—and I am certain that Marty and William[6] couldn't possibly have had—that those *Notes on the Hegelian Dialectic* would at one time become a matter in which the general public was interested.[7] So this, although difficult, I am quite certain—I have worked at it for a year or two, and though it may take ten years—is going to be something that people are very much concerned with because it concerns us today.

This is what existentialism has posed: that the form of existence, the development of the human personality, the development of activity, etc., is separate from the "they," the mass social activities into which the modern individual is entirely drawn. His existence counts, not the analysis, not the class, nor the section of society to which he belongs.

This is the beginning of a quotation from Heidegger's English language translators: "Though in traditional German philosophy it [the *Dasein*] may be used quite generally to stand for almost any kind of Being or 'existence' which we can say that something *has* (the 'existence' of God, for example), in everyday usage it tends to be used more narrowly to stand for the kind of Being that belongs to *persons*."[8] It is a doctrine of the individual, but the individual as part of a general body; "they," who eat the same food, who read the same newspapers, and who believe in the same way. The individual becomes important when he transcends that unification in which he participates with everybody else.

The *Dasein* belongs to persons, and Heidegger follows the everyday usage in this respect. But he goes somewhat further in that he often uses it to stand for any person who has such Being, and who is thus an entity in and of himself.

You are going to have a lot of trouble with this word Being. But you have to accept it along with the famous word *Dasein*, being there. Another important word, though not as important as the *Dasein*, is *Mitsein*. Do any of you know German? [*William Gorman: To be with?*] Yes, with or with it. The *Dasein*, being there, means you are there. The *Dasein* is when you can communicate and have discussion. You have emerged out of the *Mitsein*—being there with a lot of people. He never deals with an individual to begin with. The individual only becomes possible to deal with when he has emerged from the *Mitsein*, and being a representative of the *Dasein*, the being there, he is, to some degree, conscious.

Heidegger continues: "To give an example, what is philosophically primary is neither a theory of the concept-formation of historiology nor the theory of historiological knowledge, nor yet the theory of history as the Object of historiology; what is primary is rather the Interpretation of authentically historical entities as regards their historicality."[9] Now that is very confusing, but you will get it in time. He is dealing with the background, this idea of transcendence of the objective situation and the historical development of what he is treating.

"Similarly the positive outcome of Kant's *Critique of Pure Reason*," writes Heidegger, "lies in what it has contributed towards the working out of what belongs to any Nature whatsoever, not in a 'theory' of knowledge."[10] Heidegger is anxious to make clear that he is not dealing, and philosophers do not deal with strictly philosophical questions. He says, "Similarly the positive outcome of Kant's *Critique of Pure Reason* lies in what it has contributed towards the working out of what belongs to any Nature whatsoever, not in a 'theory' of knowledge."

Bertrand Russell's *History of Western Philosophy* (it's a very bad book. You should read it for that purpose; to know what the history of philosophy should not be) analyzes repeatedly the work of Kant and others as theories of knowledge. Heidegger says they are not theories of knowledge at all. They open up a means of dealing with important matters in nature and the natural development of society and the individual. Kant's "transcendental logic is an a priori logic for the subject-matter of that area of Being called 'Nature.'"[11] Do you understand that? Kant's transcendental logic is a logic that is there for the purpose of analyzing nature. What you can prove about it is not important. It achieves a certain purpose. That is how I have read and how I think of philosophy.

"But such an inquiry itself," says Heidegger, "ontology taken in the widest sense without favoring any particular ontological directions or tendencies—requires a further clue. Ontological inquiry is indeed more primordial, as over against the ontical inquiry of the positive sciences."[12]

Let me explain. The ontical inquiry of the positive sciences means the kind of sociology, the kind of psychology, the kind of economics that roams about in the universities today, and which serious professors and thinkers say is absolutely no good. Nobody knows what it is all about. Its proponents gather a lot of facts and string them together in a line. Heidegger says that that is the ontical—that they deal with material information and accumulated scientific facts—but they don't have a fundamental understanding of what is involved. He says we have to get at what is below the surface of the ontical, and that he calls ontological.

According to his English language translators, "Ontological inquiry is concerned primarily with *Being*"—that is to say, the apparent fundamental nature of what is to be investigated. And that is his concern—Being, the fundamental nature of existence. "Ontical inquiry is concerned primarily with *entities* and the facts about them."[13] I hope that is clear.

Now, I go to *International Man* by William Barrett—*Irrational Man*. (I called it *International Man*. That is very interesting to me. I will have to think about why I did that.) Barrett has written on existentialism. I am not sure that he has written very well, but I wouldn't say he has written badly. But there are certain statements that he has made that I will quote here. He says: "The momentous assertion that Heidegger makes is that truth does not reside primarily in the intellect"—you see this completely in relation Hegel, and the Kantians and the rest of them—"but that, on the contrary, intellectual truth is in fact a derivative of a more basic sense of truth."[14] In other words, you can play about with truth in the ontical analysis of things, but if you try to get down to the ontological basis of the Being of things then you have to deal with something like existentialism.

And let me stop here at once. Heidegger and some of the others have said that Plato and Aristotle laid the foundation of modern civilization and modern science. They laid this foundation through the use of logic and by being able to make the Greeks and Western civilization follow them and understand the ontical conception of investigation. They have done wonderfully well, he says, but the earlier Greek philosophers—Thales and those others, and in particular Heraclitus—when you read their philosophy, the scraps that remain, you see that they had a conception of the relation of the mind and the objective world which Plato and Aristotle understood.

What completely ruined this was Christianity. Christianity has a conception that man has a being, a moral life, etc., as well as a physical vulgarity of this life, and that there is a complete contradiction between the two. That runs right through modern philosophy, and Heidegger is against that. Heidegger wants to go back to Heraclitus and the others who said that Reason was the earth alive. They had this conception. How true all this is philosophically, I don't know. But I find that in the study of philosophy, this conception is something that produces valuable new material and understanding of the state of the world.

Now Barrett goes on to say: "It is by harking back to the primeval meaning of truth as it became embedded in the Greek language, that Heidegger takes his theory, in a single leap, beyond the boundaries of Husserlian phenomenology."[15] Husserl was the first philosopher who began arguing that you have to deal with the circumstances and facts that constitute a human being. Husserl began and Heidegger carried it forward. "Husserl was [still rooted] in the point of view of Descartes, which is the prevailing view of the modern epoch in philosophy, while the whole meaning of Heidegger's thought is an effort to overcome Descartes."[16]

Walter Kaufmann has written the following: "No philosopher should be viewed only in the context of his time, against the background of contemporary art and literature; but to see him also briefly, in his context is, no doubt, legitimate. Heidegger belongs to the contemporary revolt against representation."[17] The most notable revolt against representation in art is Picasso, and for Heidegger, this thing that we do—putting all the facts together to form something—this, he says, is not philosophy.

He goes further, and he and Jaspers are very strong on this. They say that you cannot read Plato, you cannot read Kant—you cannot understand them—unless you are actively engaged in philosophy in the way that they were engaged. You would not produce the same philosophy as theirs, but you must be engaged in a philosophical struggle or engaged in philosophical problems posed in the world in which you live, or you cannot understand Plato, Aristotle, Kant and the rest. You can read them, write theses on them and get doctorates in philosophy, but you will not know what you are doing.

This is a tremendous example of the necessity for participation. And, on the whole, I think Heidegger is right. I have seen men in politics who could quote Aristotle, Rousseau, and Jefferson and who have some ideas that correspond to Jefferson that they want to carry out when they begin to take part in politics. They are not only political bastardizers but, after a while, they are unable to understand Jefferson, Descartes, Rousseau, and the rest whom they understood some years before. Heidegger is very insistent on philosophically taking part in the problems of the world in an authentic manner.

"Even as modern prose and paintings," according to Kaufmann, "are no longer satisfied with the representation of events or things, Heidegger feels that the time has come for philosophy to break with what he calls representational thinking"—ontical thinking, digging up the facts that you can see and speculate about. He seems to depart from common sense or logic.[18] "His partisans occasionally counter criticism saying that they presuppose the competence of common sense logic, and their voices show the scorn with which a critic of Picasso might be told that he is a Philistine."[19]

Now I will go over to *Being and Time* and read certain extracts: "When resolute, Dasein has brought itself back from falling, and has done so precisely in order to be more authentically 'there' in the 'moment of *vision*' as regards the Situation which has been disclosed."[20] (Now, my friends, if you didn't have Hegel and the Hegelian period in the past, that would really be something.) "When resolute, Dasein has brought itself back from falling..." Heidegger says that ordinarily man falls into the existence of the "they," the kind of life that everybody lives; that is falling—he sinks into something. That word, falling, is a very fine one because it gives the conception of your getting out of a normal type of existence and simply flopping into something, and as it does so, *Dasein* brings itself back from falling.

You have flopped into the life that everybody lives and brought yourself back from it in order to be authentically "there." You bring in the moment of vision. In the moment of vision, a man begins to see what is his own authentic life as compared to the inauthentic life he as been living with the "they" and as regards the situation which has been disclosed. And here the man you will have to remember is Jean-Paul Sartre.

I don't know if you have seen his reference to the philosophy of extreme situations. Sartre's philosophy is very much concerned with the fact they, the French, experienced the German occupation. The German Gestapo used to take you down into some kind of cell and torture you until you spoke up, or didn't—you would have to decide. But you would know that nobody would ever know whether you had spoken or not. The result: you would be killed and disappear. And Sartre and Jaspers, but Sartre in particular, says that that was a period of the extreme situation. And it is in the extreme situation that people understand exactly what they are.[21]

Now, to do this again: "When resolute, Dasein"—the individual being there—"has brought itself back from falling"—slipping carelessly into the life that everybody lives—"and has done so precisely in order to be more authentically 'there'"—Dasein means being there—"'in the moment of vision'"—when, for the first time you are clear as to the fact that you have lived a certain way and that now something else has come and you're beginning to see your way—"as regards the Situation which has been disclosed." That can take place only in a situation or in a moment of the extreme situation. That is the kind of thing you will have to do.

Now, "the present anxiety"—Heidegger says you are always in anxiety. You are not afraid of this. You are suffering from dread. You're not afraid of this policeman or that person whom you owe money—you are permanently afraid. You have the concept of dread and Heidegger says that is part of human existence.

I have known very cautious philosophers and I am prepared to go along with them philosophically. I state that this thing was written after World War I when the concept of dread became part of the everyday life of a large majority of people in Central Europe. They understood, then, the problems of existence, so that the concept of dread about which Heidegger wrote in 1928, and the concept of anxiety, which Sartre and others have done so much work on, are part of the problems of the age.

According to Heidegger, "The Present of anxiety holds the moment of vision *at the ready*...."[22] Is that clear? Anxiety means that you are worried about the actual situation, but it "holds the moment of vision *at the ready*; as such a moment it itself, and only itself, is possible."[23]

At the moment of vision, you realize that only yourself and the kind of personality and perspectives that are suitable to your individual personality are possible. The "moment *of vision*, however, brings existence into the Situation and discloses the authentic 'there,'" the *Dasein*.[24] I think you should understand that by now. He insists on the moment of vision, and most of my quotations have centered around the moment of vision. "The moment of vision, however, brings existence into the situation"—you have been living as you like and falling into the everyday. By the way, "everydayness"—the behavior of the they—is an important word with Heidegger. It is wonderful to read what he says about the "they," what he says about idle talk, and what he says about everydayness. And he says he is not attacking anyone, abusing them, or using these words in an opprobrious sense. That is how "they" are, that is exactly how they live.

With the moment of vision you begin to see exactly what you are, you begin to know what it is you are in and what decisions you have to make. And I must say, I have been applying this, not only to ordinary existence— to ordinary behavior as Sartre does in his novels and as Wilson Harris[25] is doing in his novels to an astonishing degree—I am also in the habit of applying the moment of vision—the drifting along with everybody else and then the moment of vision and discovery of the authentic "there"—to a national unit.

I find that I can apply it as a historical method. I am not going to attempt to prove it. The only thing that proves a theoretical method is what you get from it. And if, ultimately, I use this method and get a certain amount clarification of national units, etc., I use it. That's all I can say.

Now Heidegger goes on: "The Present, which makes up the existential meaning of 'getting taken along'"—getting taken along, you're just living—"never arrives at any other ecstatical horizon of its own accord." Getting along, living from day to day, you never arrive anywhere "unless it gets brought back from its lostness"—you have fallen and you're falling into lostness, that is the life that everybody lives—"by a resolution, so that both the current Situation and therewith the primordial 'limit-situation' of

Being-towards-death, will be disclosed as a moment of vision which has been held on to."[26]

That word ontological should be seen in relation to the world primordial. The word primordial means fundamental, below the surface—ontological and primordial. Then Heidegger says something here, which Sartre, in *Being and Nothingness*, that big philosophical work, attacks. Heidegger says that the real understanding of your existence is a Being-toward-death. It is only when you understand you are going to die, and that at the end of it there is nothing, that you really begin to understand and to accept the authentic facts of the existence which you are living. Heidegger pays great attention to death, and the early attraction of his philosophy was that he dealt with death and society, etc., which, up until to then, Kant and Hegel and the rest never dealt with.

Heidegger brought these problems, these problems of the existence of the early 20th century, into philosophy and treated them as part of the philosophical understanding of the world. And today, after World War II, they are far more powerful than when he wrote them in 1928. Today people understand that anxiety, the concept of dread, living along the life into which you are falling, the "they"—with everybody else—getting out of it and the responsibility that is placed upon yourself, people understand that today this is a matter of everyday concern for everybody. Some people seem to think that this discredits Marxism. Sartre did his best to link Marxism to existentialism, but the result was that he discredited himself very much.

According to Heidegger, "Falling has its temporal roots primarily in the Present"[27]—falling, lostness, dropping into the everyday existence. And, "in the moment of vision, indeed, and often just 'for that moment', existence can even gain the mastery over the 'everyday'; but it can never extinguish it."[28] Is that clear? The moment of vision is extremely important. There, for the first moment, you see what is happening to you: "in the moment of vision, indeed, and often just 'for that moment'"—it does not remain, you can have the moment of vision and fall into the mess—"existence can even gain the mastery over the 'everyday'"—the everydayness, the behavior of the "they," "but it can never extinguish it." You get the moment of vision, you understand what you are, you understand where you are going but—and this is what is very important with Heidegger—you can never extinguish the everydayness because that is where you live. He is insistent.

Descartes took everydayness out. Kant took it out. Hegel related it to class. So did Marx. But Heidegger insists that you are there and that is the kind of life that you live. You will get out for a moment, but you never completely overcome it because those are the conditions of your existence and that is the reason for the importance of existence. You begin where you exist and that is the world "being there" and that is the world you are in.

Now comes a very important passage that Heidegger underlines and one that is very important for an understanding of what he is driving at. I will read it fairly slowly and then read it a second time: *"Only an entity which, in its Being, is essentially futural so that it is free for its death and can let itself be thrown back upon its factical 'there' by shattering itself against death...."*[29] I have spoken about death, and some of the most brilliant and most famous pages in Heidegger's work are his writing on death.

But he also has something that he calls temporality, and this word futural is part of his idea of temporality. Heidegger says that all these philosophers write about this and how this happened and how that happened, etc., and they have this succession of events (Hegel was one of them). Heidegger says that that is a lot of nonsense. (Melville has some conception of two different kinds of time in *Pierre*.[30] Work that out, I haven't had time.)

Heidegger says that there is a futural and that, at all times, man is conscious of the future, and at all times man is conscious of the past. He says that there is no actual present. Once you begin to "be there" and to understand what is happening, there is no present. He says you are always in a situation that can be calculated by what you expect, what you intend to do, what has happened to you in the past, and knowing that, ultimately, you are going to be dead. So, that is the temporality he speaks about. And I have found it in the conception of history too—people have this temporality, this uncertainty about time. Heidegger says that the time that you see on a clock is one thing, but the time that a human being lives is something entirely different, and that's what he calls temporality.

Now then, he goes on: *"Only an entity which, in its Being"*—in its fundamental nature—*"is essentially futural"*—it is thinking of the future—*"so that it is free for its death"*—it is not concerned about Being, it is free of the problem of death—*"and can let itself be thrown back upon its factical 'there' by shattering itself against death—that is to say, only an entity which, as futural, is equiprimordially in the process of having-been...."*[31] Is that clear from what

I have said? It is only futural because it is clear, it is aware, fundamentally, ontologically, equiprimordially of what has been. He says that is where you are. You are an entity, living an authentic existence, and having come out of the lostness into which you have fallen, when you are aware of where you are going and clear that, ultimately, you are going to be dead, and that is the end of it.

And having been—what has happened in the past—then you can calculate what time is, and you become a real person in the calculating. But if you measure time by the year 1966 and that you meet a ten o'clock, and that you do this tonight, etc.—he says that is no good at all. A good deal of his writing argues against thinking about time in that way.

Heidegger says, *"only an entity which, as futural, is equiprimordially in the process of* having-been, *can, by handing down to itself the possibility it has inherited, take over its own throwness and be* in the moment of vision *for 'its time'."* Only if it does that can it have a moment of vision and then be for its own time. Is that clear? The futural, time for the individual—we have known that also for the social group—is never at a particular historical time. It is only when you have a future in mind, and when you are conscious of what has been in the past, that you can take over and find out what is your own, what time is at the particular moment.

Heidegger continues: *"Only authentic temporality which is at the same time finite, makes possible something like fate—that is to say, authentic historicality."*[32] Only an authentic temporality—time that you have worked out in regard to the having been and the future, and which is at the same time finite and definitive (it begins here and it ends there)—makes possible something like fate, that is to say, something like authentic historicality. Otherwise, the history that you are trying to analyze or work is just a lot of nonsense. That's what he says.

And the point that has to be made is this: You need not accept Heidegger. You may reject him. But I suggest that you master him because he is accepted as a most important philosopher of the German historical school, ranking in the tradition of Kant and Hegel and the rest. And what is happening is that all the organs and all the methods of high philosophy are being used to examine the situation of the individual in a collapsing society. That is what he is doing, and you will have to read him to find this out.

Marxism has to develop, and this is one of the reasons that I bring Heidegger's work to you. Lenin insists that idealism can become very important and follow important lines of human thought. And everywhere citizens are concerned with precisely this because the ordinary canons of logic can no longer be applied with any effectiveness and real satisfaction to what is happening in society or to what is happening to them. Heidegger and existentialism is an attempt to be able to say: "Well, this is a method that you can use." We shall have to see.

(By the way, I don't discuss or give talks on Heidegger unless I have the book with me. Unless I have it I'm lost. It's difficult, and especially to a barbarian like me not brought up in German philosophy.)

Heidegger continues: "The Self's resoluteness against the inconstancy of distraction, is in itself *a steadiness which has been stretched along*—the steadiness with which Dasein as fate 'incorporates' into its existence birth and death and their 'between'"—and nothing else—"and holds them as this 'incorporated', so that in such constancy"—thinking of birth and death and what is in between and your particular operation there—"Dasein is indeed in a moment of vision for what is world-historical in its current Situation."[33] This is a tremendous statement. The historical method has to be dealt with in these terms. Heidegger has a conception of history that he calls historicality, and he has a conception of time that he calls temporality. You can reject them, but I have found that they both have to be dealt with.

Finally, Heidegger writes: "The Present discloses the 'today' authentically, and of course as the moment of vision. But in so far as this 'today' has been interpreted in terms of understanding a possibility of existence which has been seized upon—an understanding which is repetitive in a futural manner"—that futural is very important— "authentic historiology becomes a way in which the 'today' gets deprived of its character as present; in other words it"—the today, the authentic historiology, which we have discussed—"becomes a way of painfully detaching oneself from the falling publicness of 'today'."[34]

Now, we will stop there. I believe I have given you enough material to grapple with. I suggest you get a copy of the book itself. One of our comrades in France, a professor of philosophy called Lyotard, has written a book, *La Phénoménologie*, in which he tackles these questions in strict relation to Marx.[35] I advise you to get one or two copies. Do you have anybody who reads French freely? [*Glaberman: No, not as yet.*] Not as yet. Well, you ought to be able to find someone. Yes, get two or three copies of this Marty and spread them around. Lyotard is a very good comrade. He publishes a mimeographed bulletin. Do you get it? [*Glaberman: Yes.*] He has broken with Chalieu, and this is very much to his credit,[36] and the Presse Universitaires de France has published his *La Phénoménologie*.

I will translate certain passages from it and send them to you. He deals well with existentialism and Heidegger, and the passages that I will translate will show you how closely related phenomenology and existentialism are to a philosophy of history and a philosophy of everyday existence. And unless Marxism can incorporate these elements and still remain Marxism, we will continue saying the things that are said by Engels in *Anti-Dühring*, etc. But we are going to deal with that, and William, I suggest that you take the rest of it, and introduce your understanding of that long quotation, etc.[37]

So that's the situation with regard to that. In a few days I will send you translations of parts of Lyotard's *La Phénoménologie*, and William I recommend that you get down to work on this business. That you have the capacity I know. But don't be indifferent to it.

Rousseau and the Idea of General Will

I believe that, after Karl Marx, Rousseau is the most important figure in modern history. In his *A History Of Western Philosophy*, Mr. Bertrand Russell says that with Rousseau there began the descent into the modern world, or the descent of the modern world into barbarism—or something of the kind. There is also the attempt to make out that Rousseau's policy is the ancestor of totalitarianism.[1] I am absolutely opposed to that and I am glad to have this opportunity this evening to explain.

Rousseau's personality is worth studying, but not from the point of view that the average person does, as to how erratic a man of genius can be, but how consistent and determined a man of genius can be. He was a young man who grew up in the city of Geneva in Switzerland. Don't forget that, please. Geneva was a city-state, one of the few city-states that remained in Europe. I cannot think of another one. The great city-states of the previous centuries—of which there had been the Greek city-states and, towards the end of the Middle Ages, the Italian city-states—Venice, Florence, and the rest of them, and those remarkable city-states of the Netherlands—were famous states. Rousseau was brought up in one—Geneva. His father encouraged him to read (his mother died early). Rousseau went outside of Geneva and he lived with a lady called Mme. de Warens (he wrote it all in his *Confessions*) and later he found himself in Paris.

In Paris, there was taking place one of the greatest and most instructive movements in the history of human society and human thought. In the 18th century, a certain element of the middle classes set out to destroy Christianity. Are you aware of that? The Enlightenment, lead by Voltaire, Diderot, Rousseau, Grimm, and the rest of them, set out to destroy Christianity. (The man who has written about this best is a man called Hazard.[2]) They reached so far that I think the first four or five presidents of the United States—Benjamin Franklin, Thomas Jefferson, George Washington, and the rest of them—were not Christians; they were a vague thing they called Deists—there was some sort of god somewhere but they had no use at all for Christianity, Jesus, the Son of God, Virgin birth, and the Second Coming and all of that.

They repudiated all of it and that was done chiefly by these French writers of the 18th century. They said their basic theory was the Enlightenment and they are known as the Encyclopaedists because they organized, wrote, and published (Diderot as the editor) a tremendous encyclopaedia which was to present knowledge, learning, and to tell the world about what was going on; what was going on in theory, what was going on in science, the historical development of the world, what was taking place in industry, what was taking place in painting, what was taking place in philosophy, and so forth. You had to do that because the world was still dominated by the idea that everything of importance had been divinely revealed—the monarchy had been placed there by God and Revelation told you what was necessary. For the large majority of people, the world was run on the basis of Revelation and these men of the 18th century, the Encyclopaedists, set out to destroy it. Even Gibbon, the great historian of Rome, was a member of the Enlightenment. Gibbon wrote that history was nothing else but a record of the crimes, vices, and follies of mankind.[3] Do you know that phrase? That was the Enlightenment attitude.

They were not only successful in the work that they did. Catherine II invited Diderot to Russia. He had a good time there and she bought his book. Frederick II of Germany invited Voltaire to Berlin. The aristocracy played about with these ideas because they were advanced. They entertained no nonsense about letting them circulate among the masses of population, however, but thought that the ideas were wonderful. What is very noticeable, and what is to be observed today is that the aristocracy in France was permeated with the ideas of the Enlightenment. Diderot, Grimm, and the rest of them used to be friendly with members of the aristocracy. Every now and then the king, or those persons who were responsible for order, would put one or two of them in jail. They were getting ready to put Rousseau in jail for something extremely revolutionary that he wrote, but a member of the royal family came and told him, "They are coming for you," and he hid in the house of the prince, and eventually, the prince got him away.

Revolutionaries who are not members of the working-class or who are not able to organize the class which is to make the revolution always lead to mischief in the end. The Encyclopaedists were lead by Voltaire, Diderot, and Grimm. There were lots of them and they wrote magnificently. Lenin says that even up to today their attacks on Christianity are worth being read and circulated among the mass of proletarians everywhere. Voltaire said that if God did not exist, it would be necessary to invent him—a famous saying. They were against the monarchy, the monarchy that was there by Revelation, the Church, and the dishonest bureaucracy. Voltaire had a phrase for it. He called it *l'infâme* and he used to end all his letters with the phrase *écrasez l'infâme*—"crush the infamy," which I translate, "clean up the mess."

They had an ideal in mind. They wanted to clean up the mess in France, get rid of this rotten monarchy, get rid of the powers that the aristocracy had, and, above all, get rid of the Church with its Revelation. They had this idea and they published volumes of the *Encyclopedia*. They wrote philosophy and history, they attacked the Church, and they penetrated into the aristocracy with their ideas. Diderot would be in jail today, and stay there for a few weeks or a few months, but a month or two afterwards he would be at a party of the aristocracy and they would be listening to the flow of eloquence and wit that came forth from his mouth.

As the story goes, one day the University of Dijon[4] announced a competition: "Have the arts and sciences increased the public health, and has the restoration of the arts and sciences had a purifying effect upon public morals?" Rousseau said that he was walking along the road and he sat down. It was a beautiful summer day and he got a vision that the increase of the arts and sciences had meant the increase of the ruling elements in society and the decline and degradation of public morals. (Nowadays, people can prove anything about Rousseau and the more learned a man is, as a rule, the more reactionary he his, and the more easily he can prove anything about Rousseau.)

There is debate as to whether Diderot had those ideas first, or whether Rousseau and Diderot had them together, etc. What remains is that Rousseau is the person who carried these ideas to their extreme development, and he and Diderot split over them because, having put forward the idea that the development of the arts and sciences had tended towards the increasing degradation of public morals, Rousseau then went on to write his second essay, *Discourse on the Origin of Inequality* (1755), where he gave an analysis of the class struggle and the increasing results of the spread of economic and mechanical power and the spread of knowledge, which meant the increase in the knowledge and the power of the ruling class and the increasing degradation and exploitation of the mass of the population. You will find references to this as one of the books that enlightened people in Western Europe in Friedrich Engels's *Anti-Dühring*.[5]

Now, as you can imagine, there was a split right down the center of the Encyclopaedists and of the Enlightenment. What Rousseau was saying was this: "Don't listen to these people. In the end, ultimately, they will be no different from this aristocracy and monarchical bureaucracy that we are seeing. There is no point to it at all. Don't bother with them." Well, the split was great. Rousseau and Diderot quarrelled to the last degree. They split and Rousseau began his life of persecution. But Rousseau had broken away from them and he proceeded, in a very curious way, to stick to his own opinions. Everything that he subsequently wrote and touched, he illuminated according to these ideas.

The first point was that the development of the arts and sciences had resulted in the increasing domination of a ruling class and the lowering of the standards of social morality in the world. Then he went on to deal with *The Discourse of Inequality*, in which he proved, according to his outlook, that inequality was ruining the world and that the consequences of this would be serious; that the basis of this was the necessity of suppressing the mass of the population by those who gained more and more power. Then he developed, on the basis of this, an idea that early man, at the beginning, was everywhere born free. Primitive man had not known these qualities of the class struggle and suppression of people. Primitive man had lived according to some simple way of life, etc. (I believe that there were times when Rousseau used to go into the forest and come back and say he had seen some examples of these primitive men living in this way. You cannot say that Rousseau had not seen them—I cannot say that. But what you can say is that anybody else with him would not have, or most probably would not have, seen them.)

Rousseau developed this idea of primitive man, the native savage, the noble savage, and so forth. He did this because he was busy attacking the society that existed in the 18th century. He had written about inequality, he

had written about the restoration of the arts, and then he wrote a novel, *Julie*.[6]
It is a novel of a love affair. He was himself involved in it, or he was involved in
a love affair and he wrote on how he thought the love affair should have been
allowed to develop. It was something new: the sensibility, the refinement, and
variety of feeling were something that French writers had not known. The
great period of French writing was in the 17th century when you had Racine,
Comte, Molière, Pascal, and the rest of them. But it was Rousseau who began
the Romantic movement. Other people were doing it. Keats, Shelley, and
others in Britain were eventually to do it, but Rousseau wrote about the world
and about nature and the sensibilities of people in society in a manner that has
not been surpassed up to this day.

There were two men in French literature who marked stages in the
development, not only of French literature, but of European literature. The
first was Blaise Pascal. (Have you done any Pascal? Lord have mercy!)
Pascal was a great scientist; he was also a great religionist and one of the
creators of French prose. There was a society just outside of Paris called the
Jansenists. They were a society which got into a fierce quarrel with the Jesuits and they were finally suppressed by the Pope. This quarrel between the
Jansenists and the Jesuits was taking place and nobody could understand
what was going on. Pascal wrote some famous letters, *Lettres provinciales*
(Provincial Letters), a series of quite fictitious letters to friends in the country, telling them what was going on in Paris. That marks the beginning of a
certain stage in European prose. For the first time, religious, historical, and
philosophical matters were written in a prose which the average man could
read. Before that it had always been the preserve of educated people. That
is the first great stage in the writing of literature, and France led Europe
for many centuries. The second stage was Rousseau.

It is very strange, and it is of importance to some of the ideas that I'm
developing, that Rousseau handled the French language—it was his native
language, it was the language of Geneva—but he was not a Frenchman.
Therefore, I have developed this point (and I will have to come to it sometime) that that is one of the secrets of his work. Rousseau was a master of
French culture and civilization—he was accepted by them and so forth—
but he was not a Frenchman. In that period of crisis, catastrophe, and difficulties, he could see what the average Frenchman could not see. Rousseau's
writing in his novel, *Julie*, marks a tremendous stage in the development of

the European consciousness. It is not a question of the novel that he wrote, but the relations of people to one another, the influence that nature had on them, and so forth.

When he finished *Julie*, Rousseau then wrote another book called *Emile*, in which he took up the education of children. (Here Rousseau reminds me very much of Frantz Fanon.) Rousseau wrote about the education of Emile, a child of twelve or something, and he said, "This is the way children should be educated." But Rousseau was not a fool—it is very unwise to think that a man of genius is a fool. Rousseau would know that it was quite impossible that all the children in every part of society should be educated by a special tutor teaching him in a particular way. What he was concerned with was to make clear certain principles of education which were in harmony with his ideas of the freedom of development of the individual and so forth. That is a very fine book and is one of the great classics of education studied by people. It has played its role in the development of the school system and education generally, although Rousseau wrote of a single child who was specially educated.

For many years he had been writing a book on the political institutions of society and, when he felt he was getting old, he decided to take out some of it (I think the rest of it is still there, but I'm not sure.) He decided to take out some of it and he published it as *The Social Contract*,[7] one of the most terrific books that you can ever read. I'm glad to be able to speak about it tonight in a general way.

Rousseau begins with his whole idea: "Man is born free, but everywhere he is in chains." You know what born free means? That is his idea of inequality in the arts and sciences. He says, before all this, men lived freely together and were in harmony with one another. (It reminds me of this young man, Stokely Carmichael.[8] They asked Stokely, "What do you mean by Black Power?" He said, "I mean simply that Negroes should love one another [*Laughter*] because if the Negroes love one another—a lot of Negroes live in this neighbourhood—they would meet and love one another; they wouldn't fight and argue. They would do what they have to do and, if Negroes love one another, Whites will also love one another in the same way.")

There are a few things you have to remember. I shall say only about three: The social contract had long been a concept and method of historical analysis which writers had used from the days of Plato and Aristotle.

Certainly Thomas Hobbes, David Hume, and John Locke and others had used it. But all of them had had the idea that the social contract consisted of a contract between the population and those who formed the government. Rousseau blew that to pieces. Rousseau said that the social contract was a contract between members of the population. They had made a contract with each other and they had decided on the basis of this contract to give certain powers, which belonged to them, to the government. But if at any time the government did not satisfy them, they could take those powers back.

This was something new. We have to look at the philosophy and what that meant philosophically. This was something new, that the contract could be broken because it was not a contract between people and government. Locke and Hume, Montesquieu and the rest of them had insisted that they thought the contract was natural. Rousseau said, "No, it was a contract between different members of the population. They gave it to the government and, if they felt like it, they can take it back from the government."

Rousseau proceeded to develop certain other ideas. He said that representative government was a total failure and, not only a failure and a farce, but also a means of deceiving the mass of the population. For Voltaire and the rest of them, the British government with its political parties—Whigs and Tories—was what they wanted in France, because they thought it was better than what they had. But Rousseau said, whenever you put some people to represent you, before long, they're representing themselves. (I remember the burst of jeering laughter which arose when giving a class or talking about this in Trinidad, showing that all of them were followers of Rousseau [*Laughter*].) Rousseau said, "We don't want any representative government."

Rousseau also had the doctrine of the general will. He said, "We have to find out what is the general will of the population. The population must think, in regard to a certain matter, in the interest of the total population." I know what he means very well. I have seen it in history and I have seen it in Trinidad twice. Rousseau said, "It is true that every man is concerned with the individual, his individual necessities, but when you meet together and you discuss a social problem in social and political terms, the result is not the summation of the individual necessities and requirements of every individual; the result is a social conception and you get the general will of the population."

I have seen that in Trinidad, 1920 to 1932—Captain Cipriani—and I saw it with the PNM[9] and Dr. Williams, 1957 to 1960. When there is a general opinion that the person who is leading a particular struggle has the mass of the population behind him and the feeling is that what is taking place is not about wages or more education, not this or that, but something for the total benefit that is lifting the population to a higher stage, the minority becomes very quiet; the minority does not carry on in the way that they ordinarily do.

That is the significance of the general will and I have identified it in various historical situations and I have seen it myself in Trinidad. That is what Rousseau meant by the general will. But he is very aware that individual people have individual desires, and he said, "If a majority consists of nothing but the individual desires and wishes of the majority against the minority, then that is not the general will." Hegel, Kant, and others were also very clear about it. Most of them followed Rousseau in his conception of the general will. That is one of the reasons why I wanted you to study Rousseau and to bear him in mind.

With the West Indian politician—majority. He has a majority and he can do what he likes. He will lock you up or he is always threatening to lock you up or pass this law, or pass that law, or spend the money. In 1957, when Williams said he was going to make oil pay, look after sugar, put the Colonial Office and the U. S. State Department in their place, and he wanted Chaguaramas back,[10] there were a lot of people who felt that he was going too fast or being rash, etc. But they did not oppose it because they felt that here was somebody who was taking charge of something and doing something which should have been done a hundred years before. I remember Cipriani when he started in 1920. I talked to him and wrote his biography in 1931. He told me a lot of things. He said, "Time and again, you see me stand up in the house and say 'the government is doing this and that and that and that.' Do you know how I know? Someone in the office inside comes and tells me, 'Cip, so and so in going on and you can deal with it if you like. All I'm asking is don't say that I told you.'"

Time and again Cipriani used to come out and denounce the government for what was going on, and the government wouldn't know where he got it from. He had the sympathy of the large majority of the population, and even those who were against him felt that they couldn't really tackle him on this question. That is the meaning of studying history. You have to get some idea of what the general will means, because Rousseau knew what he was talking about.

Rousseau got himself into trouble, and this is, I think, one of the greatest examples of the really magnificent person he was. Rousseau had in mind the Greek democracy, these little states of 10,000, 15,000 and 20,000 people. Athens, the biggest, had no more than about 30,000 at most, so they could manage their democracy and work out their general will and so forth. Rousseau had also lived in Geneva and, in all his writings, you can see he had that in mind as the model upon which he was building. Rousseau also knew that what took place in a Greek city-state could not take place in countries like France, Britain, and Germany. You see him struggling to get some kind of political means whereby the general will can be expressed and, to me, his mistakes are not evidence of his incapacity or his lack of political sense. The mistakes are evidence of the clear way in which he saw what was to be done and the way he was struggling to find a way in which it could be carried through.

Rousseau went so far in places as to say, at times, in order to express the general will that a dictator would be needed. That is the basis today when they say that Rousseau is the basis of the totalitarian state. But Rousseau was looking to see how this general will could be expressed. Rousseau's conception of the general will—that you could blow this government out of sight at any time that you like—that is no dictatorship, no totalitarian state.

Well, at the end he lost his reason. People thought he was being persecuted. He went away to England and came back. Before he died, he wrote his *Confessions*,[11] another place in which he broke new ground. St. Augustine had written his confessions, some 2000 years before, but now a modern, Rousseau, wrote his confessions. He had broken out into all kinds of spheres.

There are two conclusions that I want to draw about Rousseau. One is Rousseau's influence on philosophy, and the other is Rousseau's influence in politics. We know that Kant was a great philosopher of the 18th century, a philosopher of the bourgeoisie. He made this tremendous change from Hume, yet he never made any bones about the fact that he owed the foundations of his philosophy to the influence of Rousseau. Once you have broken up Revelations and the idea of the king being sent by God and people being born to rule, and you finish with the monarchy, aristocracy, the Church, Pope, and the rest of them—the moment you are finished with that, you have to find some basis in society for the ideas of government that you have. Kant's basis was to prove that ethics were due to some instinct in the mind and that people had to obey what he called the categorical imperative.

(Do you know who has written a fine book on it? *Kant and Rousseau,* a small pamphlet by Cassirer.[12] Do you know Cassirer? He is a very learned man, but it's a small pamphlet and he is not too learned in it to upset anybody. In the pamphlet, it is very clear that a great deal of the basis of Kant's philosophy is in the work of Rousseau.) Kant was no man of God, the Virgin birth, and all that, but you have to find some basis, and Kant found his basis in an ethical system which, he said, belonged to the instincts of mankind, and man should not behave as if man was a means, but an end, and so forth.

Rousseau had been saying this. Rousseau said, "Man is born free, but everywhere he is in chains." Is that where Kant got it from? I don't know what your professor will say. One has to be careful in these matters. But the influence of Rousseau—Rousseau's sociology, historical, and political ideas, his ideas on education, and so forth—on Kant's philosophy and *The Critique of Pure Reason* is something that is a commonplace among people who are not bothered about these things at all. But your professor might be very hostile to Rousseau (Bertrand Russell cannot stand him). So that in regard to philosophy—and one of the greatest philosophical works of all time, *The Critique of Pure Reason, The Critique of Practical Reason,* and other things of the kind—they come from Rousseau. Practically everything in the 20th century that matters comes from Rousseau. He began it, even the sensibility of prose style.

That is Rousseau on philosophy, and now I come to the last and the most beautiful of them all. The French Revolution was made on the basis of the principles of Rousseau. In France, they had popular sections, and the great driving force of the French Revolution was the section of Paris. There were forty-seven, I think. (Albert Soboul has written on them, but they say that the translation is not good.[13] They have also cut short a lot that is in the original French edition, but one of you must begin to learn French.) Some of the sections called themselves "Rousseau" and, time and again, the conflict in the Convention was between the sections of Paris attacking the Convention and members from different parts of Paris which were not so revolutionary in the Convention. That is the basic difficulty.

Robespierre's problem was that he couldn't let the sections of Paris, expressing this freely through democratic participation, upset the Convention which was elected by persons from all over France. The ultimate end of that would have been a split and civil war between Paris and certain cities elsewhere which were part Parisian in sympathy, and the rest of the country. It nearly came to it. Robespierre did his best to prevent it. That is how I interpret him. That is what I see. Others play with it. Leferbvre tried his best but is not clear about it.[14] I make no bones about it. But the thing I want you to remember is the Parisian masses in particular had been reading Rousseau and said that they were the sovereign. They said: "Rousseau said we are the sovereign. We are the sovereign and therefore you have to do what we say."

It was very plain and I find it extremely profound that the greatest philosopher of the age, Kant, owed one of the most important books ever written in philosophy, *The Critique of Pure Reason*, and later, *The Critique of Practical Reason*, to the writings of Rousseau, and that the mass of the Parisians in the French Revolution also made their revolution, and carried through the revolution as far as they could, destroying feudal society (the bourgeoisie could not do it), with the belief that they were carrying out the doctrine of Rousseau.

I think it would be extremely difficult to find a man—maybe Dante, I am not sure (I don't know enough of Catholicism and the history of that period; I wish I knew somebody who did)—who has had such a tremendous influence on all aspects of human thought and society as Rousseau has had. It pains me to see the superficial way in which they write about him, the careless way in which people discuss his philosophy, because Rousseau was a revolutionary, he was against the established regime, and there is no question about that.

That is what I thought I would say to you this evening. I hope I have given you a picture of the kind of person Rousseau was and how, with every single thing he touched, he brought into existence something new which we are using up to today. I know no figure in history whom you can say had, within a few years of his death, such tremendous influence on such widely separated spheres of humanity. That is what I wanted to say about him, and now we can talk about it.

QUESTION: Was the state that he proposed the ideal state for man, where man was going to be happy?

JAMES: That's what he had in mind, but I don't think he proposed an ideal state. He was very realistic. (By the way, there's someone named Guehenno[15] who has written a life of Rousseau. I read it in French when it came out years ago. It is not a good book. He has done a lot of research but his ideas are not very bright. If it so happens that you are interested in Rousseau, he's worthwhile reading, but I would like you to bear in mind what I have said.) He didn't write of any ideal state. That's why I mentioned Fanon. Rousseau knew that a new world was coming into existence.

A few years after he died you had the American Revolution in 1776, and a few years after that you had the French Revolution in 1789. A new world was coming into existence and Rousseau was pressing in every single direction that he knew, saying what it should be. He was a new man, a sensitive man, and all the new ideas, etc., that were current at the time—they were in Shakespeare too, repeatedly—he would feel them and he wrote about them as they came to him. He didn't write a blueprint for a new society. He didn't do that.

What he was saying was, "Hobbes has written on the social contract, Hume has written on the social contract, Locke has written on the social contract. All of them have written on the social contract. I am going to say what I think the social contract should be like." In the same way as he said, "This is how I think a pair of lovers should behave, how they should take part in nature and see the landscape, and express themselves to one another; this is how a child should be educated, etc.; this is how history should be written," and so forth. That is what he was doing. He didn't write the blueprint for a new society. The man who wrote the blueprint for society was Karl Marx. Rousseau didn't do that.

QUESTION: You know Rousseau admired the state of nature. My professor said that it was after he realized it is impossible to return to this state that he posed this intermediary state where it could have an executive and legislature, and this sort of thing.

JAMES: An executive legislature? But what kind of state is Rousseau proposing? Where the sovereign is able to say, "We don't like this arrangement we have made with you. You're not carrying it out. Out you go." I don't think that Rousseau would have thought that that was the state that he had in mind. He may have had ideas, but he was blowing up the actual states that existed. That's what he was doing. Diderot and all of them were playing about with a kind of state like the British state. Rousseau was saying that as long as you have this representative government and a state with authority from above, that is no good. The only kind of state is a state where the people are the sovereign.

It is a commonplace among those of us who are studying him that, if you had asked Rousseau, "Did the state of nature exist?" he would have said "no." Kant has said it isn't a question of whether the state of nature actually existed. Get that book, *Kant and Cassirer.* I am not telling you to tell your professor that you are saying this, and if you do, you say "Professor Cassirer..." [*Laughter*] otherwise these fellows can be very cantankerous. Not all of them, but it is well to be on the safe side.

Cassirer said that Kant says, although the state of nature did not actually exist historically, it is necessary to think it was so in order to be able to deal with the problem as it is today. You have to visualize that it began that way. Rousseau would go in the forest and say he saw some people from the state of nature. Rousseau never believed that. Cassirer is quite sure of it. You see, I have to be careful here because to be saying these things means that you have to read through some thirty or forty volumes with notes and so forth. I haven't done that, but I have an instinct and Cassirer and the others say Rousseau never believed that there are people living according to the state of nature. But he built up his picture of the state of nature.

And he was not so far wrong because the basis of Marx and Engel's theory of historical development is primitive communism. There is a lot of debate about this, one way or the other. Marx never committed to it too strongly himself, but that's where they began. I would recommend to you a book called *Totemism* by Lévi-Strauss. And you will see where he says that, where no research had been made into primitive society and totemism, Rousseau, by some sort of instinct, was near to what is an essentially modern view on totemism and the function that it played in a primitive society.[16] It is worthwhile, even if you don't go on to read the whole book. But get that section and read it.

QUESTION: Neither of my professors had mentioned Rousseau, even in the introduction to Kant which we started last week. They mention Hume. The Introduction to Philosophy professor said that Hume has influenced modern philosophy. He hasn't mentioned Rousseau. They have not said one word about Rousseau.

JAMES: Now, let me tell you something which you will remember and put in your notebook, but whenever you see your philosopher, go blank. Kant says that the position Hume took in which he was saying there was no sort of dependence that could be made on the human mind, he says, well, Berkeley had started this business, Locke, with this *tabula rasa*, and Hume had carried it to the ultimate limit. Kant had been a philosopher teaching Natural Anthropology but he said that he read Hume and realized that that would not do. He now had to find something and he found it in Rousseau.

Now what must be clear is this: Hume said everything was custom. He said, "You cannot be sure that the sun will rise tomorrow morning." How do you know? It happened before so you can expect it. It is a custom, a habit that it will come tomorrow, but you cannot prove that. He said, "You cannot prove anything." And Kant said, "No, we can't accept that." But where he found the way out was with Rousseau. Hume made him realize that they could not go on in the old way, but Rousseau opened the new way to him. And I advise you to get that little book by Cassirer, *Kant and Rousseau*, and read it.

Cassirer is one of the most famous philosophical and sociological scholars on the nature of man of the 20th century. Ernst Cassirer. It is a small pamphlet (about sixty or seventy pages) on Rousseau and Kant. Lord have mercy, your professor is teaching you Kant and he does not mention Rousseau! Anyway, I am not surprised.

HARVEY: [Inaudible]

JAMES: I have given some talks on Shakespeare. I did two on Lear, one on each of the other three tragedies, and I did one on Shakespeare the man. I discussed how he arrived just at the time when a new society was being born. The Revolution began in 1629 and Shakespeare died in 1660; Rousseau died about 1770, but it was clear in all his writings that the Revolution was as much on the way to him as it was to Shakespeare.

There was a new society coming, and Shakespeare lived at a period when he could see them both. But nevertheless, there was only one Shakespeare. So, I want to make clear that there is a certain stage in the psychology of a great individual that you do not know. If you study the man's work, if you study his biography carefully, and you read up all the letters and so forth, you may get somewhere. But I am usually very scared of that.

What were the motives? I have seen people talk about the fact that his father encouraged him to read books, romances and novels, etc. When he was a boy he did not do any serious work, but he fed his imagination. I do not know. All I can say is it seems to me that he was an extremely sensitive man. He had not been brought up in French bourgeois society. Marx is very emphatic that he was a singularly honest person and could never be committed to sell his principles to the bourgeoisie or the aristocracy which, growing up in these circumstances, meant living the life of the ordinary people; reading and knowing a lot of things; going to France, working in that intellectual circle; getting in touch with the aristocracy, etc. And being a fundamentally honest man, he remained a man of the people. But he could see them for what they were, and that is why he was able to write both ways. Further than that, I could not go.

HARVEY: This is precisely what I was asking, because I remember when you gave the talk on modern politics when you were here the first time. You were explaining the clash—well not the clash—between Hegel and Marx and you said, for example, whereas Hegel believed that the concept starts in the mind and then whoever the individual may be would express this concept, Marx said the opposite in that he got the concept, not from his mind, but from what was going on. And this is precisely what I am saying. I was just asking, not of the psychology of Rousseau, but that these concepts came in his mind because he knew, saw, and experienced what was going on within French society.

JAMES: I think you would be justified in saying so with due caution. You see, what I am talking about is this: There are a lot of other people who lived in this society but who did not see it—at least nobody wrote it. And that is what we are up against. How is it that this particular fellow, this Shakespeare, saw and wrote this way? And what were the others doing? So there is a certain something there that is inexplicable. The man of genius, and the man of rare genius. And Rousseau was one.

HARVEY: I was not in the process of asking why he wrote in this way and why nobody else did. What I was stating is he managed to write that way because of a certain factor and...

JAMES: He undoubtedly lived among the people. He began living with his father who was a watchmaker, or jeweller of some kind, in Geneva. He went to live with Madame de Warens, who lived in a house outside Geneva in the country somewhere. Then he went up to Paris and he lived with some girl and maybe had five children with her. So, he lived the life of the people. But he was such a brilliant man that he moved about in this intellectual circle, and this intellectual circle was in touch with the aristocracy. So, Rousseau was seeing all. But as Marx points out, he never lost that fundamental honesty of character, and he could write about everything in that way.

He was quite a person. And you certainly should read *Inequality* and the *Arts*. Engels pays great attention to it. Engels feels that there, for the first time, somebody had begun to use the dialectic....[17]

Marx's *Eighteenth Brumaire of Louis Bonaparte* and the Caribbean

The Eighteenth Brumaire, as we have it here, is a hundred and thirty-five pages. It is obvious that I cannot attempt to go through a hundred and thirty-five pages with you. But you will have read it, and I hope you will do what I have done—read it over many times. It is, not only in my opinion but also in the opinion of even some American historians, the finest piece of history that has ever been written on such a small scale, and every page is of great value. I have selected a few, I could have added to them, I could have done less, but I think they will cover the ground.

In the introduction by Marx you will come across one of the sharpest pieces of analyses of value today. Marx says that they are dealing with the revolt, the counter-revolution of 1851—*coup d'état*. Napoleon seized power in 1798 on the 18th Brumaire, and this one, this seizure of power by Napoleon III, they called it the Eighteenth Brumaire of Louis Bonaparte. Marx makes an analysis here that covers a lot of ground. But, he says, "Of the writings dealing with the same subject approximately *at the same time* as mine, only two deserve notice."[1] Victor Hugo wrote *Napoléon Le Petit*[2] and he thought, in saying that, as opposed to the Great Napoleon, he was saying something. Marx says Hugo "confines himself to bitter and witty invective against" Napoleon III.[3] "The event itself appears in his work like a bolt from the blue. He sees in it only the violent act of a single individual" (*EBLB*, 8).

A lot of people speak about Dr. Williams[4] in Trinidad being that way. Marx says, "He does not notice that he makes this individual great instead of little by ascribing to him a personal power of initiative such as would be without parallel in world history." He says Hugo wrote well (I read the Hugo essay many years ago out of curiosity), and he says by taking this man and talking about what he did, you completely distort the historical view. (That fellow, Ivar Oxaal, is a beautiful example of this. Have you read that one, "C.L.R James versus Eric Williams"?[5] I was a bit annoyed that he put me in that. What have I to do with Eric Williams? At any rate, he made an analysis of Williams, and I have met this many times in England, everywhere else, but particularly with West Indians.)

Marx continues: 'Proudhon, for his part, seeks to represent *coup d'état* as the result of an antecedent historical development. Unnoticeably, however, his historical construction of the *coup d'état* becomes a historical *apologia* for its hero." I have met this repeatedly. Those economic determinists, they say, "this was the historical situation, this was the economic situation, this represented this, this represented that," and they give you the impression that they are using Marxism, that in reality it was inevitable that so and so should get into power and should remain in power. Then comes something without which Marxism is a lot of nonsense: "Thus he falls into the error of our so-called *objective* historians." They are all over the place, particularly in the Americas—in the United States and in the West Indies. Marx says, "I, on the contrary, demonstrate how the *class struggle* in France created circumstances and relationships that made it possible,"—there you are —"for a grotesque mediocrity to play a hero's part" (*EBLB*, 8).

Are you aware of that, of the distinction? Not the economic analysis and the economic forces expressing themselves. Marxism is essentially the question of the struggle of classes. That is one of the finest statements I know, in this introduction to the *Eighteenth Brumaire*. That is one of the finest pieces of historical materialism that I know because it not only analyzes in general, but it also takes some specific books and it shows you where Proudhon, who must have thought that he was dealing in historical analysis, made his mistake. If you do historical and economic analysis without being aware of the significance, the dominant significance of the struggle of classes based on that economic analysis, you end by looking upon and painting the actual state of events as inevitable.

Here is something for you West Indians to learn: "Colonel Charras opened the attack on the Napoleon cult in his work on the campaign of 1815." Napoleon went to St. Helena and built up a lot of ideas about himself as a man seeking to build a new Europe and so on. These ideas run around and you have to deal with them. Marx says: "Subsequently, and particularly in the last few years, French literature made an end of the Napoleon legend with the weapons of historical research, of criticism, of satire and of wit" (*EBLB*, 8).

I don't think we have many legends in the West Indies to deal with except the largest of them all—the British legend, the European legend, has to be dealt with, particularly that the British and the Europeans in general civilized us and then abolished slavery. The history of the abolition of slavery has not been properly told. They had reached a stage where slavery had to be abolished. (Williams has a sentence in his book stating that it was done from above because if it wasn't done from above it would have been done from below.[6] I told him that, in all probability.) They had reached a stage where it was absolutely impossible to go on. In addition (I spoke of that when I spoke here in Montreal[7]), long before slavery was abolished, it was clear that those societies in the Caribbean could not exist at all without slavery. So, the legend of the British educating us and helping us and then abolishing slavery is a legend that is still around. We have got to clear that out of the way. As the Napoleonic legend was terrific in France—and Marx says how they settled down and, after a number of years, they got rid of it—we have to get rid of the legend that we have of being civilized, then slavery was abolished, then we began to learn and so forth, and then they taught us to serve governments. You would not be able to do it, unless you have the method of Marxism, or some other method, if you like—I don't care—but you have to get a European conception.

The West Indies have no method of history. The Africans may have one, but that isn't going to explain the abolition of slavery in the Caribbean in 1833 and 1848.[8] So, that has to be out of the way and the way it will be abolished is by systematic historical study and having a particular method. And that is a job. Some of us have done what we could. But the work still remains to be done. If you read Williams's *Capitalism and Slavery*, you will see that he is more concerned with what slavery did for capitalism. That is a useful volume. He's a scholar and it's a fine piece of work. Elsa Goveia has written about slavery in the Windward and Leeward islands.[9] Have you read the book? Have you got the book? Well, that is a book you might read in time. She writes about the slave owners and the profits and what they did, and so forth. But she does not deal with the impact of slavery and the impact of the slaves upon the society and what the society did to the slaves.

I hear that Orlando Patterson intends to do it.[10] I don't know. But there is a great legend to be cleared up. We have the most absurd ideas about this slavery business. Don't they say that the Queen abolished slavery? Isn't that the conception? Which is most untrue. She came into power in 1837. Slavery was abolished in 1834.[11] And she had little enough power when she came to the throne. She had none before she came. The Queen didn't abolish slavery. This whole slavery abolition business is absolutely necessary to do.

I go on next to page twenty-five. I don't know what books you are using but it begins:

> During the June days all classes and parties had united in the *party of Order* against the proletarian class as *the party of Anarchy*, of Socialism, of Communism. They had "saved" society from the "enemies of society." They had given out the watchwords of the old society, "property, family, religion, order," to their army as passwords and had proclaimed to the counter-revolutionary crusaders: "In this sign thou shalt conquer!" From that moment, as soon as one of the numerous parties which had gathered under this sign against the June insurgents seeks to hold the revolutionary battlefield in its own class interest, it goes down before the cry: "Property, family, religion, order" (*EBLB*, 25).

What are the slogans in the West Indies today? They are against communism. They are for democracy. Williams says they are for free enterprise. What is it they are talking about? They are against communism everywhere. But what are they for? Democracy? Joshua,[12] all of them are for democracy. That is a slogan. But is there anything else they are for? The situation in the West Indies is beyond belief.

Speaking about the West Indian middle classes, I have written:

> We live in a world in the throes of a vast reorganization of itself. *[James: That's why you have to study Marxism: to know where you live.]* The religious question is back on the order of discussion. The two world wars and the third in the offing, Nazism, Stalinism, have made people ask: where is humanity going? Some say that we are now reaching the climax of that preoccupation with science and democracy which well over a hundred and fifty years ago substituted itself for religion as the guiding principle of mankind.[13]

That started with the French Revolution, and now we are drawing the full results. "Some believe we have to go back to religion. Others, that mankind has never made genuine democracy the guiding light for society. Freud and Jung have opened up depths of uncertainty and doubt of the rationality of human intelligence" (*PPWI*, 134). Since Freud, the people understand that what a man does and says is one thing, but below all sorts of powerful, irrational forces are working.

> Where the West Indian middle class (with all its degrees) stand on this, who is for, who is against, even thinks of such matters, nobody knows. They think they can live and avoid such questions. You can live, but in 1962 you cannot govern that way (*PPWI*, 134).

You must have some conception, some ideas, and you must guide yourself by those and people must understand where you are going, what you are doing, and what you are against. These fellows today are against communism. Isn't that so? They are against race, and the West Indies is ridden with racial antagonisms and prejudices. But they go all about saying people live together in our countries. "Are they capitalists, i.e., do they believe in capitalism, socialism, communism, anarchism, anything? Nobody knows" (*PPWI*, 134).

What does Joshua believe in? What does the other man, the lawyer,[14] what does he believe in? He believes in Catoto power. They are all very clear about that. But any policy, any program, any idea?

> They keep as far as they can from committing themselves to anything. This is a vitally practical matter. Are you going to plan your economy? To what degree is that possible, and compatible with democracy? To West Indian politicians a development program is the last word in economic development. They never discuss the plan, what it means, what it can be. If they feel any pressure they forthwith baptize their development program as "planning".

> Where does personality, literature, art, the drama stand today in relation to a national development? What is the relation between the claims of individuality and the claims of the state? What does education aim at? To make citizens capable of raising the productivity of labor, or to give them a conception of life? (*PPWI*, 134)

You ask Vere Bird[15] and all these people—they don't know. I know them well. On all these matters, they are blank. You have not talked to them. All they think about is how to get into power, defeat the other side, pick up some loans and something, and get the people to work.

What is the relation of education to a new society? To give them a conception of life, or to educate them for increasing the productivity of labor? "West Indian intellectuals who are interested in or move around politics avoid these questions as if they were the plague" (*PPWI*, 134). If you all go back to the West Indies and raise them, they're going to make you understand that the quicker you get out of there, the better.

> Some readers may remember seeing the movie of the night of the independence of Ghana, and hearing Nkrumah choose at that moment to talk about the African Personality. This was to be the aim of the Ghanaian people with independence. Is there a West Indian personality? Is there a West Indian nation? What is it? What does it lack? What must it have? The West Indian middle classes keep far from these questions. The job, the car, the fridge, the trip abroad, preferably under government auspices and at government expense, these seem to be the beginning and end of their preoccupations (*PPWI*, 135).

That's where they begin, that's where they end. "What foreign forces, social classes, ideas, do they feel themselves allied with or attached to? Nothing" (*PPWI*, 135). Where do they stand in regard to what Nyerere[16] has been doing? *Blank*. Where do they stand in regard to Nkrumah?[17] Did they support him before? Do they support him now? What? They don't know. Not one of them knows anything. At rare moments you will get Manley[18] to talk a little bit. The others—totally blank. I know them, and I know them well. They think they can govern like that. They give the people no lead, they educate them in no way. Nobody who is thinking of anything gets anything from them. He has to pick up what he can from the United States, or Britain, but they have nothing to say.

> What foreign forces, social classes, ideas, do they feel themselves allied with or attached to? Nothing. What in their own history do they look back to as a beginning of which they are the continuation? I listen to them, I read their speeches and their writings. "Massa Day Done"[19] seems to be the extreme limit of their imaginative concepts of West Indian nationalism. Today nationalism is under fire and every people has to consider to

what extent its nationalism has to be mitigated by international considerations. Of this[,] as of so much else[,] the West Indian middle class is innocent. What happens after independence? For all you can hear from them, independence is a dead end. Apart from the extended opportunities of jobs with the government, independence is as great an abstraction as was Federation. We achieve independence and they continue to govern (*PPWI*, 135).

I brought that in to show you that, even if you are reactionary, you must have some slogans, some positive proposal that you are making. And these people had one. They were defending "property, family, religion, order." Marx says, "From that moment, as soon as one of the numerous parties which had gathered under this sign against the June insurgents seeks to hold a revolutionary battlefield in its own class interest, it goes down before the cry: 'Property, family, religion, order'" (*EBLB*, 24).

The West Indian reactionaries today have no slogan. Is there anything that they put forward that has been maintained? That is the blankness of the whole place.

> Society is saved just as often as the circle of its rulers contracts, as a more exclusive interest is maintained against a wider one. Every demand of the simplest bourgeois financial reform, *[James: "Listen to this please"]* of the most ordinary liberalism, of the most formal republicanism, of the most shallow democracy, is simultaneously castigated as an "attempt on society" and stigmatized as "Socialism" (*EBLB*, 25).

Today it isn't socialism that is stigmatized, it is communism. That unfortunate human, George Beckford, goes to Cuba. They take away his passport.[20] Why? Some way or other, communism. That's what is involved. As soon as you say anything against them, it is stigmatized as communism, or you are a friend of James. It is very easy, and sometimes very stupid, to make predictions. But what those pseudo-democrats are doing in the West Indies is preparing the way, either for a tremendous movement of the mass of the population, or for some totalitarian gangster to impose his will upon the community. That is what happened to these fellows—"the property, religion, family, order."

This is a famous passage:

And, finally, the high priest of 'the religion and order' themselves are driven with kicks from their Pythian tripods, hauled out of their beds in the darkness of night, put in prison-vans, thrown into dungeons or sent into exile; their temple is raised to the ground, their mouths are sealed, their pens broken, their law torn to pieces in the name of religion, of property, of the family, of order (*EBLB*, 25–26).

These pseudo-democrats who are playing around and are telling the people nothing—and the people are getting more and more tired of them and more and more aware that there is nothing to be got from them—are preparing the way for the most violent upheavals in the Caribbean. The upheavals will take one of two forms: either a kind of Castro revolt,[21] or it needn't go that far, because what Castro had to fight against does not exist in the West Indies. Bustamante[22] and Williams and these fellows, are fake dictators. They are not dictators. They have no armies, they have no people dressed in some kind of shirts[23] who they can depend upon and call out to keep order. I know Williams well because I've been in Trinidad for the last two years. He marches three or four hundred army soldiers up and down. If you look at them, they don't mean anything. They are preparing the way either for a tremendous move forward, or Trinidad and the other West Indian islands will sink down to where Haiti is today.

We have to analyze it and learn to analyze it, and learn from what happened to other countries. We have our own history to write but we can't write that history unless we have a method, unless we have some historical principles that we work by. I am a Marxist. If there are others—by all means. But you can't just leave it alone or write whatever comes into your head. And these principles are the best I know. I'm always trying to draw conclusions for the Caribbean. What is taking place with Bustamante's nonsensical pseudo-democracy? Barrow's[24] democracy? Always certain to put people in jail. Williams is the same. What is taking place in Guyana? Jagan[25] has given a lot of trouble; Burnham[26] says he has settled it but nothing is settled there. Those islands are preparing for the most violent explosions, one way or the other. Either they express themselves fully, or it is down to where Haiti is today.

I go on next to page fifty-three. I will take various passages. This Marxism is supposed by some people to be mathematical and a method of calculation in politics. The whole point of the *Eighteenth Brumaire* is that in addition to the basic economic analysis and the class struggle, Marx insisted that there are particular periods in a political situation where it is either one thing or the other, where it is balanced on a razor's edge. I will read one passage to show you that. Marx says:

> If the *Montagne [James: "a certain part of parliament"]* wished to triumph in parliament, it should not have called to arms. If it called to arms in parliament, it should not have acted in parliamentary fashion in the streets. If the peaceful demonstration was meant seriously, then it was folly not to foresee that it would be given a war-like reception. If a real struggle was intended, then it was a queer idea to lay down the weapons with which it would have to be waged (*EBLB*, 53).

Alfie, you got that?[27] The danger is that people begin to look upon Marxism as something mathematical. It isn't. I remember Trotsky telling us one day that in 1905 there was some problem of returning guns, and they came to some decision (I need not go into it). But he said the debate ended in a decision, some were for and some were against, and they decided to do this, etc. But to this day, Trotsky said, he does not know whether the decision was correct.[28] So, Marxism does not give you a blueprint in which you know what to do every time. It creates a situation where you observe the classes based upon the economic relations and you face the decisions. They can be quite open, so I quote that passage for that reason.

People have asked me whether I think there is any fear or possibility of some ferocious, totalitarian dictatorship. I say no, not in the Caribbean. You may have a military dictatorship, you may have an autocratic regime, but a totalitarian, communistic kind of dictatorship or fascist dictatorship, that is most unlikely and I will tell you why. Let us read this passage at page seventy-four: "As in 1849 so during this year's parliamentary recess, the party of Order had broken up into its separate factions, each occupied with its own Restoration intrigues" (*EBLB*, 74).

Is that clear what is happening? The order, religion, family, and the rest of them who, as we are going to see later, are going to get it in the neck, they had broken up into their separate factions. Those regimes in Trinidad and the Caribbean will break up into their separate factions. That is certain. And there will be various processions:

Bonaparte, in his turn, was therefore entitled to make tours of the French Departments, and according to the disposition of the town that he favored with his presence, now more or less covertly, now more or less overtly, to divulge his own restoration plan and canvass votes for himself. On these processions, which the great official *Moniteur* and the little private *Moniteurs* of Bonaparte naturally had to celebrate as triumphal processions, he was constantly accompanied by persons affiliated with *the Society of December the 10* (*EBLB*, 75).

If you look at a fascist regime or an old fashioned, even a new communist regime, there is the government, there is the civil service, there is the police, there is the army. That's what you have in Trinidad. [The army is nothing.] But the real totalitarian regime is a regime in which the ruler and his friends constitute an extra-governmental body. (God, I have to say that so often.) The German fascists had the Brown Shirts. Don't you know about them? The Brown Shirts could handle the police and could go into a state, into a city, and handle the proletariat there.

Mussolini had his Black Shirts, Stalin had his party, and Nkrumah tried to form a party but he wasn't able to. It isn't easy for certain regimes to form these things, but they can be formed in an advanced country. It is an extra-governmental body because as long as you have the ordinary police, the ordinary army, and the ordinary civil service, they can always break up under your hands. But you must have a special body of gangsters who are allied to you, pay tribute to you, and whom you can call upon. All that helps to bring a lot of uncertainty your way. Nothing like that has appeared in the Caribbean so far. That is going to be very difficult for them to do. I know these boys are thinking of dictatorship and a benevolent dictatorship and the size of the dictatorship, etc., but they have a police. They have a thousand police. They tell the police, "shoot the people." The police may shoot once, but to shoot again, it's his brother he's shooting, his wife, his sister, his girlfriend, all of them. So you have to get this special body of gangsters allied to the government, or whoever is going to be dictator, which is able to act and will act in support of the governor, in support of the dictator, irrespective of the police, civil service, and army. That must be borne in mind when you are considering what is to happen in the West Indies. Somebody may attempt a dictatorship, but with the civil service, police, the army, and nothing else, that dictatorship can break up within twenty-four hours of his appointing it.

> This society dates from the year 1849.[29] On the pretext of founding a
> benevolent society, the *lumpenproletariat* of Paris *[James: "That is flotsam
> and jetsam"]* has been organized into secret sections, each section being led
> by Bonapartist agents, with a Bonapartist general at the head of the whole
> (*EBLP*, 75).

This is the origin of the fascist society. When you see that sort of grouping
appearing in a Caribbean island, danger is there. Be ready for that. We'll
take that up some other time.

> Alongside decayed *roués* with dubious means of subsistence and of dubi-
> ous origin, alongside ruined and adventurous offshoots of the bourgeoisie,
> were vagabonds, discharged soldiers, discharged jailbirds, escaped galley
> slaves, swindlers, mountebanks, *lazzaroni*, pickpockets, tricksters, gam-
> blers, *maquereaus*[30] *[James: We call them 'maco' in Trinidad]* brothel keepers,
> porters, *literati* *[James: Men of letters]*, organ-grinders, ragpickers, knife
> grinders, tinkers, beggars—in short, the whole indefinite, disintegrated
> mass, thrown hither and thither, which the French term *La bohème;* from
> this kindred element Bonaparte formed the core of the Society of Decem-
> ber 10 (*EBLB*, 75).

Now, in Germany, the Nazi party was a little more than that because the
middle classes had been ruined by inflation. Hitler did not only get this
riff-raff and this good for nothing, but members of the middle-class formed
this organization and by the time he got into power he dealt with the army,
he dealt with the police and he disciplined them and took a lot of people
from these Brown Shirts and put them there. And that is the secret of his
power. If some West Indian boys sit down and watch a would-be dictator in
Trinidad doing that and don't do anything, well, there is no use; they should
not have left Trinidad to come to study at all.

That is the way that Napoleon III built up his force, this Society of
December 10. And after he had built up this Society of December 10, he
then went to work and he got the army to become members of the Society,
and he got members of the Society, important persons, to go into the army.
Having built up the Society of December 10, which is an extracurricular
body (it is not a body that is governing), he now sets out to corrupt the
army, but on the basis of this Society. "The Society of December 10 was to
remain the private army of Bonaparte until he had succeeded in transforming the public army into a Society of December 10" (*EBLB*, 77).

That was what Hitler did, that was what Mussolini did, that was what Franco did, and that is what those boys in the Caribbean will have to do if they wish to attempt any substantial dictatorship. It is all there in Marx. Having built up his Society of December 10, he now sets out to corrupt the army. "Bonaparte made the first attempt at this shortly after the adjournment of the National Assembly and precisely with the money wrested from it. As a fatalist, he lives in the conviction that there are certain higher powers which man, and the soldier in particular, cannot withstand. Among these powers he counts, first and foremost, cigars and champagne, cold poultry and garlic sausage" (*EBLB*, 77).

It is done quite openly. But you notice he built up something that he could depend on, irrespective of the army, and then he seeks to corrupt the army. I won't say that is exactly what happened in 1933, because what happened in 1848 was very different. But you have to look out for these things.

So, establishing a dictatorship—I don't bother with it. It is not so simple. Not in an advanced social body like Trinidad or Barbados. You can't establish a dictatorship just like that. You can't do that. You will have to begin purging the police. You will have to begin motioning the inspectors of police who are determined to go with you and there must be people ready to shoot down the population.

(Listen, it looks as if it's likely to be lengthy. Do you mind? [*Alfie Roberts: Not at all.*]) I have been to Venezuela. I have been telling Harvey[31] about this. I pass in Caracas. I see a club, an officers' club. They tell me that's the finest officers' club in the world. Very good for the officers. I go another twenty miles. I see a fine savanna with a lot of splendid little huts and so forth, and everything nice, and soldiers very clean, well washed. I say, "What is this?" They say, "That is the army." I drive along another twenty miles and I see the same again. Beautiful houses, nice grass and everything, flag flying, clean soldiers—the army again. I go another thirty miles. Another—the army. I say, "Who do you all fight against?" There's nobody. "When was the last time that you had a war?" They say, "Well, about 1882 we had a war against Columbia, or Ecuador, or somebody, but we haven't had any more." I say, "What is the cause of all this?" They say, "Well, the army is built up by these dictators to be used against the population, and chiefly against the population in the urban centers."

What happens is this: When you go to a place like Venezuela, or even Ghana or Nigeria, or places like that, you have the urban centers, and you have vast areas, hundreds and hundreds of square miles, where peasants and very backward people live. They're backward because they haven't been brought into civilization; that would mean roads, schools, telephones, gramophone record shops, and all that. So they go up into these country areas, they pick up the brightest, strongest young men that they can get, and they bring them into the towns, they teach them to be soldiers, and they establish them in these military depots and can call upon them at any time to shoot down the proletariat and the urban elements who talk about democracy and freedom and liberty.

All peasants are concerned with is the peasant question and the land and the agricultural situation. So, you have the urban centers and the students at the universities; then you have these territorial areas where peasants and backward people are, miles away from urban centers, where you have the army; and you have these military settlements where the soldiers, most of them, consisting of, number one, military peasants brought in from the country, and this officer caste who takes part in that beautiful officers' club, etc. This is a special grouping. And they can continue to rule that way. Such a thing does not exist in the Caribbean anywhere.

What is the difference in Barbados between urban and rural? We can't tell. In the West Indies, there are no peasant elements which are remote and can be brought in hostility to the people living in the city. They don't exist. In the Caribbean, being able to build people up in the army to use against the proletariat, the urban people, and the students—that does not exist. Williams's army marches up and down. I don't know who he's fighting; he doesn't frighten anybody because they wouldn't shoot twice. They will shoot the first time. But the idea that an army built up in Barbados, Jamaica, or Trinidad would be so different from the rest of the population that they would shoot and keep on shooting them, I don't see it. You have to have a special kind of territory and have the people properly arranged to do that. The circumstances which make for a dictatorship and a savage totalitarian force in these advanced countries does not exist in the Caribbean—nowhere. That is the situation. And by the way, if you are paying attention to what is taking place, you will know that. Nothing happens in a Caribbean island that people don't know. It happens in advanced countries, too, but in a Caribbean island, any place where you meet secretly, everybody knows. That is one defense of the democracy.

So, Louis Napoleon builds his Society of December 10 (it is important to know what's happening and to know what is not happening) and then he set out the army and he gives them a nice list: "cigars and champagne, cold poultry and garlic sausage. Accordingly, to begin with, he treats officers, and non-commissioned officers in his Elysée apartments to cigars and champagne, to cold poultry and garlic sausage" (*EBLB*, 77). Now, here is a sentence that I find very interesting. He sends a message to the public: "'Above all things, France demands tranquility'" (*EBLB*, 79). Have you all heard that? Williams in Trinidad says that he is going to ensure stability. That means the mass of the population must keep quiet.

Now, here is a phrase which I think you will find interesting, particularly in the way you write. (I had occasion to tell you about this, Alfie.) "Whomever one seeks to persuade, one acknowledges as master of the situation" (*EBLB*, 88). When you are writing a document, you do not beg those who are in charge, you do not beg the British Government, you do not beg the Colonial Secretary; you do not seek to prove to him that you are right. You do not do that. The moment you seek to persuade him, you say he is the boss. You seek to persuade the ordinary people. This is a very important sentence, and I mention it to bear that in mind. A little later, Marx says what he intends to do, how he is going to write his documents and how documents are to be written.

Now this is for you would-be writers. The revolution took place in 1848. Bonaparte, Napoleon III took power in 1851. The *coup d'état*, known as the Eighteenth Brumaire of Louis Bonaparte, took place in 1851—I think it was December 3. Listen to Marx's analysis and you would-be writers please note:

> I. *First period.* From February 24 to May 4, 1848 …Universal brotherhood swindle.

All of them say, "Well, revolution: All of us brothers together."

> II. *Second period*: Period of constituting the republic and of the Constituent National Assembly.

1. May 4 to June 25, 1848. Struggle of all classes against the proletariat. Defeat of the proletariat in the June days.

2. June 25 to December 10. Dictatorship of the pure bourgeois republicans. Drafting of the constitution. Proclamation of a state of siege in Paris. The bourgeois dictatorship set aside on December 10 by the election of Bonaparte as President.

3. December 20, 1848 to May 28, 1849.

III. *Third period.*

1. May 28, 1849 to June 13, 1849

2. June 13, 1849 to May 31, 1850.

3. May 31, 1850 to December 2, 1851.

(a) May 31, 1850 to January 12, 1851 (*EBLB*, pp. 116–117).

After the three divisions, he puts another three or four. When you are analyzing a political situation, you don't just write and say you don't like that fellow and what he did, and so forth. You say this thing began—for instance, the business of the Industrial Stabilization Act[32] in Trinidad and Tobago—it was first stated, and so and so; it went on from so and so to June. Sometimes it's only twenty days. Something happened in June, a new phase then begins. From June 23, 1965 to May 2, 1966. Then enters a new stage. That is the way the analysis is done. That is done not only when you are writing history; when you are making politics, you are watching it stage by stage. And you are watching the economic basis, you're watching the class struggle, you're watching the events and what events are taking place, and what forces have gained by this, and what they have lost, etc. It is a serious, systematic, strictly logical, and almost geometrical business, except that you are dealing with people and individual characters.

There come times when you don't know what is happening, you can't tell. Even long after, you don't know. There are things we know in politics long after; three or four years after, we begin to see that this was really taking place three or four years ago. I could give you instances of that, but I'm not going to bother with that now. When I resigned in Trinidad in 1961 from editing the *Nation* newspaper, told Williams good-bye, and resigned as secretary of the West Indian Federal Labour Party, I could see what was going to take place. You are not in politics and you are able to see this. As a serious political person, I didn't keep it to myself or tell my friends. I wrote it down. I said, "such, and such, and such." That is the only way.

Before you read this, were you aware that Marx was so systematic in the way that he dealt with these things? No. It is most systematic, most close and active, and concerned about the different shades. And I particularly read that one for you where he said, "if you wanted to do that, you shouldn't have done that; if you wanted to do this, you shouldn't have done this." That happens all the time. And we must get into the habit—particularly when writing, but even when taking part in politics—of watching these questions as closely as ever. Here is the foundation of what is taking place in Africa (I wrote an article on Africa and Nkrumah[33] the other day) and what is taking place in Caribbean countries as a whole. Marx says what is happening to the state, the government.

This is France in 1848, a somewhat backward country:

> This executive power [*James: "the state government"*] with its enormous bureaucratic and military organization, with its ingenious state machinery, embracing wide strata, with a host of officials numbering half a million [*James: "Within the Caribbean and Africa it may not be half a million but they number plenty"*], besides an army of another half a million, this appalling, parasitic body, which enmeshes the body of French society like a net and chokes all its pores, sprang up in the day of the absolute monarchy, with the decay of the feudal system, which it helped to hasten (*EBLB*, 121).

What is happening in Africa is you had a semi-feudal system and with the decay of the system, there is taking place this enormous proliferation of the executive power, the state, so that the state—as you have seen in the Caribbean—now becomes an enormous, powerful body in the body politic. "The seigniorial privileges of the landowners and towns became transformed into so many attributes of the state power" (*EBLB*, 121). That is the significance of the underdeveloped countries today: the enormous power of the government. So the privileges that people had previously people now become attributes of state power: "the feudal dignitaries [*James: "Those fellows who used to have authority before"*], into paid officials and the motley pattern of conflicting medieval plenary powers [*James: Justice of the peace and all of these*] into the regulated plan of a state authority whose work is divided and centralized as in a factory" (*EBLB*, 121–122).

Tell me, are you all aware that that is taking place in every Caribbean island? And when they become self-governing, it will be worse. That is what is taking place. This is a process, a historical process. Williams is not responsible; Grantley Adams is not responsible; Bustamante is not responsible enough to talk to the people in these terms. What they say is, "All right. If Bustamante is a scoundrel, well let's put in Manley. But we put Manley in. He wasn't much better …. Well, we don't know." You have got to get them to understand what is taking place. These men are merely the subjects of an objective movement.

> The first French Revolution *[James: "the work is divided and centralized as in a factory"]* with its task of breaking all separate local, territorial, urban and provincial powers … was bound to develop what the absolute monarchy had begun: centralization, but at the same time the extent, the attributes and the agents of governmental power (*EBLB*, 122).

That is running wild over all the underdeveloped countries today, and if you watch in the Caribbean carefully you will see that happening. Have you seen it?

> Napoleon perfected the state machinery …Every *common* interest was straightway severed from society, counterposed to it as a higher, *general* interest, snatched from the activity of society's members themselves and made an object of government activity, from a bridge, a schoolhouse and the communal property of a village community to the railways, the national wealth and the national university of France (*EBLB*, 122).

By the way, in Britain, in France, in the United States, in Holland, and in Belgium, the governments have not got the power that the government of an underdeveloped country government has. Take, for example, Trinidad. When they used to have the railway, they were in charge of it. In Britain, the government is not in charge of the railway. When, in Trinidad, they finished up with the railway, they put in the buses; the government is in charge of the buses. In Britain, you have Oxford, Cambridge, York University, and the rest of them. They run themselves. In the West Indies, in Trinidad, the government runs the university. In Britain, you have Eton, Harrow, Rugby, and these colleges; they are run by individual groupings of people. Not in the West Indies. The government runs every one of the secondary schools. Even Saint Mary's College, the government says, "We're going to send eighty percent of your students to you and we are going to pay the salaries." And the secondary schools that are being established—the government is doing it. The telephone—the government is in charge of it. The government is not in charge of the telephone in England.

So, that's the situation in all these underdeveloped countries. This state power, which, it seems, Marx is trying to say, once you are changing over from the old feudal regime to a modern regime, once you are changing over from an underdeveloped colonial country, and aim at being a modern country, straight away you have this enormous concentration of power in the hands of the state. That is what we face. Not Eric Williams, not Busta-mante, you are facing an objective thing that would take place under any circumstances. The only way it does not take place and doesn't overwhelm you is if the people who are taking charge of the government are aware that this is the danger and take steps to moderate it and keep it in order.

These fellows do nothing at all. They know nothing at all. They don't know what is happening. If you told this to Bustamante, he would won-der what country you are talking about, whether you come from heaven or hell or something. He wouldn't know what you're talking about. They know nothing. They are really ignoramuses. You could be an ignoramus in Britain, you could be an ignoramus in the United States, you could be an ignoramus in Holland. You know why? Because they have a long tradi-tion of government. They have been doing that for centuries; they have a lot of history books and so on. We know nothing. All we know is, well, we have independence; a flag goes up and now I am the boss. There is nothing established there. Nobody is teaching anybody anything. Nobody knows anything to teach anybody except, "If you're not with me, you are against me." Do you have that Calypso here by Sparrow?[34]

Now, the national wealth, the national university of France. Marx says, "Finally, in its struggle against the revolution [*James: In their (the West Indian politicians') struggle against the people*], the parliamentary republic found itself compelled to strengthen, along with the repressive measures, the resources and centralization of governmental power" (*EBLB*, 122). You either have to be an extremely acute observer—and it will take you a year or two to understand this—or if you have studied some serious historical and political writings you are sensitized and you can see and recognize this for what it is. That is what is taking place in the Caribbean.

I'm coming to the end. Karl Marx says, well, he's got into power, but if he makes himself emperor, as the old fellow did, "when the imperial mantle finally falls on the shoulders of Louis Bonaparte, the bronze statue of Napoleon will crash from the top of the Vendôme Column" (*EBLB*, 135). Marx says: That fellow, if he makes himself emperor as the first Napoleon did, that will be the end of him. He waited a few years, but that actually happened. The Vendôme Column[35] was torn down, and they chased out Napoleon and France established the Republic.

I have one more sentence to talk about. Marx, writing a letter to a friend of his in America says, "Your article …is very good, both coarse and fine—a combination which should be found in any polemic worthy of the name" (*EBLB*, 136). In a polemic, you do not try to persuade the colonial officer. You can try to persuade them if you are sending a deputation to ask them for something; they say five million dollars; well, you make it six million and you try to persuade them. That's something else. But if you are writing politics, you don't try to persuade them. You are writing to the population and you say: "This is what we have got for you. These rascals have such and such power, we have got to break it. We can't break all the power now but we can…." But Marx says both sides: You can let them have it sometimes, with good elements of coarseness. So you let him have it, coarse remarks and so forth, and at the same time, a little later, you give some first-class analysis. He says any polemic should have both. You need not write history that way but any polemic should have both.

Well, I think, if you don't mind, ladies and gentlemen, we have covered the *Eighteenth Brumaire*. I haven't gone into it in detail—that would have been quite absurd. But I have selected certain points in it which stand out, and I have rather crudely made the application to the Caribbean. It may sound a bit crude, but it isn't. Do you know why? Because in 1848 and 1851, France, a backward country—underdeveloped, so-to-speak—was making the transition to a modern state. We in the Caribbean are making the same transition, so that what he writes here has an extraordinary application to what is happening to us and you cannot understand what is taking place in the Caribbean in particular, and in various other underdeveloped countries, unless you have a proper view of economics, historical analysis, and political developments.

Well, I would like to stop now for a bit and then we'll go over to the other one later.

Marx's *Capital,* the Working-Day, and Capitalist Production

I am selecting one chapter of *Capital,* and I want to put off the rest for another time. I hope to be back here in 1968, and that session will be a very serious examination of *Capital.* I asked you to do the chapter on the working-day because we can only do one. A serious look at *Capital* means six sessions and you have got to get the books and spend a lot of time on it.

Now, on page 233, Marx insists on what he has to say, what he says every time: "capital has one single life impulse, the tendency to create value and surplus-value, to make its constant factor, the means of production, absorb the greatest possible amount of surplus-labor."[1] It is difficult to find out how many people will read this, will read it in every ten pages of *Capital,* and yet not understand it. "Capital is dead labor, that vampire-like, only lives by sucking living labor, and lives the more, the more labor it sucks" (233). That is what is meant by labor-power is a commodity. Everything is a commodity. My glasses are a commodity, cigarettes are commodities, tea is a commodity, the gramophone is a commodity, the tape recorder is a commodity—everything is a commodity. The important thing that I want you to remember in your study of *Capital* is Marx's insistence that the particular commodity that is important in the study of capital is the labor-power of the individual. In all societies that are in any way developed, there is commodity production. But that the man sells his labor, his labor-power—a commodity—to the capitalist, Marx says, once you begin there, the whole of capitalist society grows from that; that the labor-power of the human individual is sold as a commodity. Because if capital sucks, it is from him that it sucks these things.

Now Marx is a very funny man, very comic in a very profound way. "Suddenly, the voice of the laborer which had been stifled in the storm and stress of the process of production, rises: The commodity that I have sold to you differs from the crowd of other commodities, in that its use creates value, and a value greater than its own" (233). Marx says, you buy some leather to make shoes; you put the leather in the factory, but, he says, even the leather that you get from that is the same as what you put in there. The leather has not improved. The leather has not increased in value. That it has increased in value is because changes are taking place because a man worked on it. (If it was worked in the factory alone, men were needed to make the factory.) He says, without a human being exploited, capital is nothing. That is why you bought it.

> That which on your side appears a spontaneous expansion of capital, is on mine extra expenditure of labor-power. You and I know on the market only one law, that of the exchange of commodities *[James: And it appears that you have got money and you buy my commodity, the labor-power.]*. And the consumption of the commodity belongs not to the seller who parts with it, but to the buyer, who acquires it. To you, therefore, belongs the use of my daily labor-power. But by means of the price that you pay for it each day, I must be able to reproduce it daily, and to sell it again.(233–234)

In other words, when you buy it you must give me enough to live by and to have some children so that when you want some more people to work then, of course, I can produce them for you. I don't know if you can see it in Canada—maybe, but I know Detroit pretty well.

I know the American working class, in some respects, better than I know the English. America is a highly organized country. The wife of the American working-man says, "He works in that factory. I don't work in the factory. He brings money home on Fridays and he gives it to me." The American workingman brings the money home (takes so much for cigarettes) and gives it to his wife. But she says, "My whole life, and the life of the children, is governed by the fact that he is working in that factory and has to work under certain conditions. When he leaves here in the morning, we have to get up and arrange everything and get his food. His clothes have to be washed. When he comes home, he has to eat, and we have to see about this and that and the other. We don't go to the factory to work, but that factory governs our lives as much as it governs his." Such is the organization of production in the United States. That is what Marx is saying.

I must be able on the morrow to work with the same normal amount of force, health and freshness as of to-day. You preach to me constantly the gospel of "saving" and "abstinence." Good! I will, like a sensible saving owner, husband my sole wealth, labor-power, and abstain from all foolish waste of it. I will each day spend, set in motion, put into action only as much of it as is compatible with its normal duration, and healthy development [James: That is what the worker is saying]. By an unlimited extension of the working-day, you may one day use up a quantity of labor-power greater than I can restore in three. What you gain in labor I lose in substance... I demand, therefore, a working-day of normal length, and I demand it without any appeal to your heart, for in money matters sentiment is out of place.(234)

One of the most tremendous social battles that have been fought over the centuries is this battle that Marx is insisting upon. When he comes to the very end of it, he makes a stroke that comes home to those of you who have got an ordinary secondary education. Marx says that one of the great battles that has been fought in society is whether the worker is able to say that the working-day is to last from this time to that time, and the employer ensuring that the working-day is to last longer. He says that for centuries they fought it out, and he goes into detail. But you will go to a university and you will not hear this. The battle over the length of the working-day is a tremendous battle.

We in the West Indies, we inherit that. In other words, when they come to write our constitution, or they come to write something about labor, they say, "Well, the working-day will be this, and that and that." But we have not fought for it. We know nothing about that. What we are doing is transferring to the Caribbean something that has been fought for and arranged in an advanced country, Great Britain, and the point is, it isn't only that the worker does not know the background, but even those men who went to the University of Cambridge or went to McGill University, they don't know what the working-day means—they don't know that at all. To them, the working-day is something that workers do. That is all. The history of the working-day is one of the greatest battles that have been fought for democratic rights for working people. It has lasted centuries, and you must be aware of that, otherwise you don't understand it at all. That is the significance of this chapter.

Marx goes on:

"What is a working-day? What is the length of time during which capital may consume the labor-power whose daily value it buys? How far may the working-day be extended beyond the working-time necessary for the re-production of labor-power itself?" It has been seen that to these questions capital replies: the working-day contains the full 24 hours, with the deduction of a few hours of repose without which labor-power absolutely refuses its services again.(264)

You will see in reading these chapters that this question of the working-day has been a tremendous impetus in the development of production itself. The British have led the struggle. Do you know that? They have also lead in games. They were foremost in cricket, football, and other games of the time, international athletics, and so forth. With regard to labor problems and labor rights, the British have been foremost. They have been very backward in many things, but nevertheless, we are not dealing with that now.

This is what Marx says, and you have to understand it. He says that somewhere about 1848, the extension of labor-power reached such a stage that the civilization, the level of physical and intellectual development of the working-class was falling to pieces, it was going to nothing. These circumstances, and by the struggles of the working-class, not for an eight-hour day, but to defend its very habits of life, resulted in people passing laws. The British factory inspectors and the rest of them introduced legislation to limit the hours of labor because, otherwise, British society would have been destroyed. You will find that here. Under these circumstances, having been blocked at extending the hours of labor of the persons who were working, capital then began to develop machinery in order to get as much profit out of production in as much as the extension of the hours of labor was blocked. So that the development of profit by means of machinery was the direct result—Marx makes no bones about it and it has never been challenged—of the battles that the working-class fought in order to save the civilization, health, and general intellectual and moral development of the working-class.

Now, how many people in the West Indies know that? You see, when you are educated in this and you know it, then the working-class and people who are speaking on behalf of labor get a certain confidence. Civilization as it is, we have built it up. We not only built it by putting in our physical labor, but the things that we have done have made the situation what it is. When those who are educated know that, the relations between them and the mass of the population become different. Each is aware of certain past developments and so forth. But in the Caribbean, the workers don't know. Some of the greatest convicts and gangsters that I know are labor leaders in Trinidad. Undoubtedly, in regard to fundamental matters, I can't imagine men more ignorant than some of the politicians in Trinidad and Tobago. They know nothing at all about this. They go to university; they get a Ph.D., but nobody tells them anything about this. The society that they have, the production that they have, and the possibilities that they have are due to the action of the working-class. They don't know that.

If you have been educated on the idea of the working-day and the working-class has been educated on that—in Britain and these advanced countries, but more in Britain than elsewhere—a certain relation then begins. It does not exist in the Caribbean, and if it is to exist and progress is to be made, you will have to tell them. We have got to make them understand that that is the reality. I was a number of years old before I understood that this question of machinery and the development of machinery was due to the obstinacy with which the working-class fought what was taking place under the conditions of ordinary manufacture.

What is a working-day? What is the length of time? This is what Marx says:

> Time for education, for intellectual development. *[James: Follow me please.]* "For the fulfilling of social functions and for social intercourse, for the free play of his bodily and mental activity. Even the rest time of Sunday (And that in a country of Sabbatarians!)—Moonshine! *[James: Capitalist attitude.]* But in its blind unrestrainable passion, the were-wolf hunger for surplus-labor, capital oversteps not only the moral, but even the merely physical maximum bounds of the working-day. *[James: Please listen carefully—page 265.]* It usurps the time for growth, development, and healthy maintenance of the body. It steals the time required for the consumption of fresh air and sunlight. It haggles over a meal-time, incorporating it where possible with the process of production itself, so that food is given to the laborer as to a mere means of production, as coal is supplied to the boiler, grease and oil to the machinery. It reduces the sound sleep needed for the restoration, reparation, refreshment of the bodily powers to just so many hours of torpor as the revival of an organism absolutely exhausted, renders essential. It is not the normal maintenance of the labor-power which is to

determine the limits of the working-day. It is the greatest possible daily expenditure of labor-power, no matter how diseased…(264–265)

Marx goes on with this in great detail. He spends pages and pages on it, and then he ends. Mr. Harvey,[2] listen to this please. Everybody listen:

It must be acknowledged that our laborer comes out of the process of production other than he entered. In the market he stood as owner of the commodity "labor-power" face to face with other owners of commodities, dealer against dealer. The contract by which he sold to the capitalist his labor-power proved, so to say, in black and white that he disposed of himself freely. *[James: I have my labour-power, you, Mr. Capitalist, you have the money and we enter into a freely arranged contract.]* The bargain concluded, it is discovered that he was no "free agent," that the time for which he is free to sell his labor-power is the time for which he is forced to sell it, that in fact the vampire will not lose its hold on him "so long as there is a muscle, and nerve, and drop of blood to be exploited." For "protection" against "the serpent of the agonies," the laborers must put their heads together, and, as a class, compel the passing of a law, an all-powerful social barrier that shall prevent the very workers from selling, by voluntary contract with capital, themselves and their families into slavery and death. (301–302)

Is that clear? You see the contract is, in theory, an absolutely equal and fair contract. That's what Marx is saying. It isn't only in this case that he is saying that; repeatedly, you find it. The contract is fair. The law is passed. But when you get down to the actual concrete reality, there are contradictions there which create a situation that was not taken into consideration by the contract, so that the worker has got to pass and see that laws are passed to prevent the workers "from selling by voluntary contract with capital, themselves and their families into slavery and death."

Now comes this tremendous sentence: "In place of the pompous catalogue of the 'inalienable rights of man' comes the modest Magna Charta of a legally limited working-day, which shall make clear 'when the time which the worker sells is ended, and when his own begins.' Quantum mutatus ab illo! *[James: 'How much change from the former.']*"(302) That is a tremendous sentence. What are these inalienable rights? The French Revolution took place on July 14, 1789 and they established these inalienable rights in the Declaration of Rights of Man. The Americans established their Declaration of Independence and said, men are born free and equal and are entitled to certain inalienable rights—life, liberty, and the pursuit of happiness (we used to say life, liberty and the pursuit of profit). Marx is saying this: This battle that the workers fought for centuries to decide that the working-day should begin at this time and should end at that time is far more important in the life of members of the community than these famous documents— the French Declaration of Rights and the American Declaration of Independence. (If you not only understand that but, continually, as you investigate politics and history, look down beneath what is on the surface and what is actually taking place, then you begin to see, you begin to really study Marxism.)

Marx says these inalienable rights, the Declaration of Independence, man's right to life, liberty, and the pursuit of happiness, everybody knows that and the French Declaration of the Rights of Man. But, he says, "What I'm talking about are the rights that have been fought over for centuries, for the worker to say: 'Look here, I begin work at such a time, and I finish at such and such a time, and after that I am my own boss." He says that is one of the great battles, infinitely more important than these inalienable rights of man. You have to learn that Alfie.[3] It isn't easy to learn. You will say "yes" and then go straight over it and then see another thing and say "yes."

These countries today, they are giving Africa and the colonial territories independence. Marx would say Independence in Trinidad—where I have just been for two years—what independence? There are six banks there that are masters of the country: Tate and Lyle who have the sugar estates there; Texaco, BP, and Shell—they have the oil and they have the gas stations. Lord Thompson owns the paper, the *Trinidad Guardian,* owns the radio station. He has large shares in television. Everything that matters in the country, they own. But the British still tell you about independence, freedom, liberty, equality, constitution, etc.

That is what Marx is talking about. He says the working-day, that battle—the day begins at 7:00 and ends at 3:30—that is one of the greatest victories for human life and human development that has ever been won. I can tell you something, Mr. Alfie—it takes some time to get that in your head, the habit of looking at things that way. Independence or Africa independence—independence, my eye!

Now I want to show you something else. Do you remember what we talked about on page 265? Do you remember that? I want you to bear these in mind: "It usurps the time for growth, development, and healthy maintenance of the body. It steals the time required for the consumption of fresh air and sunlight. It haggles over a meal-time, incorporating it where possible with the process of production itself." (265)

Now go to page 409. Pardon me, now I'm going to read:

It is self-evident, that in proportion as the use of machinery spreads, and the experience of a special class of workmen habituated to machinery accumulates, the rapidity and intensity of labor increase as a natural consequence. Thus in England, during half a century, lengthening of the working-day went hand in hand with increasing intensity of factory labor. *[James: They lengthened the working-day at first.]* Nevertheless the reader will clearly see, that where we have labor, not carried on by fits and starts, but repeated day after day with unvarying uniformity, a point must inevitably be reached where extension of the working-day and intensity of the labor mutually exclude one another, in such a way that lengthening of the working-day becomes compatible only with a lower degree of intensity, and a higher degree of intensity, only with a shortening of the working-day. So soon as the gradually surging revolt of the working-class compelled Parliament to shorten compulsorily the hours of labor, and to begin by imposing a normal working-day on factories proper, so soon consequently as an increased production of surplus-value by the prolongation of the working-day was once for all put a stop to *[James: Are you following me?]*, from that moment capital threw itself with all its might into the production of relative surplus-value *[James: That is to say surplus-value by machinery]*, by hastening on the further improvement of machinery.(409)

Is that clear? The working class resists and it says, "You are killing us! We can't continue to intensify labor in this way. You have to shorten the working-day." They were busy lengthening the working-day and intensifying labor then the working class said, "It can't be done, we cannot continue." Once the working class, by fighting, got the government to pass the law to limit the working-day, then capital started to use the intensification of machinery to get as much surplus-labor as possible out of the worker. That's that Marx calls relative surplus-labor. Did you know that that is how things developed? I know you didn't, unless you have read this before.

I'm going somewhere, ladies and gentlemen. Page 487 in this edition, the line before the bottom:

> Modern Industry, on the other hand, through its catastrophes imposes the necessity of recognizing, as a fundamental law of production, variation of work, consequently fitness of the laborer for varied work, consequently the greatest possible development of his varied aptitudes. It becomes a question of life and death for society to adapt the mode of production to the normal functioning of this law. *[James: And then Marx writes badly, which is the only place that I have caught him.]* Modern Industry, indeed, compels society, under penalty of death *[James: That repetition 'under the penalty of death' comes too quickly. He doesn't do that sort of thing; but he must have been very serious]*, to replace the detail-worker of to-day, crippled by life-long repetition of one and the same trivial operation, and thus reduced to the mere fragment of a man, by the fully developed individual *[James: Listen please]*, fit for a variety of labors, ready to face any change of production, and to whom the different social functions he performs, are but so many modes of giving free scope to his own natural and acquired powers. (487–488)

Do you understand what Marx is saying? The kind of person you need to deal with modern industry is a person who will be able to give free scope to his own natural and acquired powers and not subject it to the discipline of capitalist production.

You will have noticed that I showed you a passage on page 265. I showed you another passage on page 405, I showed you another passage on page 487. Now, I am going on to page 645:

> We saw in Part IV., when analyzing the production of relative surplus-value: *[James: That is to say surplus-value that is produced by machinery.]* within the capitalist system all methods for raising the social productiveness of labour are brought about at the cost of the individual laborer; all means for the development of production transform themselves into means of domination over, and exploitation of, the producers (645) .

Do you get that point? All the means that improve, intensify, the amount of surplus-labor, dominate the workers and the assembly line and mean further domination, even automation of the workers:

> They mutilate the laborer into a fragment of a man, degrade him to the level of an appendage of a machine, destroy every remnant of charm in his

work and turn it into a hated toil; they estrange from him the intellectual potentialities of the labor-process in the same proportion as science is incorporated in it as an independent power.

To the extent that science is incorporated into the labor-process, the worker has less and less to do with it. He is not educated by being in the factory. I will read that sentence again, it's a magnificent sentence:

> they estrange from him the intellectual potentialities of the labor-process in the same proportion as science is incorporated in it as an independent power; they distort the conditions under which he works, subject him during the labor-process to a despotism the more hateful for its meanness *[James: Is that so, Alfie? You were telling me about some despotism that they subjected you to in New York⁴];* they transform his life-time into working-time, and drag his wife and child beneath the wheels of the Juggernaut of capital. But all methods for the production of surplus-value are at the same time methods of accumulation; and every extension of accumulation becomes again a means for the development of those methods. It follows therefore that in proportion as capital accumulates, the lot of the laborer *[James: Then comes that tremendous phrase]*, be his payment high or low…(645).

God have mercy! To get people to understand what Marx is saying—if he gets some extra wages, you tell him, well, you have ten days holidays, free of charge, instead of five. Instead of getting $1.20 an hour, you get $1.25 and in three years time I give you $1.30. Marx says that that has nothing to do with the well-being of the worker.

Marx says:

> But all methods for the production of surplus-value are at the same time methods of accumulation; and every extension of accumulation becomes again a means for the development of those methods. It follows therefore that in proportion as capital accumulates, the lot of the laborer, be his payment high or low *[James: It has nothing to do with how much you are paying him. There is nothing happening to him as a human being in this whole process]*, must grow worse. The law finally, that always equilibrates the relative surplus-population, or industrial reserve army, to the extent and energy of accumulation, this law rivets the laborer to capital more firmly than the wedges of Vulcan did Prometheus to the rock. It establishes an accumulation of misery, corresponding with accumulation of capital. Accumulation of wealth at one pole is, therefore, at the same time accumulation of misery, agony of toil, slavery, ignorance, brutality, mental degradation, at the

opposite pole, *i.e.*, on the side of the class that produces its own product in the form of capital (645).

I want you to know something. I took those four passages, one at page 265, one at page 405, one at page 487, and one at page 645. (Alfie, are you able to understand that what Marx is concerned with is not the selling of the product, whether they can sell the product or not, or the advantages that the worker has to get by forming a trade union—what he's saying is the mere process of capitalist production drives this fellow down, down, down and mutilates him into a fragment of a man. Do you get that?) You will listen to people giving you lessons on *Capital* from now until 1984 and they will not tell you that. They say that he misunderstood the market. They say today that they can sell the commodity. The government can intervene. J.M. Keynes says the government can introduce capital, start production, and, therefore, employment is increased and so forth. Marx is not talking about that. That's not his main point. That's why I chose those four passages and told you at the beginning, a third of the way through, half-way through, and two-thirds of the way through, that he is concerned with what is happening to the members of the working-class as living human beings in a factory. Marx says that as long as the employer is buying the worker's labor-power, this business must go on because he has to accumulate, and so forth. He says that the production of relative surplus-value, the increase of machinery, was the direct result of the power of the working-class in putting an end to a system that was carrying into destitution the whole of society. Did you understand that capital meant that in the past? I'm asking you, Alfie. [*Alfie: No.*] No, I know you didn't. It would have been very strange if you had. Unless you knew somebody who knew me and knew my friends, that is the only way.[*Laughter*]

Now to the last point. Volume Three. I won't keep you much more. (The next time I come here I will go through *Capital* with you, but I must read this section for you.) I want to read another passage here for you in Volume Three. Now here it is. Marx says that the first distinctive feature of capitalist production is that the labor-power of the worker is sold as a commodity. Then, he says:

The *second* distinctive feature of the capitalist mode of production is the production of surplus-value as the direct aim and determining motive of production. *[James: To get this profit, this surplus.]* Capital produces essentially capital, and does so only to the extent that it produces surplus-value. We have seen in our discussion of relative surplus-value *[James: That is to say, the value of surplus that comes from the introduction of machinery]* and further in considering the transformation of surplus-value into profit, how a mode of production *[James: Listen, please]* peculiar to the capitalist period is founded hereon—*[James: Now I wish I could say this ten times by saying it once]* a special form of development of the social productive powers of labor...(880–881)

Capital is "a special form of development of the social productive powers of labor." You had feudal society which organized its forms of production in a special way; you had slave society which organized the forms of production in a special way; capital is "a special form of development of the social productive powers of labor, but confronting the laborer as powers of capital rendered independent, and standing in direct opposition therefore to the laborer's own development."(881)

What happens to capital is that the powers of the social productive system are placed into a situation where they become persons, individuals, the human element, which are in opposition to the development of the working-class. It will take years, but there are some people whose heads cannot get into it. They see capital as essentially private property and the question of the improvement of capital as wages, hours of labor, times of vacation, and all this business. Marx goes on to say:

> [It is] a special form of development of the social productive powers of labor, but confronting the laborer as powers of capital rendered independent, and standing in direct opposition therefore to the laborer's own development.
>
> The authority assumed by the capitalist as the personification of capital in the direct process of production, the social function performed by him in his capacity as manager and ruler of production, is essentially different from the authority exercised on the basis of production by means of slaves, serfs, etc. (881)

Marx says, when you have production by means of slaves, production by means of serfs, even peasants and so forth, what happens is that you have a system of production and you have somebody who owns. Because he owns, he places some people in authority and he takes the profits and goods away. He says the capitalist system of production places this owner or the man who is in charge in a situation in the process of production itself where he stands dominant over the man who is working. As the process of production improves, etc., he gains, Marx says, more and more power in this position of ruler and suppressor of the fellows down below. That is the capitalist system. I promise you, you could get a hundred people who claim to know Marxism, some of them have been to Russia and have studied *Capital*, and they still don't understand. They say, "private property, and if you abolish private property and nationalize then …Of course, you get a harder job than before and you are getting less money but you are working for the state, don't grumble. Marx may not have used the word 'nationalization' exactly, but that is what he meant." I have seen them say that for some twenty years. This is Volume III and Marx is very particular about that: "The authority assumed by the capitalist is the personification of capital in the direct process of production."

Now, in the direct process of production, the slave-owner or the serf-owner or the man who owns the land and gives it out to peasants, he does not occupy a position of dominance in the direct process of production. He doesn't. But with the capitalist, this fellow is in the direct process of production and "the social function performed by him in his capacity as manager and ruler of production, is essentially different from the authority exercised on the basis of production by means of slaves, serfs, etc."(881)

Now Marx goes on:

> Whereas, on the basis of capitalist production, the mass of direct produc-ers *[James: That is the workers]* is confronted by the social character of their production in the form of strictly regulating authority and a social mechanism of the *labor*-process organized as a complete hierarchy—this authority reaching its bearers, however, only as the personification of the conditions of *labor* in contrast to *labor*, and not as political or theocratic rulers as under earlier modes of production—among the bearers of this authority, the capitalists themselves…(881)

I will read that again, for I want you to get it clear. Marx says, in capital-ist production, the direct producers, the workers, meet an authority that is organized and knit into the very process of production and the people who own, the people who are in authority, the people who manage, are in direct authority over the ordinary laborer. He says that that takes place in no other kind of economic society. Let me read it again:

> Whereas, on the basis of capitalist production, the mass of direct produc-
> ers is confronted by the social character of their production in the form of
> strictly regulating authority and a social mechanism of the *labor*-process
> organized as a complete hierarchy...

A hierarchy in other societies was when you went to work and you came out, then you met people in authority over you. But Marx says that capital-ist production insists that the hierarchy of those above you takes places in the very process of production itself so that it is bound to be so outside of the process of production, and that is not easily changed.

If Marx does not mean this as the fundamental part of his analysis of capitalist society, then the volumes of *Capital* are nonsensical. You will find it all through, except perhaps in Volume II where he is dealing with com-modity sales and so forth. But that is the essential thing. This is a very seri-ous business. He says, the more they accumulate and the more they expand, the greater this authority becomes and the greater the subordination of the direct producer. (Have you seen the Charlie Chaplin film?) Marx says that that is the process of production. He says it is bound to be so. Do you take Marxism at the university? [*Alfie: No, nothing at all. They have courses on Marxist economics...*] They tell you how he said the revolution is going to take place in an advanced country, and that he said there would be increas-ing poverty. Marx never said anything about increasing poverty. He said increasing accumulation of misery, slavery. He said, when you put a man on an assembly line and he spends the day doing that—he derives no job sat-isfaction at all. For the mass of the population, that is the result of the form of capitalist production. Marx is very clear about all of that.

The thing that I want to make clear this afternoon is that you can listen to any number of people, some of them who can take *Capital* like anything and quote a lot of Marx, but they don't know anything about this. What I read to you from Volume Three makes nonsense of the idea that in Russia there is socialism because production is nationalized. Marx says that the whole structure is a fundamental social mechanism of capitalist production which builds up a constant number of people who are in direct opposition to the workers. It does not take place in any other form of production.

I think we'll stop there. I intended to stop at about 5:00 and we have reached to 5:14. So I can say to myself, save one minute, I might have gone to 5:15 but I stopped at 5:14. [*Laughter*]

All right my friends, there we are. I wanted to get something clear: in your studies of *Capital*, as you read, never lose sight of the worker in the process of production. Alfie, you never lose sight of him. If you lose sight of that, you are losing sight of Marxism. Now Marx wrote a lot about the selling of this and pricing and all that, but that is where he began and that is where he stayed all through. He went into various aspects of production, commodity exchange, prices, the level of prices, ownership, and so forth—he went into all of this, but he never lost sight of what is happening to the worker. The increase of capitalist production meant the greater suppression of the worker, and Marx says you cannot keep doing that to human beings.

Alright there fellows, I think we will stop there for the time being. Any questions? Questions never tire me. Sometimes they make me more lively. Go right ahead, please. Any question you like. If I don't know the answer, I will tell you so.

FRANKLYN HARVEY: [Inaudible].

JAMES: Sir, that is a fundamental question. The beginning of the problem is the selling of labor-power, and the selling of labor-power as a commodity and capital means the production of surplus-value. He says the day must come when production means the development of the worker as an individual and not the production of surplus-value. But as long as you pursue purely surplus-value you are suppressing the worker and creating this division. But, he says, when you reach a certain stage and you begin to develop the worker as a person, the production of surplus-value then will go beyond what you think about. He says, when that happens, the production of surplus-value will increase beyond belief.

And he says man must be paid according to what is required to develop him. Now, can we do that today? (I'm sorry, this will take us very far, but I am prepared to go there.) How many billions do they spend going to the moon? The Americans spend 70 billion a year on the war in Vietnam. They spend any number of billions going to the moon. They spend a vast number of billions—they want to leave London and go to New York in two hours. (I don't know if the vast majority of people will want to go from London to New York in two hours. I don't think so.)

In other words, between 1935 and 1945 they spent hundreds of billions on this war. They did the same thing, 1914 to 1918. With half of that money, it is perfectly possible to build, to develop the population and educate people to take advantage of all the accumulations of science that have been discovered. But they are busy going to the moon and they are not going up there to see the moon. Not at all. It is to get up there before the other fellow. That is what they are after: to get up there first, and get there so as to dominate in this merciless competition.

They have enough guns or satellites to destroy two-thirds (that was what I read two or three years ago) of the population of Russia. But the Russians have enough of these things to destroy one half—we'll assume that they are a little behind—of the population of the United States. So, now the Russians are busy working out a means of stopping these satellites coming in. They say it will cost a lot to prevent the satellites from exploding before they reach. And these fellows are busy making a lot of explosives and things to prevent the satellites from coming. But very soon that fellow will discover a new kind of satellite, and this fellow is busy discovering another new kind of satellite, but you also have to discover means to be in time to stop the new kind of satellite.

Pardon me, I am not making fun. That is exactly what they are doing. That is the billions in money that they are spending every day on all of this, and that is why they cannot devote themselves to the development of the ordinary person. The average man today can learn anything. Anything they teach us, we can learn. We have learned Western civilization. We were freed in 1833. It isn't a hundred and fifty years. These fellows are spending the money on all this kind of business. They put people in high positions, even if they don't pass their degree.

And my last point is this: They are not stupid, they are not frivolous, but they are in a certain situation. They have certain powers and so forth. And the idea that you can have a new type of society in which the large majority of the population is highly educated and taking part in it, that is fantastic to them. But if you have this high development of education on a worldwide scale—a lot of Black people highly educated, a lot of Chinese people highly educated, Indians highly educated—they say, "No, leave it alone please."

That is the situation. But there is enough money in the world today, and there has been for the last fifty years, to make tremendous developments in education, in the way that Marx and Lenin have taught. That is a fact. That is what is required today. I don't see any need to go to the moon. I don't know if anybody does. What are they going to the moon for? They have a lot to do in Africa; they have a lot to do in India; they have a lot to do in the United States in the South. But they are busy going to the moon. (If I said that in Trinidad or Barbados, they would want to put me in jail.)

Marx insisted that the socialist society was going to be an internationalist society. As long as Russia and the United States are fighting and people join in and so forth, then it will go on.

Well, Harvey, there we are.

HARVEY: Would you say, sir, that, for example, the enlarging rate of the unemployment situation in the modern world, generally speaking—particularly in the Caribbean—that it can never really be solved because in the very process of what they are trying to develop in industry, these industries are being highly, very intensely victimized and can never absorb the amount of labor that is available; that even though one is thinking or trying whatever method you may use in trying to develop, unemployment would continue at an even higher rate so that eventually the workers would get totally fed up, that they would see no other way out than to themselves barge into the whole decision and process of...

JAMES: But that wouldn't help the situation. If the workers take charge, the workers are not taking charge to lessen the labor intensiveness of industry. The workers take charge to improve the situation. And if the basis for labor taking charge is an improvement in the level of the development of the economy, then that means increasing unemployment as sure as day.

There are two things that are involved here. Number one, you cannot take the West Indies and make it a kind of conceptual model by which you judge the rest of the world. It is the rest of the world that has to be taken, and if they stop this nonsense about going to the moon and building satellites; if they say the first thing to do is to develop the person, then you have a different kind of an economy. But what is obvious is that the West Indian economy cannot settle itself, Harvey, irrespective of what is taking place in the world economy. However, the situation need not be in the same miserable situation that it was under colonialism, with all these people taking oil and running away. That change can be made. But that the situation can be settled indefinitely when the rest of the world has gone the other way, that is out of the question.

HARVEY: I wasn't talking about the question of settling one's self. I wasn't just talking in the sense of the workers taking charge through the developmental sector of the economy. What I was talking…

JAMES: That is the only serious basis for the working-class to take power. The workers must take charge and convince people that—especially in an underdeveloped country—they cannot take charge everywhere, but they can take charge of a place like Texaco or bauxite in Jamaica. And that is the only basis for that taking place…

HARVEY: Yes, but what I was concerned about was this point: My main point was that the workers, particularly the unemployed, have become so fed up with their own condition, the misery that they face, that the only way they can see to better respect themselves as men is for them to take charge. That was my point.

JAMES: They might think so, but I don't know what would happen. If they take charge, what do they propose?

Now, let me tell you what I am thinking of. I believe that the sugar estates should be taken over because you can develop the same amount of sugar and have greater diversification of production. We [The Workers' and Farmers' Party] have put all that forward in facts and as time goes on we shall be able to prove that statistically. But for workers to say that they are going to do that with bauxite… It means a total change in the economic life. Now, you can't sit down and wait for total change. You can make certain advances, but if the unemployed in Trinidad, for instance, take over Texaco—we have our eye on it and we are carefully calculating what would be the benefit if we take over; if we buy the sugar estate, because we are going to get it in any case, we cannot give the impression that if the workers or unemployed take over, thereby unemployment would be solved. I am very concerned about that because it will not be. Do you accept that?

HARVEY: Yes, but you are concerned with the question of whether there will be change when the workers take over. I haven't reached that far. All I was saying is that, for example, you say you have put forward that the estates should be bought over and so on. That is assuming that you are there to do it. The point is that you may not get the person who would be there to put forward this—not to put forward but to actually implement such a program—and that the workers would get more and more fed up of their own situation.

JAMES: They may. That I have to agree. They can do that today. Marx says, "Well, they should have done that and this should have been done and so forth."[5] That is part of politics. Although I don't believe in workers just taking power.

HARVEY: No, but in any case, whenever there is a group of people, a mass of people, or a section of a population, people emerge as leaders of that certain section.

JAMES: This is what I believe with regard to the point that you are making. I don't know what is going to happen. In politics, you don't know. You cannot be certain. But I believe that the land, for example, is the first thing we have to take over. And I believe the land is going to be taken over. Whether it will be done constitutionally or not, I don't know. For the time being, I am saying, let us see if we can do it constitutionally.

If, however, it cannot be done constitutionally, the fact that every democratic means was tried is one of the surest ways of making the idea of a
revolt spread widely and be accepted by large sections of the population.
And that is all you can do. There is a famous expression of Napoleon: *on
s'engage et puis s'en voit*. You engage and then you see. That's all you can do.
As Karl Marx makes clear in *The Eighteenth Brumaire*, politics is not an
exact science. It is a science but you cannot be sure.

I am going to be talking about that when Bobby[6] and the rest come
down. We will have one day on the actual concrete art in which this question could be tackled. And I will go into those questions. But before you
go into that, it is good to have a clear theoretical-historical conception so
that you know how to approach the question. Because unless you approach
the question in general correctly, you can't get the tactical points right. You
must have some idea of how you approach the question and then you get to
know what to do.

Lenin and the Trade Union Debate in Russia
Part One

I will have to move with a certain freedom, but, nevertheless, the general line will be clear, especially once you have the whole thing.

I'm starting on page seven of Volume IX,[1] where we will find the important speeches that took place in the trade union debate in Russia. In Volume IX of Lenin's *Selected Works*, Lenin is talking about a row that has broken out in Russia. (This whole discussion, preliminary to and at the Tenth Party Congress, and immediately after, is one of the finest political discussions that I know of—anywhere. The other one is the discussion between Cromwell and Ireton[2] and the Levellers in the seventeenth-century at the high pitch of the English Revolution.[3])

On page seven, Lenin is attacking Trotsky and Bukharin, and he says— "Why cannot we achieve that team work of which we stand so much in need? Because of our differences on the question of the method of approach to be adopted towards the masses, the method of winning the masses, of contacts with the masses. That is the whole point."[4] Politicians don't say that. You don't hear any of them saying that. That was Lenin's basis.

Lenin continued—"And in this precisely lies the peculiar feature of the trade unions as institutions which were created under capitalism, which must inevitably exist in the period from capitalism to Communism, and whose future is doubtful." The future of the trade unions is doubtful, Lenin is saying, because the trade unions represent a backward type of society and they occupy a special function in this backward type of society. "This future," says Lenin, "in which the existence of the trade unions will be doubtful, is a remote one, our grandchildren will talk about it."

Lenin must have said, at least once a month, "We do not have and we cannot have socialism in Russia." Lenin now says—"At present, however, the question is how to approach the masses. How to win them, how to establish contact with them, how to get the complicated system of transmission belts to work." There is the government, there is the party, and there are the trade unions. The party and the government have to work together, and work in the trade unions; and the trade unions have to influence the great majority of the population. It is a very complicated method.

> At the moment I am only speaking in the abstract, and in principle, about the relations between classes in capitalist society; there we have a proletariat, non-proletarian toiling masses, a petty bourgeoisie, and a bourgeoisie. From this point of view, even if there were no bureaucracy in the apparatus of the Soviet government, we already get an extremely complicated system of transmission belts as a result of what capitalism created.[5]

Now we go to the bottom of page eight. Lenin is attacking Trotsky: "And yet, while betraying this lack of seriousness, Comrade Trotsky commits a mistake himself."[6] You know what that debate was about? Trotsky had said, "We are a workers' state, therefore, we will make the trade unions part of the government." Lenin said, "No, we are a workers' state, but we are not a proper workers' state, and we have to allow the working-class organization to fight the workers' government on behalf of the interest of the working class." That is one of the most delicate and the most powerful pieces of Marxism that you can or will find.

Now, Lenin goes on to say:

> According to him [Trotsky], it is not the role of the trade unions in the workers' state to protect the material and spiritual interests of the working class. This is a mistake. Comrade Trotsky talks about the "workers' state." Excuse me, this is an abstraction. It was natural for us to write about the workers' state in 1917; but those who now ask, "Why protect, against whom protect the working class, there is no bourgeoisie now, the state is a workers' state," commit an obvious mistake. Not altogether a workers' state; that is the whole point. This is where Comrade Trotsky makes some of his fundamental mistakes. We have now passed from general principles to businesslike discussion and decrees, and we are being dragged away from the practical and businesslike. This will not do. In the first place, our state is not really a workers' state, but a workers' and peasants' state.[7]

The moment you are dealing with peasants in any country, particularly a backward country, you are away from the fundamental principles or possibilities of socialism and genuine planning. Is that clear? You cannot do that with a lot of peasants. The Russian population was 175 million—10 million workers and the rest were peasants. Lenin was always aware of that. We shall see that running through his whole policy and we shall see the application we can make from that to the states of Africa and China today. Lenin goes on:

> And from this follow many things. [*Bukharin:* "What kind of state? A workers' and peasants' state?"]. And although Comrade Bukharin shouts, 'What kind of state? A workers' and peasants' state?' I will not stop to answer him ...

> It is evident from our Party program—a document which the author of the *ABC of Communism*[8] is familiar—It is evident from this program that our state is a workers' state with bureaucratic distortions ...Here you have, then, the reality of the transition. Well, the state has in practice taken this form; does that mean that the trade unions have nothing to protect, that we can dispense with them in the protection of the material and spiritual interests of the entirely organised proletariat? No. That is an entirely wrong argument theoretically. It carries us into the sphere of abstractions, or the ideal which we shall achieve in fifteen or twenty years time, and I am not sure that we shall achieve it even in that time. We are confronted with reality, which we know very well—that is, if we do not allow ourselves to become intoxicated, to be carried away by intellectual talk or abstract arguments, or by what sometimes seems to be "theory," but what in fact is a mistake, miscalculation of the specific features of the transition. Our present state is such that the entirely organised proletariat must protect itself, and we must utilise these workers' organisations for the purpose of protecting the workers from their own state and in order that the workers may protect our state.[9]

I hope that is clear. Turn over now to page fifteen. There, Lenin, the practical man of politics, the practical man of affairs, is speaking. The second paragraph on page fifteen begins: "We must study practical experience. I have signed decrees and orders containing practical instructions on coalescence [our coalescence with our trade unions], and practice is a hundred times more important than any theory." The greatest political and theoretical leader we have known is Lenin, but now, in the organization of the state, he is instituting a different attitude:

That is why when people say, "let us talk about 'coalescence,'" I reply, "Let us study what we have done." I have not the least doubt that we have made many mistakes. Perhaps a large number of our decrees will also have to be amended. I agree, I am not in the least infatuated with decrees. But then give us practical proposals: change this and that. That will be a businesslike presentation of the question. That will not be unproductive labour. That will not lead to bureaucratic project-hatching. When I turn to part VI of Trotsky's pamphlet, "Practical Conclusions," I find that this is exactly what these practical conclusions suffer from.

And now comes a very important section:

There we read that one-third to one-half of the members of the All-Russian Central Council of Trade Unions and of the Presidium of the Supreme Council of National Economy shall be members of both bodies, and that in the case of collegiums, the inter-representations shall be from one-half to two-thirds, etc. Why? Just like that: "rule of thumb." It is true, of course, that such proportions are repeatedly laid down in our decrees precisely by "rule of thumb"; but why is it inevitable in decrees? I do not defend all decrees, and I do not want to make the decrees appear better than they really are.

Now, follow this carefully, Alfie:

In them conventional magnitudes like one-half, one-third of the total membership, etc., are very often put in by rule of thumb. When a decree says that, it means: Try to do it like that, and later on we shall weigh up the results of your "trying."[10]

Lenin used to quote Napoleon's maxim *"on s'engage ... puis on voit."* You decide to say one-third, one-half, when you begin, and at the end of the time, you check what the results have been. Lenin explains: "Later on we shall see what exactly came of it. And when we have seen what came of it we shall move forward."[11]

Now go over to page sixteen, to the middle of the third paragraph: "Trotsky's theses speak about production propaganda. This was unnecessary because, in this case 'theses' are already obsolete." If you are not doing propaganda, you haven't to write theses. Is that clear?

We do not yet know whether these institutions are good or bad. We shall try them, and then we shall express an opinion. Let us study them and investigate. Let us suppose that at a congress ten sections of ten men each are formed; they will ask: "have you engaged in production propaganda? What has come of it?" After studying the matter we shall reward those who have been particularly successful and cast aside what has proved to be useless. We already have practical experience; it is slight, not much, it is true, but we have it, and we are being dragged back from this to "theses on principles."[12]

Now, I want to go on to page twenty-three. This is going to be a rough one. I'm going to read two or three pages because I want you to absorb what these pages are saying. Lenin says, "We are in crisis." Do you know where this crisis comes from? They have just won the Civil War. They were now victorious and they settled down in this debate to find out what they were going to do with the Russian Revolution. That is what this debate is about: "Where are we and what are we going to do?" Exactly the same thing took place in England sometime around 1648. They defeated Charles and all the royalists and the debate was "what are we going to do with this country now?" That situation is going to face every revolutionary body.

Lenin made it clear that the only way we can do that is by practical experience and involving the mass of the population. Any other attempt— what they are attempting in Africa, in the Caribbean and all these former colonial places today—is bound to end in disaster.

So Lenin picked up an old conference document, "The Fifth All-Russian Conference of Trade Unions," in which Rudzutak[13] had made a report on the tasks of the trade unions in production.[14] Now, you must remember there were only about 10 million workers in a population that was somewhere near 175 million. You can understand the situation that faced the Bolshevik Party, having to carry out socialist ideas and so forth. Lenin used to say (he said this until the day he died), "If we can manage state capitalism in Russia, we would have done wonderfully."[15] What happened was that the workers seized the factories. So, he said, "You're going to take the factories?" They said, "Yeah." He said, "Do you know what to do with them?" They said, "We've come to you to find out." He said, "I don't know, so you go and see about it." But you can't quarrel with workers who seize factories. We have that document dealing with the workers' councils in the factories[16] and we are waiting for the translation.[17] That is going to upset all the ideas and so forth that people have of the development of the Russian Revolution.[18]

I will tell you what happened. It seems—this is a speculation, but I think it is correct—the trade unions, to a substantial degree, were supporting the Russian Revolution, but the leaders of the trade unions were, to a substantial degree, Mensheviks. You follow what I mean? You can have a right-wing Bolshevik and a left-wing Menshevik. They were Mensheviks and they were very hostile to the idea that the Russian workers wanted to carry through—to fix workers' councils to run the industry.

Now I am being very cautious here, but this is why I am waiting to get that document, to see what is in it. It seems that the Bolsheviks suppressed the workers' councils and supported the Menshevik leadership of the trade unions because to have supported the workers' councils would have blown everything sky high.

So, that was the situation. We have the "Fifth All-Russian Congress of Trade Unions" with Rudzutak's report. What I am concerned with is that many of the things that Lenin was working on from 1921 to 1923 when he died—and he made analyses and proposals that are of a standard that have never been touched since—are problems which today face the bourgeoisie even under the bourgeois state. I hope that is clear. The problems that he dealt with, which were facing the Russian Revolution after three or four years, are problems which face those who are in charge of the trade union movement, even under the bourgeois regime. That, we will work out.

Now let us see Rudzutak's theses quoted by Lenin:

"1) Immediately after the October Revolution the trade unions proved to be *almost the only* bodies which, in addition to carrying out workers' *control,* could and had to undertake the work of organising and *managing production.*["][19]

Is that clear? Immediately after the October Revolution, they not only carried out workers' control, but they had to undertake the work of organizing and managing production. We are going to get the details of that when that document, which we want translated, is translated. Nobody has touched that document yet.[20] Deutscher referred to it in a footnote.[21] He has read it, but he doesn't understand it at all. We are going to impose that as we imposed Marx's *Economic-Philosophic Manuscripts.*[22] I am waiting patiently.

Let us return to Comrade Rudzutak. He continues with his opening thesis:

"A state apparatus for managing the national economy of the country had not yet been organised in the first period of existence of the Soviet government *[James: Is that clear?]*, and the sabotage of the factory owners and the higher technical personnel very acutely raised before the working class the task of preserving industry and restoring the normal functioning of the whole economic apparatus of the country.["][23]

The working class saved the economic apparatus of the country in the moment after the October Revolution. The working class came to the rescue and they formed the organizations and they ran it—that's how they were able to win the Civil War.

"2) In the subsequent period in the work of the Supreme Council of National Economy, when a considerable part of this work consisted in liquidating the private enterprises and organising the state management of these enterprises, *the trade unions carried on this work side-by-side and jointly with the state economic management bodies.*["]

"The weakness of the state bodies not only explained but also justified this *duplication*; historically it was justified by the establishment of full contact between the trade union and the economic management bodies.["][24]

Do you see what happened now? The state starts to organize, to take over from the workers and the trade unions.

"3) The management of the state economic bodies, their gradual mastery of the apparatus of production and management and the co-ordination of the various parts of this apparatus—all *shifted the centre of gravity of the work of managing industry* and of drawing up a production programme *to these bodies*. As a result the work of the trade unions in the sphere of organising production was reduced to *participation in the work of forming the collegiums* of the Chief Committees, Central Boards and factory managements.["][25]

The workers had started it and they kept it going when it was going to fall apart. Then, when the state bodies came in, they and the workers worked side-by-side and then the state management took over completely. That is the fundamental problem of the Russian Revolution. (Have you read Hannah Arendt's book, *On Revolution*?[26]) Then came the situation of appointing people to the boards that run production. Whereas formerly the trade unions used to run it and at the second stage they worked side-by-side, after this stage the state took over.

> "4) At the present time we are once again squarely faced with the question of establishing the closest ties between the economic bodies of the Soviet Republic and the trade unions; it is necessary at all costs because to make expedient use of every unit of labour and to enlist the masses of the producers as a whole for the purpose of taking a conscious part in the process of production; *[James: I will give up politics and study psychology, if an African socialist says this]* the state apparatus of economic management, gradually growing and becoming more complicated, has become transformed into a huge bureaucratic machine out of all proportion to the size of industry, and is compelling the trade unions to take a direct path in the organisation of production not only through the persons representing them on the economic bodies, but as organisations.["][27]

Now, if the trade unions were a solid body, dominant in the economy of the country and had had so much freedom, they could never have lost it. Is it clear why the Russian Revolution failed? If some sixty or seventy per-cent of the workers and peasants in Russia were trade unionists with some experience of managing the trade unions, etc., and when the Revolution began they had taken over that bit, they could never have lost it. That was the problem. And bear Africa, India, and China in mind all the time. This is the same situation that they face. In fact, a little worse, but in some respects better.

It is magnificent, the honesty—the absolute plainness, the regard for truth—which you find in these documents. This is an education not only in politics, but in the moral approach to a political situation. There is nowhere you can find as serious and as comprehensive an attitude towards the problem of the Russian Revolution as in the statements of the Russian government itself. I have read plenty. These are the people who know what happened, because they spoke the truth.

That is the problem that the Russians were facing—not democracy and all that kind of nonsense that people talk about. Lenin knew that was happening and why it was taking place. You can get no clearer statement of that anywhere else. Now we go on:

> "5) While the Supreme Council of National Economy approaches the question of drawing up a general production programme from the point

of view of *the availability of the material elements of production* (raw materials, fuel, the condition of machinery, etc.), *[James: That is what a body has to do. You know that is an official activity]* the trade unions must approach this question *from the point of view of organising labour* for the task of production, and of the expedient utilisation of this labour. Therefore it must be an absolute rule that the general *production programme, in its various parts and as a whole, be drawn up with the direct co-operation of the trade unions* in order that the utilisation of the material resources of production and of labour may be combined in the most expedient manner.

"6) The introduction of genuine labour discipline, the successful combating of labour desertion, etc., are conceivable only if the whole mass of participants in production take a *conscious part* in the fulfilment of these tasks. This cannot be achieved by *bureaucratic methods and orders from above*; every participant in production must understand the need for an expediency of the production tasks he is carrying out; every participant in production must not only take part in the fulfilment of tasks given from above but also take an intelligent part in remedying all technical and organisational defects in the sphere of production.["]28

May I say this, and imagine that I am saying it a hundred times, although I am saying it once: "This cannot be achieved by *bureaucratic methods and orders from above*". You cannot get the working class to take a conscious part in production and assume responsibility for what is taking place "by *bureaucratic methods and orders from above.*" That is an absolute statement. You cannot do that. That is a socialist society. This is what they proposed. Lenin said you can't do that from above. If you are going to insist on doing it from above, you are going to have a brutal dictatorship, which is what they got. Lenin never at any time, as we are going to see, thought it could be done otherwise than by the party and the leadership instilling into the population that "this is a responsibility that you must start out. It cannot be done from above." Stalin set out to do it from above, and to do it from above, he had to destroy the Bolshevik Party and rewrite the whole history of the Russian Revolution.

Now, I hope that you're beginning to understand what happened in Russia. This is the problem as it faced the Russian Bolshevik Party in the days when it was still the socialist, civilian party. Let us go on:

"The tasks of the trade unions in this sphere are enormous. They must teach *their members in every shop*, in every factory, *to note and take into account all the defects in the utilisation of the labour power that result from the improper utilisation* of technical resources or from unsatisfactory adminis-tration. The *sum total of the experience of the individual* enterprises and of every industry must be utilised in a determined struggle against red tape, laxity, and bureaucracy.

"7) In order to especially emphasise the importance of these production tasks they must organisationally occupy a definite place in definite current work. In developing their work, the *economic departments* of the trade unions[,] organised in accordance with the decision of the Third All-Russian Con-gress[,] must gradually clarify and define the character of the whole of trade union work. For example, under present social conditions, when the whole of production is directed toward satisfying the needs of the toilers them-selves . . .["][29]

This is Lenin all the time. He would put forward an idea of the most exalted kind and then immediately seek practical ways and means to carry it out. To do this they must "occupy a definite place." Do you get the sig-nificance of that? You know why the trade unions were not functioning properly. They were going to the countryside to get some food. Lenin was saying, in effect, "the whole business of the production today is to give the workers some food to eat, some clothes to wear, and something to put up in their house. That is where they have reached in 1921."

"...*wage rates and bonuses should be closely connected with and dependent upon the degree of fulfilment of the production plan.*"Bonuses in kind and the par-tial payment of wages in kind must be gradually transformed into a *sys-tem of supplying the workers* in accordance to the degree of productivity of labour.["][30]

In other words, the wages and bonuses must be in kind; that is where you give the worker so much for potatoes, you give him so much for bread, you—give him a piece of cloth, you give him a piece of wood. That is the way to develop the economy, but, despite the poverty, do you notice the insistence upon the factories? The workers have to do it. What they pro-duce you must give them so that they have something to eat, something to wear and something to burn. You will not find this thing anywhere else, you know. You will not find it. Let us go on:

"8) The organisation of the work of the trade unions on these lines should, on the one hand, put an end to the existence of *parallel bodies* (*political departments etc.*), [*James: He said "finish up with that." The trade unions now must deal with the economic development of the country*] and, on the other hand, should restore close contacts between the masses and the economic management bodies.

"9) After the Third Congress, the trade unions failed in a large measure to carry out their programmes of participating in the work of building up national economy owing to *wartime conditions,* on the one hand, and owing to their *organisational weakness* and their isolation from the leading and practical work of the economic bodies, on the other.

"10) In view of this, the trade unions must set themselves the following immediate practical tasks. a) to take a most active part in solving the problems of production and management; b) to take a direct part jointly with the corresponding economic bodies in organising *competent management* bodies; c) to carefully register various *types of management bodies* and their influence on production [*James: The working class are to be the decisive element in the development of production*]; d) unfailingly, to take part in drafting and laying down economic *plans* and production programmes; e) to *organise labour* in accordance with the degree of urgency of economic tasks; f) to build an extensive organisation for *production agitation and propaganda.*["][31]

If I went to any African state or any state in Eastern Europe, and even some of the advanced countries, and said that, they would put me in the lunatic asylum for fifteen days.

This was the basis on which the Russian Revolution sought to build a new society.

"11) The economic departments of *trade unions* and trade union organisations must be transformed into swift and powerful levers for the systematic participation of the unions in the organisation of production.

"12) In the sphere of planned material supplies for the workers, the trade unions must shift *their influence to the distributing bodies of the Commissariat for Food Supplies,* both local and central; they must take a practical and businesslike part in the work of and *control* all the distributing bodies and pay particular attention to the activities of the central and *gubernia* [city council] *workers' supply commissions.*["][32]

The trade unions have to watch the distribution of the food. This is in their hands. Could you imagine if, out of a 175 million population, there were 75 million workers carrying out a program like this? What would happen to the Russian state? That's what you have to bear in mind. What killed them was they didn't have the trade unions to do it. The workers were perhaps only 10 million and starving. But the point I want to make here is that Lenin never lost sight of what a socialist society and a socialist objective of a party was to be.

> "13) In view of the fact that, owing to the narrow departmental strivings of certain chief committees, central boards, etc., so-called 'preference' has dropped into a state of confusion, the trade unions must everywhere become the champions of genuine preference in industry and of revising the prevailing system of defining preference to correspond with the importance of the industries and the material resources available in the country.["][33]

They were giving preference to workers in the important industries. Lenin said, the Bolshevik Party said, in effect, "No, the trade unions have to decide who will get preference and what they get. Whatever the significance of the industry in the country, that does not matter. The workers themselves will decide who will get and what they will get."

> "14) Special attention must be paid to the so-called exemplary group of factories in order to transform them into genuine exemplary groups by creating competent management and labour discipline and stimulating the work of the trade union organisations.

> "15) In organising labour, in addition to drawing up regular wage rates and thoroughly overhauling rates of output, the trade unions must firmly take into their own hands the whole work of combating the various *forms of labour desertion* (absenteeism, late-coming, etc.). The disciplinary courts to which insufficient attention has been paid up to now, must be transformed into the genuine means of combating violation of proletarian labour discipline.["][34]

Did you know of their disciplinary courts? The workers were to institute courts and they were to decide who should be punished and what was to be done in the industry. Disciplinary courts, preferences, bonuses: the trade unions and the workers were to take charge of that. Now, I want to tell you something. You will hear people talk and write about the Russian Revolution. This doesn't matter to them. They say, "Oh, Lenin is crazy." But this is how the revolution was made and this is what he tried to do. Trotsky didn't understand this at all.

> "16) The fulfilment of the tasks enumerated, as well as the drafting of a practical plan of production propaganda and a number of measures for improving the economic conditions of the workers, should be imposed upon the economic departments. Therefore it is necessary to instruct the economic department of the All-Russian Central Council of Trade Unions to convene in the near future a *special all-Russian conference* of economic departments to discuss practical questions of economic construction in connection with the work of the state economic bodies.["][35]

That is the basis of the socialist society. If you have sixty or seventy percent of the population trained in the union movement and working in industry, they must take complete control. Now, Lenin said:

> I hope you will now see why I had to call myself a fool. This is a platform! It is a hundred times better than the one Trotsky wrote after thinking it over many times and the one Bukharin wrote without thinking at all. All of us members of the Central Committee who have not worked in the trade union movement for many years should learn from Comrade Rudzutak, and Comrades Trotsky and Bukharin should learn from him.[36]

Do you see where that came from? They had not worked in the trade union movement for many years. Rudzutak was a genuine unionist and, being a Bolshevik, he wrote this.

Now, Lenin compares Rudzutak's theses with the theses that Trotsky submitted to the Central Committee. In making the comparison, Lenin says:

At the end of thesis 5 I read:

> "It is necessary immediately to proceed to reorganize the trade unions, i.e., first of all to select the leading personnel from this point of view."

> This is a perfect example of bureaucracy! Trotsky and Krestinsky will select the "leading personnel" of the trade unions![37]

This was absolutely foreign to what had been written in Rudzutak's thesis, which the Committee carried.

Now go on to page twenty-eight, the last paragraph on that page. "What must be done to achieve the most rapid and surest cure?"[38] The Party is in crisis. The Party is shaking with fever. Do you understand that? The Party was the government. The Party meant something and the Party was shaking with fever because of the tremendous debate and the problems, and the crisis and the conflict between leading members—Lenin on one side, Trotsky on the other. That is the way in which the Bolshevik Party lived. The Party was in crisis over what was to be done in the situation that faced the country. They had to decide what kind of society was Russian society going to be.

"What must be done to achieve the most rapid and surest cure?" Lenin asks. His answer will indicate to you the kind of things that have to be done in any political party:

> *All* members of the Party must with absolute coolness and the greatest care *study* 1) the essence of the disagreements and 2) the development of the struggle within the Party. Both the one and the other must be done, because the essence of the disagreements unfolds, is explained and becomes concrete (and often undergoes transformation) *in the course of the struggle*, which in passing through various stages does *not* always and at every stage reveal the same combatants, the same number of combatants, the same positions in the struggle, etc. Both the one and the other must be *studied*, and we must unfailingly demand very exact, printed documents capable of being verified from all sides. Whoever merely believes what is said is a hopeless idiot whom one can only give up in disgust. If *no* documents are available, witnesses on *both* or several sides must be examined, and it must be "examination under ordeal," examination before witnesses.[39]

Do you know what you are listening to here? All talk about the dictatorship and Lenin in the Bolshevik Party is a lot of nonsense. Isn't that clear? Isn't it obvious? Where could you get a more serious, democratic personality? You cannot anywhere. The British Labour Party did not carry on discussions like that. This is a man who is determined that the party should work out the problem, because he knows that there is no other way of getting a really genuine understanding which will appeal to the mass of the population, except by getting what the Party at this particular stage thinks, and he wants everybody to understand what is taking place. It is not mere talk. That is the way he conducted his affairs at all times. This business about one-party dictatorship is a lot of nonsense, a lot of lies and stupidity which they stick into the minds of the public. This is the Bolshevik Party, and if people do not want to take that, then leave them alone. They do not want to listen to Lenin at all.

Now, look at what Lenin proceeds to do. I'm not going to go into the details of this. Lenin said: "I will try to draw a synopsis of what I understand to be the essence of the disagreements as well as of the successive stages in the struggle." First stage, second stage, on page twenty-nine; third stage on page thirty; fourth stage on page thirty-one; fifth stage on page thirty-one. Lenin tells everybody to discuss and evaluate, and, by the way, this thing is printed in the Party press and circulated all over Russia. Every Russian worker or peasant would hear what was going on.

That was the Bolshevik Party—the finest political Party ever heard of. What Stalin introduced into it afterwards had nothing to do with Bolshevism. There are people who say (this is their great argument): "Well, it is true that Lenin was like that, but what Lenin was doing led inevitably to Stalinism." I don't buy that. I don't buy that, not if you know what Lenin was doing.

Now, Lenin continues. On page thirty-three: "I summed up the substance of Rudzutak's thesis on December 30, in four points." And he goes into the points, etc. I will go next time into the second part of the debate, "The Trade Unions and the Mistakes of Trotsky and Bukharin,"[40] where you will get a view of what Lenin and the Bolshevik Party were like. It is the finest political party the world has ever known. That is what is characteristic of it.

However, there were a lot of working class and peasant people who were not touched by the trade unions. This great debate was about what was to be done with the trade unions. Trotsky proposed that it was a workers' state. Therefore, the workers' state will take over the trade unions, the trade unions will become part of the government, which they are today, and Lenin said, "No, you can't do that. The workers will see about bonuses, the trade unions must do this, and the trade unions must do that, etc., and in time they will be able to set up a system, in twenty years—I don't know when—when we have a socialist society in the sense that we have unions, trade unions which represent the mass of the population. Then things will be different, but, meanwhile, you have to go on as best you can." But he knew where he stood.

Now, what about the rest of the population? Look on page 457. You remember my statement in that last essay as to what Lenin proposed in 1923. That is clear. But it was 1920 when Lenin wrote "A Letter to J.V. Stalin on Drawing Up Regulations for the Workers' and Peasants' Inspection."[41] This is what Lenin wrote to Stalin on 24 January 1920. Stalin had made such a complete mess of it—not made a mess of it, he hadn't done it at all. You will understand, therefore, that when Lenin wrote about the change for the Workers' and Peasants' Inspection in 1923, he was merely repeating what he had already written in 1920.

I'm going to go through this with you in detail so we can understand what he had in mind for the trade unions and for the rest of Russia. Here it is:

> To Comrade Stalin, *copies sent to* Avanesov, Tomsky and Kiselev, *member of the Presidium of the All-Russian Central Executive Committee*
>
> On the basis of the instructions given by the Central Committee I think the three drafts should be worked up into one.
>
> I think the following should be added:
>
> 1) The "Department" of the Workers' and Peasants' Inspection of the State Control should be a temporary one. Its function should be to introduce the Workers' and Peasants' Inspection in *all* the departments of the State Control, and it should then cease to exist as a separate department.
>
> 2) Objects to enlist all the toilers, men, and particularly women, in the work of the Workers' and Peasants' Inspection.

Is that clear? Are you following? It should introduce the Workers' and Peasants' Inspection in every section of the State Department and then a Department for Workers' Control should abolish it. In other words, it should be rooted in every section of the work itself. The workers and peasants, they were to inspect what was taking place in the government. You could not control what was happening in all the departments of production; a man has a little business here, another has a little place there. It could not be done. But in the business of the government, all the workers and the peasants were to be involved. Let us go on:

3) For this purpose the local authorities should compile lists (according to the constitution), exempt office employees, etc.—all the rest to take part in the work of the Workers' and Peasants' Inspection *in rotation.*

You know people say that all this was utopia. That is OK with me; if you think it is utopia, that is fine. If you do not have that, then you have what they have in the Stalinist regime.

4) Participation in this work should assume various forms in accordance with the abilities of the participants—from the function of 'informer', witness, or learner, or pupil *[James: "Something is very wrong, you bring them in. Now listen to this Alfie"],* in the case of the illiterate and uneducated workers and peasants, to all rights (or nearly all rights) for the literate, the educated, those who have been *tested* in one way or another.

Lenin conceived, even in that backward society, that all persons, even the illiterate, the uneducated, should be involved to the extent that they could be. They could be involved in the investigation and checking of production. They could do a little bit of that. But in the state affairs, that is what the Workers' and Peasants' Control had to do.

5) To pay special attention to (and to draw up strict rules for)—and the Workers' and Peasants' Inspection to exercise *wider* control over—the accounting of products, *goods,* stores, tools, materials, fuel, etc. etc. (particularly dining rooms etc.). *[James: Workers and peasants were to go and see what was going on]*

Women, all women, should be enlisted for this purpose, without fail.

6) In order to avoid confusion arising from the enlistment of masses of participants, lists indicating the order in which they are to be enlisted should be drawn up. It is also necessary carefully to [sic] think out the forms this participation is to assume (two and three at a time; to enlist a large number of participants only rarely and then on special occasions, so as not to distract employees from their work unnecessarily).

You can't have a lot of people going to inspect the government and the process. Stalin never organised this at all, so Lenin said at the end, "Get rid of that fellow and put somebody else there," and he instituted new methods whereby the Workers' and Peasants' Inspection should be organised.

7) Detailed instructions should be drawn up.

8) It should be the duty of the officials of the State Control (in accordance with special inspections) first to enlist the co-operation of the representatives (or group) of the Workers' and Peasants' Inspection in all of their operations *[James: Now Alfie, this is for you]*, and second to deliver lectures at *non-party* conferences of workers and peasants…

Is that clear? This is not the party. This is every single worker and peasant; involve them in doing this work, both non-party workers and peasants—"(popular lectures according to a specially approved programme, on the principles and methods of the State Control. Instead of lectures they may arrange for the reading of the pamphlet we shall publish…)"

9) Gradually invite peasants *[James: Every section of the Russian society, he says, not only the women, not only the non-party people but, "gradually invite peasants"]* (unfailingly non-party peasants) from the local districts to take part in the work of the State Control in the centre. Start at least with one or two from each gubernia [city council] (if it is not possible to start with more) and then *extend* it as transport facilities and other conditions permit. *[James: And, by the way]* The same to apply to non-party workers.

This one-party state or this one-party that they imitate from Bolshevik Russia …none of them could debate me on any serious platform. I know what that fellow was after. I understand it completely. That last passage that you read, that last section of the essay in *Nkrumah Then and Now*[42]—do you understand that this began from the beginning? All through his work you will see that. Let me read the last paragraph:

10) Gradually introduce the verification by the Party and the trade unions of the participation of the toilers in the work of the State Control *[James: In other words, the Party and the trade unions have to verify if bodies of workers are being brought into this verification of the State Control of the government of the country]*, i.e., they are to ascertain whether all the toilers participate in this work, and the results of this participation from the point of view of the participants learning the art of state administration.

That is the socialist society and Lenin never lost sight of that, however backward Russia was: the poverty, the misery, the absence of food, etc. He always put before the Party what was required, because he was a socialist. He was not a socialist who came to power, then forgot about it.

I sent a copy of this to Kwame Nkrumah thirty-six years later. I don't know if he read it. I saw him and asked him and he said he did not receive it. But even if he read it, he could not understand it. Lenin always stated that the two things that matter are bonuses to be controlled by the workers and disciplinary courts to be controlled by the workers. He says, "Without bonuses and preference and disciplinary courts, you have nothing."

Now, what was the Workers' Opposition[43] proposing instead of this? Lenin got very impatient with them, very savage against Shliapnikov,[44] in particular. (I am sorry I have not got the books here. I am in a little difficulty. That is why I was so glad to get that speech by Trotsky reporting on the conference. It is perfectly obvious that Trotsky either did not understand or did not agree at all. He did not understand. Did you get any conception from him that he understood what was taking place here? Nothing.) It was very difficult for the Workers' Opposition to get it. Lenin was very impatient with them. He said, "This is what I propose, this is what I suggest, this is what was proposed before, this is what the union has failed to do, this is what we must get it to do. What do you suggest?"[45] The response was: "We will have more democracy."

I am in a little difficulty here. I know quite well what they were talking about, but I have picked it up second hand. I can't really publicly debate an issue where I am not able to read and quote from the Opposition. You follow what I mean? I am in difficulty, but I have read enough of Lenin to know that this is exactly what he was saying from the beginning. These people that began to say, "We want more democracy, we want freedom, we want authority of the workers against the bourgeois capitalists who are in charge," Lenin was very angry with them—"Get these god-damned people out of the way!" I would have been the same because it was a very serious problem that they faced: what was to be done?

There are many other points that come up. I can't go into all of them. In thinking over the situation, what constantly comes up is what will happen in Trinidad. This kind of policy could go like that [*James snaps his fingers*] in Trinidad and any West Indian island. *Any West Indian island.*

I will always keep the distinction between trade unions and the population. Do you remember what Lenin said at the end when he was dying?

Make a note of what he was referring to. He said two things are needed: One, to fix the government (do you remember that?), and to fix the government, the people, the workers must fix it—and the trade unions. Nobody else can fix it. That is what he saw from the beginning. Secondly, Lenin says the peasants must be organized in co-operative societies. The trade union could take care of itself. What happened was the peasants outweighed the trade union movement. Anyway, that's enough for now.

ALFIE ROBERTS: What happens when you don't have a trade union?

JAMES: If you haven't got a trade union then you have nothing. What country hasn't got a trade union? If you haven't got a trade union, you make one.

FRANKLYN HARVEY: Or what if you have a trade union dominated by certain elements in the community?

JAMES: Who are the elements dominating the trade unions?

HARVEY: In Grenada, for example, let us say you have people in the trade union movement who are not concerned with the trade union movement and workers and...

JAMES: A trade union consists of members of a union, workers and people whom they have elected. That is the trade union. If there are people who dominate, this lawyer or that one, you throw him out. You say, "He has no right there," and you will get the workers to support you if you propose that.

I have not heard of backward workers. The Russian workers were ready to take over. At the beginning, they kept it going when the thing was falling apart. But then the government bodies took over. I am waiting patiently for that account of the Workers' Conference. It has been stated that the Russian Bolshevik Party suppressed them. I am not going to sit here and say what they should or should not have done. I want to know what happened. But, then, so many Mensheviks were in charge of the union movement and to have gone in favor of the small body of workers would have upset the whole business and the Bolshevik trade union. You follow what I mean? That's the situation.

But you begin to understand, I hope, that the Russian Revolution was a very serious problem, and this business of a one-party dictatorship and that Lenin couldn't understand democracy—that is a lot of nonsense. They have not gone into this question and that is my situation. I have read and translated Souvarine;[46] I have read E.H. Carr. I have his book at home;[47] I have read Trotsky repeatedly; I have read Deutscher. They don't seem to understand what was involved.

ROBERTS: But to get back to something. I don't believe this is the impression you really want to give or impart: that trade unions have to be the prerequisite for any meaningful socialist construction?

JAMES: Not the trade unions, but the proletariat, the organized proletariat.

HARVEY: They must be organized in some sort of movement. It is not bound to be a union.

JAMES: No, it must be a union. What is the strength of the Oilfield Workers Trade Union? They are united, disciplined, and organized by the very mechanism of capitalist production. That is the strength of the Oilfield Workers Trade Union. They are not organized by Weekes[48] and union organizers. It is the fact that they are working in a large industry, coming to work every morning, and working together. That is the basis of the organization. And that is what Marxism means.

ROBERTS: Therefore, then, if we take—well, I do not think it is a special case—the situation that prevails in St. Vincent, where there is no real trade union movement. What you then say is this: If there is any serious effort to develop the economy, a trade union movement would begin to grow and the workers will then be organized in that trade union movement.

JAMES: But in addition to that, you have got the second part of the program where people can be involved in the structure of the government. And you will have in St. Vincent, or wherever it is, a body of people who are ready to take part from a progressive point of view.

There is something else. In any community which approaches a modern community, you have some sort of industry. And in the West Indies you have the bauxite industry, you have the sugar unions, you have the Oilfield Workers Trade Unions. They will set the tone for the whole of West Indies. They will decide and it is from what they go around and say, etc., and from what they do, that workers who are not in any kind of industry will be able to follow them and take part. Have they not got a lot of fisheries?

I cannot understand. You have the domestic servants industry, you have plenty of workers. Now the dominant feature in any economy is large-scale industry and the proletariat which corresponds to it. That is why I keep on insisting, number one, to talk about socialism in the West Indies is a lot of nonsense, and this African socialism is more nonsense than ever, because you haven't got any basis to work on. Maybe they can work out something, I don't know. I haven't heard any of them. They believe that, in nationalizing the economy, that there is socialism.

ROBERTS: When you say there is no basis...

JAMES: There is no social basis for the construction of a socialist society. Lenin envisages a situation in which the trade unions would not be such a dominant section and so separate from the rest of the population: "Maybe in fifteen or twenty years time. Maybe then, I do not know." That is what Lenin calls for as a socialist society. In England that could take place tomorrow. Twenty million workers in trade unions and everybody knows all about the trade union. There would be no problem in England.

ROBERTS: I believe when you make the point that there is no social basis for building socialism or a socialist society, I think this is what Harvey was arguing, trying to get at that point some nights ago—there does not seem to be this lack of a social basis upon which we can build a socialist society.

JAMES: A socialist society to an educated person must be a socialist society. Note something which I am going to tell you. I never in the Caribbean speak about Marxism. Never. I make the analysis, etc. I never say Marx. There is no need for me to do that. None whatever. In their eye, Marxism is a communist who is going to shoot everybody. When we are talking, I can go into that, and it does not prevent me from writing as I like about Marxism in an internal party magazine or journal. It does not prevent me from writing an article in the paper. But I do not go to the public saying, "Marx says therefore..." I say this: "All these foreign parts, they should go."

HARVEY: There is a difference, and a very big difference, to a certain extent, between small islands, the islands of St. Lucia, Barbados, Trinidad. As I have mentioned before, you have not any working class as such in any one of the smaller islands and, as far as I know, there is no industry, no manufacturing complex. It is strictly a peasant society.

JAMES: Haven't you got small workers, a man making shoes, artisans, etc., women domestic servers, sewing and so on and so forth?

HARVEY: A woman sewing, for example, is simply like Alfie coming to me and telling me to sew a dress at my house. They do have these private, as they call it, individuals.

JAMES: And they form a certain basis for the creation of a special set of people organized in a certain way. You do what you can. It is obvious that, in the 20th century, that is a special type of society. You do what you can, but what is going to be dominant in their minds, and what is going to guide them is the kind of activity that is taking place in all the advanced countries of the world, and what is taking place in a separate section of the Caribbean itself. You admit that you haven't got it, so you do the best you can. You have got the teachers, you have the civil servants and so forth.

ROBERTS: For example, sir, with the Party that you were in.[49] I suspect that you may have had a certain concept and view of the type of society you would like?

JAMES: We used to put it forward. I lectured to the Oilfield Workers Trade Union and I said to the workers, "we cannot create any socialism here." There is nothing that I wouldn't tell a worker.

ROBERTS: I imagine that, knowing your philosophy and so on, you would still have a certain conception of the type of society that you would like to see. Lenin, for example, said you have to be very practical and realistic. But yet you have a certain social vision...

JAMES: Which he always put forward. Yes, he had a vision and I have put forward the type of society that we can have in 1967. I always make clear, however, that if we form a party, a mass party involving the mass of the population, and we have a daily paper, I don't know what we could do in 1970. But if we work this out properly, then we can go further, depending on the mobilization of the population. But there are certain things that we could do at once, and that is this, that, and that—and for the rest, we will see.

And by the way, I wrote in the *Guardian* that Africa has quite a fate. And I said, I don't propose to nationalize the banks. On that I will wait until Britain and these nationalize. And then I put in brackets, "If, however, the British nationalize today, you look out for us tomorrow." I put that in the paper.

But meanwhile, we want to know when this money is going away. Girvan[50] and these boys have taught me how deceitful the foreign interests can be. These fellows can put money in their pockets and go. We know there are problems but we do what we can. And we will have, in the course of a year or two, far more control of the money that is going abroad, etc.

ROBERTS: I am not saying this has to happen...

JAMES: Why are you so hesitant about what you're saying?

ROBERTS: You may get the impression that...

JAMES: I won't get a bad impression of you. Except with regard to Cuba. [*Laughter*][51]

ROBERTS: Let's assume we don't have any short-range plan of really taking over the banks. How could you guarantee that, over a certain period of time, the force of the banks won't defeat you in the end?

JAMES: They cannot defeat you in the end. If the population, the voting population, is 500,000 and I get a majority of 450,000, I don't want a one-party state. I would prefer the opposite: the other part divided into twenty parties and I have 400,000 out of 500,000—those banks cannot defeat me. You see, the problem for the bank is that there are a lot of other banks ready to come in. And I have written it in the *Guardian:* "If you [the banks] don't want to play then you can go. Here are your passports. Because if you leave in one plane, another comes in the other plane." You don't know the enormous advantage you have in the Caribbean.

These fellows have no support in the population. With that, you have everything. Girvan and these boys state, "Boy, you don't know the difficulties." I said, "Girvan, you all will lead the way and if you can't lead them, furthermore, you must understand this: there are a lot of people abroad who are very sympathetic to what is being done here. Plenty."

There is a man who has written two or three books on the oil companies. The oil companies, they did not do anything to fool him. We have a lot of people everywhere who are ready to work with anybody. And if you have a daily paper and proper people in charge, a proper editor... Of course, there will be trouble. One should always expect that there will be trouble. But I am not scared of those boys.

Lenin and the Trade Union Debate in Russia
Part Two

Now, gentlemen, we are doing our last session of this particular work. I am insisting on my Volume IX.[1] I live by it. What I will do now is the third and last section of this tremendous debate on the trade union problem, a debate in which the fundamental principles of, number one, Bolshevism, of Marxism in the 20th century, were made very clear; and, number two, the difficulties under which they lived.

At the present time, we are in a serious situation, because, for thirty or forty years, there has been nothing to speak of that calls itself Marxism. Therefore, in going over this debate, I am very much aware of that. Furthermore, in going over this debate properly, we shall find out what is really fundamental, even in bourgeois society today, although they were first posed in the revolutionary society in Russia in1921. It is to page forty of Volume IX, "Once Again on the Trade Unions, the Present Situation and the Mistakes of Comrades Trotsky and Bukharin," that I will now turn.[2]

I am going to take various sections, and these you will be able to look at over time. The first one that I'm taking is Lenin's introduction to this section of the debate. I want to read it because there is, in the minds of many people today, and even some of us that are sympathetic, some feeling that Stalinism was in reality a continuation of Leninism; that the distinction between Leninism and Stalinism was not sharp. They keep insisting on that. I want to read certain passages which show you that, objectively, it was not so, and in theory, analytically, it most certainly was not so. That comes out very clearly in this debate.

Now the first section: "A party discussion and a factional struggle of a pre-congress character, *i.e.*, before the elections and in connection with the forthcoming election of delegates to the Tenth Congress of the R.C.P.

[Russian Communist Party], has flared up."[3] Is it clear to you what that means? There is a party discussion and a factional struggle has broken out of a pre-congress character. Now, that is entirely different from what Stalinism used to do. There you have, quite clearly, the profound democracy of the Bolshevik Party under Lenin. "The first factional pronouncement, namely, Comrade Trotsky's pronouncement 'in the name of a number of responsible workers' in the 'pamphlet-platform' ('The Role and Tasks of Trade Unions,' preface dated December 25, 1920), was followed by the sharp pronouncement of the Petrograd organization of the R.C.P. and by a statement by the Moscow Committee in opposition to the Petrograd organization …"[4] In other words, Trotsky is taking part in the discussion. There is absolutely a free party discussion, absolutely free. "Then appeared this stenographic report published by the bureau of the R.C.P. fraction of the A.C.C.T.U."— which was a trade union—"of the discussion that took place on December 30, 1920, at a very large and very responsible Party meeting, namely, the meeting of the R.C.P. fraction of the Eighth Congress of Soviets."[5]

When the Soviets met—the Soviets were made up of one worker to every five-hundred in a factory—when the Soviets met, the Russian Bolshevik Party met as a fraction of the Soviet. This may seem superficial—not to me. That shows how they considered themselves and how democratic the procedure was. "This stenographic report bears the title 'The Role of the Trade Unions in Production.' This, of course"—Lenin at his best!—"is not all the discussion material by far. And party meetings at which the questions in dispute are discussed are being held almost everywhere."[6]

This discussion was widely circulated, some of it in the Party press and some of it in the general press. Do you get the significance of that? If you have to debate what Bolshevism was, this alone would suffice. This is what used to go on. They were always that way. "On December 30, 1920, I spoke at a meeting under conditions in which, as I expressed then, 'I violated the rules of procedure,' *i.e.*, under conditions in which I could not take part in the discussion or hear the preceding and subsequent speakers. I will now try to restore the violated order and express myself 'more in order.'"[7] That is the way Lenin concerned himself and took part in the discussion. Everybody took part freely and Lenin begged pardon and said, "I wasn't able to be there also. I beg your pardon. And now I will tell you what the situation is, as I saw it." Then he goes on. (I am not going into the debate as such. I'm taking a particular part.)

Now look at page forty-two. Lenin says about one of the documents (you have to think of Stalinism and the murderous attitude Stalinism has always shown.): "This is not all. Look at the factional attacks with which this pamphlet is replete." Do you get the significance of that in the light of what Stalinism was to become? Lenin says that the pamphlet in the discussion is full of factional attacks against the others. That is not the way you carry on a discussion.

Now look at page forty-three: "Let the reader carefully re-read these arguments and deeply ponder over them. First of all, appraise this pronouncement from the point of view of its factionalism!" Trotsky has said something. "Imagine what Trotsky would have said and how he would have said it, had Tomsky published a platform accusing Trotsky and 'many' military workers of cultivating the spirit of bureaucracy, of fostering the survivals of savagery, etc."[8]

Do you get the spirit of the discussion by the founder of Bolshevism? What I'm trying to point out is the spirit of the discussion, the way in which the founder of Bolshevism approached these problems. Even in writing these documents against one another, you were not to write in a factionalist spirit, far less sending people to Siberia and shooting them because they confessed. That was totally foreign to Bolshevism. You have to get that clear.

Lenin then says: "Does the essence of the controversy lie in the fact that someone does not want to understand 'new tasks and methods'? Or is it the fact that someone, talking a lot about new tasks and methods, is clumsily concealing the defence of certain unnecessary and harmful excesses of bureaucracy? Let the reader fix this *essence* of the whole controversy in his mind."[9] What this debate was about was the question of bureaucracy, particularly in the trade union movement. This bureaucracy that developed under Stalin was something that was a problem when they began. When they began the discussion about what the revolution was, although the discussion was as free as it could be, it was about the nature of bureaucracy. That is what this debate was about. If you want to know about bureaucracy, study this debate.

Now, page forty-five. Lenin says that there is a dispute in the trade union movement and (follow the analysis and note the absence of personality): "Clearly, in a country which is experiencing the dictatorship of the proletariat, a split in the ranks of the proletariat, or between the proletarian party and the masses of the proletariat, is not only dangerous, but extremely dangerous, particularly if in that country the proletariat constitutes a small minority of the population."

That was the problem. The proletariat is a small section of the population, so that if there is a split in the proletariat—small as it is—it is now divided against itself. If there is a split between the proletariat and the Party, he says, the whole thing will fall apart. That is the problem, and that is the problem that you must bear in mind about Russia today. This was the great debate. As I say, along with the debate between Cromwell and the Levellers,[10] this is the most important political debate that I know, and I'm only choosing some special points.

I go on to page fifty-three. Lenin says:

> Thirdly *[James: He is a great man for giving the arguments first, second, third, and so forth]*, it is wrong to look only to the elected persons, only to the organisers, administrators, etc. These, after all, are only a minority of prominent people. We must look to the rank and file, to the masses. In Rudzutak's theses this is expressed not only more simply and intelligibly, but theoretically more correctly, as follows (thesis 6) *[James: Franklyn,[11] you pay careful attention to this because of a question you asked me the other day]*:
>
> > "Every participant in production must understand the need for and expediency of the production tasks he is carrying out; every participant in production must not only take part in the fulfilment of tasks given from above but also take an intelligent part in remedying all technical and organisational defects in the sphere of production."[12]

That is what the debate was about. Lenin could foresee the state that was coming, if things were allowed to go on. The Stalinist state would have been no surprise to him, none whatsoever, because that is what this debate is about. You will remember that it was said emphatically in Rudzutak's thesis, "We cannot organize the proletariat from above." You remember that? You cannot do that. He said: "It can't be done." You could pass a wage freeze on them; you could put men with guns in the factory, as Stalin did, but you cannot organize them from above. You can't take 20,000 workers in a factory and organize them properly. That's impossible. You could say, if he comes late in the morning, send him to jail for three months; if he keeps on coming late, send him to Siberia for five years. But that is not organizing.

Now, on page fifty-four. What is the whole debate about? "But the whole point is that we must speak to 'the masses of the workers,' to 'their very depths,' in the language of Rudzutak's theses, and not use words like 'production atmosphere,' which cause perplexity or raise a smile." Lenin goes into some theoretical discussion: politics and economics. He says, "It is strange that we should have to raise such an elementary A B C question again."[13] He says: I am putting forward a political analysis of the situation; Trotsky and Bukharin are saying that they are watching the economic question and that I am introducing politics. Lenin said, "You all are absolutely wrong." He said:

> The theoretical incorrectness is most striking. Politics are the concentrated expression of economics, I repeated in my speech, because I have already heard this totally unjustified—and from the lips of a Marxist totally impermissible—reproach about my 'political' approach before. Politics cannot but have precedence over economics. To argue differently means forgetting the A B C of Marxism.[14]

Now take note of this:

> Trotsky and Bukharin try to make it appear that they are concerned about increasing production, whereas we are only concerned about formal democracy. This presentation is wrong [James: And this is the point], because the only way the matter stands (and this is the only way the matter *can* stand from the Marxian point of view) is that without the proper political approach to the subject the given class cannot maintain its rule, and consequently cannot solve *its own production problems*.[15]

Is the point clear? For any kind of economic analysis, economic program, you first have to begin by a political analysis of the general situation because, if you don't get that right, you cannot get the economic questions properly. These may be simple things, they may seem simple to us, but they are absolutely profound.

On page fifty-six, again I get down to what is fundamental to the debate and I want to tell you that I had read this for years and I didn't understand it.

I was like the other fellows, but after grappling with it for a number of years, I began to see the things standing out. We talked about the workers forming courts. Now look at Lenin's solution. He says: "For, I repeat, bonuses in kind and disciplinary comrades courts have a hundred times more significance for mastering economy, for managing industry and for raising the role of the trade unions in production than absolutely abstract (and therefore empty) words about 'industrial democracy,' 'coalescence,' etc."

That is why he was so sharp on Shliapnikov and Kollontai. This is the basis of the debate. He says, "This is what I'm proposing. I am proposing that bonuses be given to the workers who are in industry, and not [only] in heavy industry, but wherever it is needed we give actual bonuses for what they produce." That is to prevent them from running to the country in order to get some food and things of that kind. He says, "Make the industrial courts of the workers; they are to decide. It must be understood that it cannot be done from above." Shliapnikov and Kollontai said, "No, we haven't enough democracy." Lenin got very angry with them.[16] He said, "To hell with these people and their democracy. Bonuses, concrete bonuses, and disciplinary courts by the workers themselves; the trade union should settle their own affairs. To come and talk to me about democracy and we haven't enough democracy and formal democracy, this is nonsense." He said, "We have had enough of this business. You all are upsetting the workers." He was very sharp to them and this is why. But it is not easy. Trotsky never understood this, and E. H. Carr[17] and the rest of them—blank. I know because I was like them once.

Now we go right on. On page sixty-one you get his general attitude to the problems that we have to face:

> Comrades, a real "businessman" (permit me also to engage in some production propaganda!) knows that the capitalists and organisers of trusts, even in the most advanced countries, have for years, and sometimes even for ten years and more, been studying and testing their own (and others) practical experience, correcting and altering what was started, going back, correcting things many times, in order to obtain a system of management, a selection of higher and lower administrators, etc., that would fully suit the given business. That is how it was under capitalism, which throughout the civilised world has relied in its business affairs *upon the experience and habits of centuries.*

We must have some perspective. In doing so, I am speaking about Africa. I say, for God's sake, they have been there for ten years only, some of them not for the whole ten. We must have some understanding. Lenin says capitalism has reached that pitch after building and shifting the experience of centuries. He says we have just begun. "We are building on new ground which demands long, persistent, and patient work on the remolding of habits which capitalism left us as a heritage, and which can be remolded only very gradually." One must have some sort of perspective, some sort of understanding. Capitalism, which began after the Reformation—a hundred years after, it is still not complete. They had to learn. It took them centuries to learn. Lenin said, we have just begun. But what he insists upon: "If we are beginning now, all that we have to learn, we have to understand that—it is not administration, management, that we have to learn—it is the working class which has to learn, just as the capitalist class had to take over from the feudalist and learn to build capitalism." That is what Lenin is saying. We must understand that it is the working class that has to build socialism. That is what this great debate is about.

Now, page sixty-two. Lenin says you have to be careful. "Measure your cloth seven times before you cut," he often said.

> Persistent, slow, careful, practical and businesslike testing of what this thousand has done; still more careful and practical correcting of their work and advancing only after the usefulness of the given method, the given system of management, the given proportion, the given selection of persons, etc., has been fully approved—such is the basic, fundamental, absolute rule of "industrial training."

That is what is required, and it is required far more in an underdeveloped country than in a country that has some experience with this business.

What experience in the development of capitalist production have countries in Africa got? China in 1951 had an industry which was equivalent to the industry of Belgium. Mao Tse-Tung made The Great Leap Forward and he fell flat on his face—he and millions of Chinese—and the thing went to pieces and they had to begin again. You can't make a leap in regard to tens of thousands or tens of millions of people. Lenin didn't make any leaps. He said the leap was to overthrow the bourgeoisie. "But now," he said, "we have got to be careful. We have to settle down to build the socialist society in the same way that over centuries the capitalists did. We start off with what capitalism has, what we have." But it is an elementary business and a slow, careful business. No great leaps. No great leaps in the development of industry and production, none at all. One has to bear that in mind when looking at Africa and various underdeveloped countries. You can make a leap to throw them out, but when it comes to developing what you have, you have got to watch and study carefully.

Lenin now goes into the dialectic thing, which is very useful. This is the reason for the sharpness against Kollontai, Shliapnikov, and against Trotsky. Page sixty-eight:

> Let us approach the question still more concretely. Let us see what the present trade unions are as an "apparatus" for the management of production. We have seen from incomplete returns that about nine hundred workers—members and delegates of trade unions—are engaged in the management of production. Increase this figure tenfold if you will, or even a hundredfold; as a concession to you and in order to explain your fundamental mistake, let us even assume such an incredibly "rapid" advance in the near future—even then we get an insignificant number of those directly engaged in *management* compared with the general mass of six million members of trade unions. And from this it is still more clearly evident that to concentrate all attention on the "leading stratum" as Trotsky does, to talk about the role of the trade unions in production and about managing production, without taking into account the fact that 98 ½% *are learning* (6,000,000 − 90,000 = 98 ½% of the total) *and will have to learn for a long time,* means committing a fundamental mistake. Not school *and* management, but *school of management.*[18]

Look at the number of people who are there. Then comes the most profound statement of the lot, in which the whole Russian economy, the whole development of the economy, the whole question of the one-party state—all the modern problems are there—in backward countries and advanced countries. This is what Lenin says:

> In arguing against Zinoviev on December 30 and accusing him, and quite wrongly and without foundation, of denying the "appointment" system, *i.e.,* the right and duty of the central Committee to appoint, Comrade Trotsky inadvertently drew an extremely characteristic contrast. He said:

"Zinoviev approaches every practical question too much from the propaganda point of view, and forgets that here we not only have *material* for agitation, but a problem which must be solved administratively."[19]

Then Lenin makes what I think is the key sentence to all this business:

I will explain in detail in a moment what an administrator's approach to the present question *could be*. But Comrade Trotsky's fundamental mistake lies precisely in that he approached (or, more correctly, rushed at*) the very questions* he himself raised in his pamphlet-platform, *as an administrator*, whereas he could and should have approached *these* questions *exclusively as a propagandist*.[20]

I wonder if you understand that? Lenin says, you do not organize the workers, because you cannot do that. That is the administrator's approach. He says, as a propagandist, to teach them and tell them, that you can do. You will read and see where he says, "If we get a hundred of them who get together, or ten in a conference and say what has been done—and what has been done properly here and what hasn't been done properly there, and so forth, and then we go and tell the other workers the experience of these— then we are getting on, we are approaching the question as propagandists. But once you approach it as an administrator," he says, "you are going to break up the state that we have here." You will see quite often in these theses where he says, "This worker's state that we have, this Soviet state, if you approach these questions in these ways, you are going to smash it to pieces." He was quite right. Lenin's analysis of the Russian problem is one of the greatest intellectual developments and discoveries that there is in history.

Now, on page seventy, you get a glimpse of Bolshevism. Here again, when you have to argue with people as to whether Leninism is Bolshevism, you cannot do that unless you approach it in fundamental matters. Look at page seventy: "The state belongs to the sphere of coercion." Lenin is saying that you cannot use coercion in the trade union movement. Do you follow that?

Now let me give you some idea of what happened. They were discussing and the men in charge of the railway in the midst of the civil war said to them, "These are accounts, here is the statement and on such and such a day, the railway system is going to break down." If the railway system had broken down, Russia would have been wide open to invasion from everybody. What to do? So they decided that Trotsky had shown wonderful organization when in charge of the army. They took him and put him in charge of the railway system, the Cectran, and told him to run that business, to save the situation. Trotsky went over to the Cectran and organized the Cectran on a military basis. When he finished organizing the Cectran on the military basis, he brought over many of the soldiers and those who had worked with him. It is on that basis that he proposed, "Let us organize the whole trade union movement on a military basis. Let us make the trade union a part of the state."

Lenin said, no, and he said, "You fellows in the military business, you have learned a lot of military, bureaucratic habits and you want to translate that into the working class; that will not do." Lenin fought them all the way. Now, he says: "The state belongs to this sphere of coercion. It would be madness to renounce coercion, particularly in the epoch of the dictatorship of the proletariat." Now follow please: "Here 'administering' and the administrator's approach are essential."[21]

Is that clear? In organizing the party and political activity, the administrator's approach is essential, because they have to govern the country. That's their job. Do you see what administration means? "The Party is the directly ruling vanguard of the proletariat, it is the leader." Do you know the worse punishment that could be given to you? Listen to it: "Expulsion from the Party and not coercion is the specific means of influencing the membership, the means of purging and hardening the vanguard."[22] That is all Lenin is to do. That was the only punishment—expulsion from the Party. They didn't put you in prison; they didn't send you to Siberia. Expulsion from the Party. But he's making a clear difference. He says, "There we are administrating, we are the ruler, we are the special section of the country that is ruling. But you can't treat the trade union in that way." That is what he is saying throughout the debate. You can't treat the trade union that way, which is precisely what Stalin went and did, and what Trotsky wanted to do. Trotsky was in a nasty situation when Lenin died.

Now we go to the trade unions:

> The trade unions are reservoirs of state power, a school of Communism, a school of management. *[James: Where they are prepared to become the rulers of industry and of the country.]* In this sphere the specific and main thing is *not* administration but *"contacts" "between* the central" (and local,

of course) "state administration, national economy and the *broad masses* of the toilers."[23]

Is that clear? That is the debate. He says, politically, we have to exercise a certain amount of coercion, i.e., expulsion from the Party. That is all. But the trade unions, the labour movement, cannot be handled in this way. That is what this whole debate is about.

Now, there is something that I want you to take note of here because it is a very important political analysis. Then I have a point to deal with in regard to the points that you, Harvey, have raised. I expect you will take these things and study them closely. There you will find out all that you have to read about your approach to the political situation. I am not doing that. But here is an important point in politics:

> That is why, when the "scrap started" at the Fifth All-Russian Conference of Trade Unions, November 2–6, 1920…when immediately after that conference—no, I am mistaken, *during* that conference—*[James: Listen carefully to this]* Comrade Tomsky appeared before the Political Bureau in a high state of extraordinary excitement and, fully supported by Comrade Rudzutak, who is the calmest of men, began to relate that Comrade Trotsky at that conference had talked about "shaking up" the trade unions and that he, Tomsky, had opposed this—when this happened, I immediately and irrevocably made up my mind that the essence of the controversy was one of policy (*i.e.,* the trade union policy of the Party) and that Comrade Trotsky was entirely wrong in his dispute with Comrade Tomsky over his policy of "shaking up" the trade unions…[24]

In other words, you must deal with personality in politics. It happens all the time. Lenin says, at that conference, Tomsky came in a tremendous tizzy and, following him, was Rudzutak, who is a very calm man. When Tomsky said that Trotsky had started this business about "shaking up" the trade unions, Lenin said, "I immediately came to the conclusion that the essence of the dispute was between 'shaking up' the trade unions and developing the trade union movement in the only way that it could develop." But he did not come to them and say this is what happened.

Lenin uses this as a means of analyzing profoundly and putting forward a political, philosophical analysis of the problem—although he is leaning to his conclusion—because of his contact, his respect for certain people and their personality, etc. But he doesn't take that to the Party. You can't take that to the Party. Over and over again, you will see where he says, "something happened, and there I saw what had happened," but he doesn't make that the center of the debate. That tells him what the issue is, and then he proceeds to analyse it economically, politically, and philosophically. Is that clear? So the personality business is not to be entirely excluded. You may come to your conclusions about it, that may help, but you don't go to the Party with the personality analysis, that "he's a very calm man and when he comes in and I saw he was all upset, I saw that..." No, no, you don't do that. He gets down to the basis of the administrator vs. propagandist, etc.

Now, this is for you in particular Harvey. Lenin is talking, I want you to take note of this because he, number one, never babbled and, number two (it is a most astonishing thing), he always said what he thought. If he made a mistake, he says so loudly and clearly, and if he did not know what was happening, he said so also, over and over again. I will give you one example. He used to say, and he said it over and over: "If we have state capitalism in this backward economy, then we have done well." He regularly said that from 1917 to 1924. However, during the Civil War they found themselves carrying out War Communism,[25] and Lenin used to say, "Whether we were forced into it by means of the necessities of the war, or whether we were mislead into theoretical experiments that were not justified, that I do not know." In other words, he was not afraid to say, "I don't know." That is a tremendous problem, but he said, "I don't know." At other times he would say, "Well, this is a serious matter. We will appoint a committee to look at it and in ten years they will make a report and we'll know all about it." [*Laughter*] Very shrewd.

Lenin and the Trade Union Debate in Russia
Part Three

Now, we are going to get down to this thing. Lenin is complaining about what Trotsky is saying. He quotes Trotsky who had said:

> "Having lost the old basis of their existence—the class economic struggle—the trade unions …owing to a number of circumstances, have not yet succeeded in collecting in their ranks the necessary forces and in working out the necessary methods by which they could become capable of solving the new problem, *viz., of organizing production*, with which the proletarian revolution has confronted them and which is formulated in our programme" (Trotsky's italics).[1]

In reply, Lenin says:

> This is not true, it is a hasty exaggeration: the trade unions have lost the basis of the *class* economic struggle, but have not by far lost, and, unfortunately cannot lose for many years to come, the basis of the *non-class* "economic class struggle," meaning by that, the struggle against the bureaucratic distortions of the Soviet apparatus, the protection of the material and spiritual interests of the masses of the toilers by the ways and means that this apparatus cannot employ, etc.[2]

That is Leninism to the last degree. Lenin said: "This is a lot of nonsense. What you are saying that the proletariat must do, the proletariat cannot do. That is not the Party program." He says:

> This is again a hasty exaggeration which contains the embryo of a serious error. The programme does not contain such a formulation and does not set before the trade unions the problem of 'organising production.' Let us trace step by step every idea, every proposition contained in our Party program in the order in which they run in the text of the programme:

1) "The organisational" (not any kind) "apparatus of socialised industry must in the first place" (and not exclusively) "rely on the trade unions." 2) "The latter must to an increasing degree free themselves from the narrow craft spirit." *[James: Backward industry.]* (How can they free themselves? Under the leadership of the Party and under the educational and every other influence the proletariat exercises on the non-proletariat toiling masses) "and become big industrial associations embracing the majority and gradually all the workers in the given branch of industry."

It must rely on the trade unions in the first place. In other words, it has many other things to rely upon. He says: We haven't got that. So, to be talking about the trade unions managing the industries is a lot of nonsense. Trotsky was not only saying that; he was saying, make them a part of the state, to manage industries. You cannot do that. Lenin says: "This is the first part of the section of the Party program that deals with the trade unions." As you see, this section immediately lays down very "strict conditions" demanding very prolonged work for the next thing. Lenin then returns to the program:

"Since, according to the laws of the Soviet Republic and by established practice, the trade unions already participate" (As you see, the words are very cautious: only participate) "in all the local and central organs of management of industry, they must eventually actually concentrate in their hands the entire management of the whole of national economy as a single economic unit." (Note: must eventually concentrate in their hands the management, not of branches of industry, and not of industry, but of the whole of national economy, and moreover, as a single economic unit: this condition, as an economic condition, cannot be regarded as being really achievable until the number of small producers in industry and agriculture has been reduced to less than half the population and of national economy.)[3]"

The small producers and the rest of them must become less than half. In other words, the dominant section of the mass of the population must be those workers organized in industry and trained in the trade-union movement. Marx made it clear that the preparation for socialism meant training in the trade-union movement and the practice of parliamentary democracy. Do you know that? The practice of parliamentary democracy, knowledge of the trade-union movement—that prepares the workers for socialism. (This

African socialism is a lot of nonsense. You could call it socialism, if you like, but you destroy completely any sort of theoretical basis.)

Now here is another one. This is the program:

"At the same time the participation of the trade unions in the management of the economy and their drawing the broad masses into this work are the principle means of combating the bureaucratisation of the economic apparatus of the Soviet government and render possible the establishment of genuine popular control over the results of production."[4]

Now, Harvey, this is for you. Says Lenin:

Thus, the last sentence also contains the very cautious words "participation in the management of economy," again a reference to the need of drawing in the broad masses as the principal (but not the only) means of combating bureaucracy; and, in conclusion, an extremely cautious statement: "*render possible*" the establishment of "*popular*," *i.e.*, workers' and peasants' and not only proletarian, "control."[5]

That is the significance of the word "popular." Do you see the point you raised? He was extremely correct, and not only he, but it was in the Party program. That is the education of the working class. The Party program is very precise and you expound the Party program—they all have copies, so they could go home and read it—and you take part in discussions. You form factions, you get ready, and you elect your delegates on the basis of the factions that you form. All of this is the debate in preparation for the Tenth Party Congress.

The idea that Bolshevism is totalitarianism or Stalinism is entirely false. You can prove that by asking somebody: "Have you been through this? Is this totalitarian?" That is why Stalin had to destroy the Bolshevik Party. This was the Party. Lenin used to say, "No party in this world has the democracy that we have." When he said that, he meant it. In order to make himself master and organize these workers as he thought it was necessary, Stalin had to destroy the Bolshevik Party and rewrite the whole history of Bolshevism. That, he was able to do. I don't think that I need to go any further with this. I am not going to do that.

Now, on page eighty is the last statement that I want to cite. Lenin says:

Events in one month in Petrograd, Moscow and a number of provincial cities show that the Party responded to the discussion and rejected Comrade Trotsky's mistaken line by an overwhelming majority. While there undoubtedly were vacillations in the "upper ranks," and in the "periphery," in the committees and officers, the really overwhelming majority of the rank and file members of the Party, of the mass of the working class membership of the Party, expressed their opposition to this mistaken line.

It was a free and open debate and discussion. Lenin insisted upon that. He said that, up there, in the offices, there were people against, but the rank and file of the party rejected this attitude towards "shaking up" the trade unions. It is a tremendous debate. When you study this, you understand which side ultimately won when he died and which side took over—the administrative attitudes.

Do you know about the *Testament*[6] that he left about the Party members? Lenin wrote a testament, and the man was so careful. After some weeks, he wrote an addition. What does he say in the testament? He never said, "I suggest that Comrade Trotsky should be the leader of the organization." (I did that, stupidly, when I left the organization in the United States. I told them Raya Dunayevskaya should be the leader.[7] I will never do that again. I would say, "You all decide who will be the leader. You decide." I left Dunayevskaya as the leader and it hit the organization with a terrific blow.)

What Lenin said was this: "Trotsky is undoubtedly the ablest man on the Central Committee," but he didn't say choose him as the leader. He said Trotsky was "undoubtedly the ablest man on the Central Committee. But," he said, "he is too much given to the administrator's approach."[8] You remember that? Bureaucracy.

The thing about Stalin in Lenin's *Testament* is absolutely magnificent. Lenin says: "That fellow has concentrated too much power in his hands and he's rude. Send him out."[9] Number one, administrator's approach: he is organizing from above. The other fellow is rude, rough. Don't appoint him at all. But for the rest, work it out yourself. Those are tremendous statements, both of them.

We can understand when he says that Trotsky has too much of an administrator's approach—we can understand from this debate what he meant, and in the course of the discussion you will see where he said that Trotsky learned it in the administration of the army and when he left the army and was put in charge of the Cectran, he organized and saved the situation. But then he and that bunch of soldiers and the rest of them wanted to do that to the whole country. Lenin said—you can't do that. That became one of the last great battles that he fought. Although you don't read Russian, you can understand—by carefully studying this volume—you can understand what happened and you can understand the method of approaching the question.

By the way, what I have found in studying history is this: It doesn't matter if you study Roman history or Greek history or the history of primitive society. If you get a first-class historian, the study of any period, particularly a modern period from the Reformation on, puts you right in regard to the approach to fundamental political problems of the day. Rousseau knew. You have to read him carefully. (Do you know who is backing Rousseau as one of the first anthropologists? Guess. Claude Levi-Strauss.) Rousseau had got rid of the habit of paying attention, as all the people of the Enlightenment also did, to those who rule. Voltaire and all of them hated them. "*Écrasez l'infâme,*" said Voltaire. Finish up with them.

But what Rousseau was saying is in a lot of Lenin. Rousseau was saying: "Don't substitute another set of administrators. Be aware of that. The people who are the sovereign are the mass of the population," and that is why we did Rousseau. Study him, and if you study *King Lear*, you will see that Shakespeare was aware of it. Shakespeare was very much aware of it, but was careful and he did not want to give any theory. But he made Lear give the theory. He said the person who will rule is the man who understands. That was a tremendous step to make. A man who has been through all that of the mass of the population, who knows all about it—he is the man to rule. It is such a tremendous thing to do. When he was finished with that play, Shakespeare said, "I am done," and he wrote the last comedies, and so on. He had been working at it all the time, but now he says that is that.

So, there you are with that debate. If you want to do some work, Mr. Book-getter,[10] you get Woodhouse's *Puritanism and Liberty*[11] and get that debate at Putney between Cromwell and the Levellers. Those Levellers understood politics more than any British politician for the last three hundred years. You will see the proof of it. I am sorry that I cannot go through it with you. If I come back again, that is the one I will do with you. We will spend two sessions. Do you know that debate? Ireton, Cromwell's man, says,

"Everybody is equal." He says, "When you have the law of nature, everybody is equal, everybody might have a vote. That means you are attacking the property system." Ireton is something. He says, "You are attacking the property system." There was Rainborough,[12] who said, "What have we been fighting this war for? We've been fighting against the King, we've been suffering, we had a lot of trouble; we win and now you come to tell us we are attacking property? What kind of nonsense is this?"

All of that is there, and when you read that business, you realize that those fellows who say today that the workers do not understand—they are crazy. The workers understood everything. The question has to be posed properly and they will know. Read that debate. Woodhouse has done a splendid piece of work.

Well, gentlemen, that is where we are now. I don't think there is anything more that is to be said except in the way of questions, if you have any question to raise on that. I recommend this debate to you. I recommend to you *Lear*—Shakespeare in the 17th century. Rousseau in the 18th century. Marx in the 19th century. And Lenin in the 20th century. Then you have to master and tackle the West Indian problem. We will go into that.

(When are we going to have a meeting? Saturday? [*Franklyn Harvey: I don't know if Bobby*[13] *is coming up.*] In any case, if he doesn't, we will do our business on Saturday, because on Sunday I am to go to the Universal Negro Improvement Association.)

What I have been reading for you are examples of how the Bolshevik Party functioned. I started by reading what Lenin said on what is to be done, the stages of the debate, and how Trotsky and the workers in Moscow and Petrograd entered into it. You will say, "How is this a totalitarian party?" I say that this is the best proof: we have the stenographic report of the internal Party discussion, which is widespread all over the Party press. Bukharin is under attack, Trotsky is under attack, and everything is being discussed in preparation for the votes for delegates to the Party Congress. That is the Bolshevik Party.

HECTOR: And the debate took place in public.

JAMES: In public. There is no secret.

HARVEY: But would you then say that the Bolshevik Party in that society was a mass party?

JAMES: It was a mass party.

HARVEY: It incorporated within the party itself the masses? Not the masses, but a significant number of the masses?

JAMES: It didn't. The real body which represented the population was the Soviets. Then there were peasant Soviets and there were proletarian Soviets, and the Bolshevik Party took its place in the Soviet Congress as a faction. That is very clear?

HARVEY: So the Bolshevik Party was in actual fact a small party?

JAMES: The Bolshevik Party could not help but be a small party. Do you know how many Bolsheviks there were? In 1917 there were about 20, 000 Bolsheviks, no more than that.

HECTOR: And it was largely of the workers...

JAMES: The large mass of the population knew nothing about it. But it is when the Soviet was formed that Lenin said, "All right, let's go." And he had in mind the world revolution in general. He never attempted to say that the Bolshevik party was a mass party. As a matter of fact, have you got Volume VII or VIII here? No. You will find (take this down Alfie) this in Volume VII, I think. At a speech at the Bolshevik Party conference in 1919 Lenin said, "We have introduced democratic procedures, etc., far more than in any other country, but in the specific matter of the working class helping to govern the country—there we have failed completely. They are not doing it." Absolutely plain. And he used to say these things from a public platform, on the radio, and print them for everybody. He says: "The working class has not been able to take over. That is due to backwardness and the difficulties we have been suffering and so forth."[14]

HECTOR: 1917, Sir?

JAMES: 1919. I think it was the Eighth Party Congress. Now Harvey, there is this other point. Lenin kept on saying, "In fifteen or twenty years our children's children will see socialism" because of the narrow, limited basis with which the party could function. He never hid it. I have calculated. He must have said it once a month from 1917 to 1924: "We have no socialism here. We will never have any socialism here," and so forth.

ROBERTS: Now I would like to ask a question.

JAMES: Go ahead.

ROBERTS: Lenin made the point that politics is a concentrated expression of economics...

JAMES: Yes. That is the tradition in the Party, in Marx.

ROBERTS: In relation to the West Indies, for example, with the collapse of the West Indian Federation, you have now a lot of people who are saying that you have to begin by economic integration and to arrive at a political solution.

JAMES: They are wrong. The question of the federation and the question of the economic development of the West Indies is primarily a political question. It has to be approached politically.

ROBERTS: Well, this seems to be a new thing now. Everybody is saying...

HECTOR: Economic integration and the politics after.

JAMES: Yes, we know that we cannot establish a socialist order now. He dreamt that it may be established in their children's time, or perhaps in their grandchildren's time. Lenin kept on saying that. And that is the great debate, the great discussion—political education in the departments. You have got to teach them how to read.

And if you are aware of what is taking place in Africa, you will realize those fellows are not serious. They are not getting down to it because Lenin's only way of settling these questions was to tell everybody what was going on. The proletariat in an African state is able to play a tremendous role, but these fellows tie up the proletariat with the government. Lenin split the proletariat and the trade unions from the government. He said these two must be kept apart.

HECTOR: To me, that is the most important statement.

JAMES: That is one of the most important things about Leninism. There are many others.

HARVEY: Continuing that same question—I will not talk about socialism now at all—my question is a question of the party. Was the basic reason why he did not attempt to create a mass party at the time, was it, would you say, as you mention so often, the question of the education of the people, that they could neither read nor write?

JAMES: I wouldn't say that, because it has to be a proletariat party and the majority of the country, of the working class, must be proletarian. You can see that in Trinidad. If you watch the Oilfield Workers Trade Union, that has been there fifty years, and how they function, and compare them to the other parts of the population, it is like an advanced country against a backward one.

HARVEY: That might be so in Trinidad, but in the case of the smaller territories where you have a large proliferation of the—well, I can't call them peasants, but let's say the peasantry—and you have actually no working class (except for the small number of people around the town and one or two who work for the small landowners), then you will say we are in a similar position to Russia at that time and therefore you...

JAMES: I could not say so. What is the situation? The situation is this: When I went through Barbados in 1932, in St. Michael's alone there were 2000 motorcars. In Russia in 1926—a place about a thousand times the size of Barbados, if not 10,000—there were 11,000 motorcars. In the whole of Russia in 1926 there were 11, 000 motor cars. In the whole of China, this tremendous continental territory in 1951, the industrial structure was equal to the industrial structure of Belgium.

That is not so in any small island. You have the ease of communication. You can cover those islands in a whole day. We must understand. In Africa you go miles before you see a few villages and some peasants and then they tell you that the cocoa estates are fifteen or twenty miles inside. You haven't got that problem in the small islands. You can build something, although you cannot build a genuine proletarian party in the small islands.

There are elements of the proletariat, and you notice that Lenin said the proletariat can lead the others. He was absolutely certain that they had to be involved to the last man, to the last woman. I read that section for you. You can find certain elements in the small islands and form a party without a proletariat because it is so concentrated and the population is so well developed. The population understands the same language; you have no peasants living a thousand miles from anywhere who still have icons and live in camps. They do not exist in the Caribbean.

So, you have the basis of a party. In every island you have the basis of a party, none more so than in Barbados. Barbados has only agricultural workers, but you can form a political party in that small island. In fact, they actually formed one, but they let it go. Look what they had in Barbados: Grantley Adams was chairman of the political party and Hugh Springer was secretary of the political party, and Grantley Adams was chairman of the trade union movement and Hugh Springer was the secretary.[15] They sat there, both of them, but they threw it away. They threw it away. In other words, there was no proletariat but they were able to form something.

There's an ease in communication, a facility in knowledge of the English language, etc., in the West Indies. You may have more trouble in St. Lucia,[16] but I do not think there is any serious problem. And in any case, those West Indian islands have got to federate. But the federation is a political matter. My position is very simple. I do not go to the West Indies and take part in a debate or discussion and say we have got to federate, "I am for federation." That is what Albert Gomes[17] says. That is to lay yourself wide open to people saying, "The federation just broke up." What we have been insisting upon is that we are going to break up that old colonial system. That is what we are attacking. And if any other West Indian territory shows the same readiness to tackle the old colonial system, we will federate with them at once. That is a political question. The economic details, that is a matter to be arranged

HECTOR: Yes, Sir. I have some observations. I don't have any questions, I just want you to correct me if I am wrong.

JAMES: You want me to correct you?

HECTOR: I want you to correct me if I am wrong. I find, Sir, from reading the trade union debate, that Trotsky is where Lenin was at in 1905 when he wrote *What Is To be Done?* I think Lenin's attitude then would be the same thing—to get some more revolutionaries into the trade union leadership and shake it up. It seems to me as if Lenin recognized the difference between the party and spontaneous mass activity in the other period. And he said, in the trade union, this is where this activity takes place.

JAMES: You must remember something that you will find in Trotsky's life of Stalin.[18] Lenin realized, long before 1917, that he had overstated the case about the vanguard party. But he soon got rid of that. In 1921, Trotsky was way off. And the debate shows you what ended in Stalinism. That is what this debate is telling you about—and what is going to take place in all the states in Africa and in China and the whole lot of them. That is what they are aiming for.

HECTOR: I was wondering what actually happened to the soviets up to 1924?

JAMES: Lenin says the government is too much the government of the old tsarist regime. In other words, the Soviet government was not in reality a Soviet government. And if you read those last essays of his, he isn't paying so much attention to the soviet. He is trying to reconstruct the apparatus on fundamental grounds. He has very little to say about the soviets there, but he was putting forward what can be said to be a subjective and possibly a utopian procedure. But that is exactly what they said about him in 1917 and he brought the Revolution off tremendously because he went to the Party with it.

When he came in April,[19] he did not have a majority and so forth. This time, in 1923, he had greater authority by far and if he had been well, or if Trotsky had followed him, they would have swept the Party and the Party would have been mobilized. If you want to know the strength of the Party, you have to see what Stalin had to do to destroy it.

ROBERTS: Could you explain the soldier's deputies?

JAMES: The army was, to a large part, a peasant army. That was one of the strengths of the Revolution. The peasants were most organized. They were organizing the army. When Lenin told them to seize the land, the peasants in the army said, "If the revolution is giving land, I must also go and seize." [Laughter] So, when the army sent them, that is what began to shake the army. All the peasants, the young peasants and the people were organized in the army. So, when he spoke of soviet deputies, the army soviets—that was the peasantry. That is one of the tremendous events in the history of the world, and they do not write about it. They cannot do that.

By the way, that debate, the Levellers and so forth, the British keep away from that debate. They don't interfere with that. They keep away from that because the moment you know what those workers are saying, you realize that they are way beyond the democracy that they have today. They keep properly away from that. But I want to publish that. If I get going at all, I will publish that debate with an introduction of my own.

Annual parliaments, payment of members of parliament, King and House of Lords—to hell with them. And today, there are people who are saying that if the revolution could have been saved, the only way it could have been saved was Lilburne's way. Do you know that? There are two fellows called Haller and Davis. They publish extracts from the writers of those days. Remember the two of them. Take them down. Haller and Davis. They are in the United States.[20] And they have now come to the conclusion that if the revolution could have been saved, it would have had to be Lilburne's way.

Have you studied Oliver Cromwell's life seriously? It's worthwhile if you are interested in personality. The British people were willing to accept Cromwell as king. The House told him, "Well, look here. Monarchy is rooted in the whole structure of Britain. It isn't only in the minds of the people; all the procedures and so forth are rooted in the monarchy. So, you have to be the monarch. And we know that he said O.K. Britain was going to have a king. Cromwell was going to be the king. But some of the old boys of the new Model Army told him, "Never mind this king business." [*Laughter*] So, that's when Oliver went down to the parliament, when they were expecting to pass the resolution and for him to say yes. He said, "No, I can't do that." The population was ready to accept it. He had won such brilliant victories, and he was obviously a distinguished person and an honest man. He was a genuine puritan. He had defeated everybody. And there he was, master of the country, master of the army. That is history, my friends. That is history.

HECTOR: Sorry to switch over to the literary field. What is Milton's attitude to Cromwell?

JAMES: Milton was Parliamentary Secretary to Cromwell. His attitude? He was Latin secretary to Cromwell. There was a fellow who attacked the Cromwellian regime and Milton replied to him in Latin and he cursed him from page one to the last part. But by 1657 or 1658, he had lost his sight and things became very difficult. But I believe that Milton, in *Paradise Lost*, was saying, "Look here boys. This man of great power and authority, Cromwell, upsets the regime." He had been with Cromwell all the time but in the end he was doubtful.

I believe that Satan in *Paradise Lost* was developed from his knowledge of Cromwell and the rest. That is what I think. I cannot prove that. I will have to spend ten years at it. I cannot do that. But somewhere I am going to write that down so that it will be left for somebody to take up. In other words, he saw, as Rousseau saw, and as the Levellers saw, that you can't substitute one set of rulers for another set. The whole system has to be changed, and Lilburne and the Levellers saw that. Have you read that debate?

HECTOR: Which one, sir?

JAMES: *Puritanism and Liberty*. The Putney Debate.

HECTOR: No, I have not read it.

JAMES: Well, I am sorry, but we could not do everything. But read it and spend some time talking about it. Mr. Professor of books,[21] get two or three, of that volume, not only one. If I see any in England, I will send them. But there will be some around, in Canada in particular. You have one?

HECTOR: And Alfie has one too.

JAMES: There must be some about. I wrote from America to Woodhouse for one and he didn't have any. I sent Chapman and Hall a cable telling them to send me one and they told me that they only had the office copy but that they would send it to me as I seemed very anxious. I thanked them and they sent me the office copy that they had. So, they haven't got an office copy now. That is O.K. with me. I have one. [*Laughter*]

HECTOR: They are at the University of Toronto Press, I understand, lying around.

JAMES: For Christ sake! Why not pester them and pick up some half a dozen copies or something?

JAMES: Anyway, gentlemen, I have to go now.

PART III

INTERVIEWS

On Literature, Exile, and Nationhood

HILL: Mr. James, in 1932 you left the West Indies for Britain to launch your writing career. Your whole career has been closely associated with the historical evolution of the West Indies ever since. In 1967, how do you see yourself personally in relation to the history of the West Indies in this fairly lengthy period?*

JAMES: Well, when I left in 1932 I had the idea to write. And to do those things in which I was interested, I had to go to London. It is very unfortunate that in 1967 anyone wishing to write or to take part in general social affairs from a basis of world civilization would have to go to London or Canada too. That undoubtedly is the same. On the other hand, the general sentiment, the general tempo of West Indian life has very much changed. I am very much aware that people today are interested in things that in 1932 they were not interested in.

HILL: While in England you published in 1938 the classic study of the Haitian Revolution and the life of Toussaint L'Ouverture. Would you like to say something about how the book was written and the perspective that governed the writing of the book?

JAMES: That book was written in the company of George Padmore, Jomo Kenyatta, and those of us who were concerned with African emancipation at the time. I don't say that was the cause of it, but I know we lived in an atmosphere in London in which we devoted ourselves in the fullest sense

---

* C.L.R. James was interviewed by Robert A. Hill for "Towards a New Culture," a special program on the Caribbean that aired on Canadian Broadcasting Corporation's Tuesday Night Program. Other guests on the February 13, 1967 broadcast included Derek Walcott and Jan Carew.

possible to African emancipation. As a matter fact, George Padmore has been called the "Father of African Emancipation," and people who have studied Africa and been in touch with the African revolution would not deny him that name. That was the atmosphere in which I wrote *The Black Jacobins*.

And I want to say that because over and over in the book you will see that the people I have in mind and the ideas that I am trying to put forward as valuable are the African people. So, *The Black Jacobins* was written about the West Indies but with the idea of African emancipation in mind and the slaves of San Domingo and their struggle for freedom as a kind of model, and even a moral incitement to the Africans to do the same. But in that same 1938, or I think the following year, appeared a book by Aimé Césaire, the famous *Cahier d'un retour au pays natal* (*Statement of the Return to My Native Country*[1]) in which he writes about the West Indies too, but he has in mind Africa. And all the ideas about African civilization show a West Indian writer who, in writing about the West Indies, is concerned to paint a portrait of Africa. And I find that, personally, very strange that both of us should have been writing with the West Indies in mind, but with Africa as a kind of immediate and historical perspective.

I want to say, without having any national pride or national faith or anything of the kind, that a great deal of the West Indies is in every book that I have written, although I have written as widely as a history of the Communist International, a book on cricket, a novel, and so forth. But I left the West Indies late. I was already thirty-one years old and everything that I write has its origin in the West Indies. Maybe I can tell you, if you ask me, why I am so sure of that. Shall I?

HILL: Well, would you like to, sir? Certainly.

JAMES: Yes. I went to the West Indies in 1958. I had written a book on cricket and the philosophy around the game of cricket. I said cricket was not a game alone, it was an art. And I wrote every chapter of that book in Spain. At that time, I had been abroad for twenty-six years. I had lived in England and I had lived in the United States. But they asked me to stay in the West Indies and do some political work, so I stayed. And every chapter of that book had been written. And then, when I left the West Indies after staying there from 1958 to 1962, I began to read the book again to see how much of the West Indies was in that book after twenty-six years abroad and not going back to the West Indies. And I have been reading it steadily since and I am absolutely amazed to find how much of the West Indies remained in me and was transferred into that book after twenty-six years abroad and not visiting the West Indies. That is what that book, *Beyond a Boundary*, means particularly to me.

HILL: The study of Captain Cipriani that preceded the study of Toussaint in Haiti shows, I think, a general tendency in West Indian history for the evolution of very sharp and very notable historical figures. In relation to the political and social entity, how does the historical figure, the historical personality, strike you?

JAMES: West Indians and people of West Indian origin are extremist. They are extreme to the right and extreme to the left. If they are not, they are extreme "middle of the roaders" in that they wobble about between the right and the left in a manner that is very objectionable to anybody who has ideas of social progressiveness. And that is because there is not much room in the West Indies, as the economic structure and social relations are today, for anybody in between. You either have to be with those on the right, usually foreign powers who own everything; they completely control the territory—you are either with them, either actually or subjectively, or you are on the other side against them, which means you are way on the left. Maybe you may not say much about it, but that is the situation with which you are faced. There is not much of an independent middle-class. That does not exist in the West Indies and, therefore, it does not produce the kind of politician and the kind of parliamentary democracy which takes care of both the dominant elements and the progressive elements and maintains a certain level. They are extremists, either the one or the other.

HILL: Your experience abroad has ranged very widely, from reporting on cricket in Britain, writing books, to the Negro emancipation movement in the United States…

JAMES: Political activity abroad also.

HILL: Yes. After the Second World War, [you had] very close contact with the rise of the Caribbean writer in Britain. Looking back on all of this, do you find anything very peculiar about the West Indian traveling abroad to gain this experience and to articulate it?

JAMES: I'm afraid that question needs some answering, needs some time because the two things that I have to say about it are very sharply opposed. I recently wrote a review of Patterson's book, *The Children of Sisyphus.* And I ask the question, here is this young man, Jamaican, obviously a natural writer. His novel wasn't a great novel but it was a very fine novel, especially [for] a young man [just] beginning. And I say, what is going to happen to him? Is he going to continue living in London writing about the West Indies? That is the situation in which West Indian writers find themselves. And I don't believe that a genuinely national literature can be built up by persons, most of whom are living in London and writing about the West Indies, not for a West Indian but for a British audience.

And while I will not go into it, I feel already that this situation in which they find themselves, an unhealthy situation, is beginning to affect their work. Not noticeably, and I don't want to say anything about what a writer is going to do because writers are most extraordinary people, they will do anything. But I feel that it is a bad situation. However, I would like to say, on the other hand, that the fact that they are West Indians, that is to say members of an underdeveloped country, is one of their great strengths. And if you allow me, I will say a few words about English literature and the literature that they are contributing to. I hope you don't mind.

When I look at English literature for the last sixty years, I notice that, before the end of the 19th century, Kipling began in some part of India. He wasn't an Englishman in the ordinary way. Then we have three Americans: Henry James, T.S. Eliot, Ezra Pound, men without whom you cannot write the history of English literature. Then you have in a different sphere, Bernard Shaw, James Joyce, J.M. Synge, and Sean O'Casey. Those are Irishmen using the English language, being able to participate in the British civilization, but they are essentially outsiders. One of the finest of them all, Joseph Conrad, was much more than an outsider. He had to learn English as a foreigner had to learn another language. And except for D.H. Lawrence, I find through the 20th century that it is the outsiders, men who can participate in English society but who are looking at it from the outside, who are the most distinguished writers in English literature.

That, I believe, is that strength of the West Indian writer. So that, on the one hand, they suffer from writing about home for the British public. On the other hand, being outsiders in England, they owe a great deal to it. What is to be the result? I don't know. I don't know at all because you never know what a gifted writer will do, and some of those men are very gifted writers indeed.

HILL: A very new and startling phenomenon in the pantheon of West Indian writers is Wilson Harris. I think that you have lectured quite widely on the work of Wilson Harris.

JAMES: Yes, Wilson Harris fascinates me. Wilson Harris was not educated abroad. He was not educated in Germany, and yet he is today writing in the way that I think Heidegger and Jaspers would write novels if they had to. In many respects, he reminds me of Jean-Paul Sartre. He is an existentialist in outlook, but he is an existentialist who makes the Caribbean the basis of his work. And you cannot be abstract in the Caribbean. The class relations there are too sharp. Harris is an existentialist to his fingertips to the point of his pen. His attitude to society is that of the individual and the attitude that he [the individual] makes for the society he is in, the memory he gets of past societies, and the moment when he begins to live an authentic instead of an inauthentic life.

But he has the virtue of dealing with a society which does not allow you to play. And Harris, if I may say so, is on the right side. That is the only side you can be on in the West Indies. So, his existentialism has a firm basis and he is a man of a wide knowledge of both the external society and the internal areas of Guyana, so that both together make one of the most remarkable of modern writers. I am glad to see that some critics in England understand that. He is not so easy a man, but he is a very fine writer in addition to which he is a most charming person. I know him personally and I have a great deal of confidence in him, not only as a writer, but as a man. I am glad to be able to say that.

HILL: You are, I think, on your way back to Britain, sir, after some eighteen months in the Caribbean. What is the perspective now for yourself?

JAMES: I have been away, by and large, for two years—away from my family, away from my home. I think that is long enough. Two years is too long a spell. I have some work to do in England. I have to finish a book called *The Memoirs of George Padmore*, a very important book that will show, among other things, what the West Indian politician is like when he is abroad, and the origins of much that Nkrumah has brought into the world. In addition, I knew him [Padmore] personally. As boys together, we used to go to the Arima River to bathe and to me it is an extraordinary thing that we used to play about in that river during vacations and that the years passed and both of us were up to our eyes in the preparation for the emancipation of Africa. I want to write that book.

    I also prepared another book before Nkrumah fell. It was called *Nkrumah Then and Now*.[2] And I want to write a book on *King Lear*,[3] Shakespeare's *King Lear*. I don't know how I will be able to do that but I want to finish those books because I have been working at them for a number of years. That is how I see my future for the time being.

HILL: Very recently in Trinidad you published a review of Ralph Ellison's recent volume, *Shadow and Act*. You went into some detail there about the controversy of Richard Wright, Ralph Ellison, and James Baldwin. Is there anything that you would like to say about the present stage of the Negro American writer and the kind of society he is participating in?

JAMES: Well, I would first like to say something about American literature on the whole. I lived in America for fifteen years. I have traveled all over America except the Northwest and what amazes me is this: between 1918 and 1945, or 1939, there were three American writers who were foremost of their class in the world. There was Hemingway, there was Faulkner, and there was Edmund Wilson. Now since 1945, I don't know what has happened, but I don't know of anyone in the United States who occupies my attention, and occupies the attention of the world the way those three did, except perhaps James Baldwin.

I knew James Baldwin many years ago, I knew Ellison, I knew Wright. And I believe they represent a definite stage in the development of writing about Negroes in the United States. Wright's *Native Son* said, "Look at how you are treating us, look at the situation we are in. And if this is the way we behave, you are responsible." That was Richard Wright. And now today, Baldwin is quite different. Baldwin is saying, "That is the way you are treating us, but look at the result of the mess we all are in."

Now, Ellison is a rather strange writer. I remember when I used to see him in New York. We all knew that Ellison was writing a book. Well, it was years that he was busy at it and, when he produced it, it was *The Invisible Man*, this extraordinary book. I read that book very carefully. It is a book about Negroes, it is a book about Negro life, and yet *The Invisible Man* seems to me a picture of American society that will only be settled as far as I am concerned by Ellison's new book. And it is remarkable that Ellison and Baldwin today are the two writers in the United States whom I find most interesting. It is not a matter of race. Not at all. Faulkner said a lot of things and even wrote a lot of very stupid things about the racial question, but that does not matter. I think he was a magnificent novelist. He was aware of American society and the tremendous forces that were at work under the surface. I think he was splendid but I don't see anyone like that around today.

HILL: In the field now of Caribbean writing, is there anyone who is particularly worth watching, anybody of the newer generation of West Indian writers?

JAMES: Here I begin to get somewhat nervous. There are two Trinidad writers. One wrote a book, *When Gods Are Falling*, and another one wrote a book called *The Games Are Coming* and another book, *A Year in San Fernando*.[4] The book *When Gods Are Falling* was a prize novel written by a young man called Earl Lovelace. I watch their writing and they are West Indian writers in a way that Lamming, Naipaul, Wilson Harris, and the others are not. They are not people whose style of writing and view of the world is based upon a general knowledge of literature.

I don't say they are uneducated, but they write in a manner that shows that they spring from the people. Their attitudes and ideas are of what I would call the Negro lower middle-class. Not that their ideas are lower middle-class. Not at all. But the persons they are watching and the persons they are describing, I know them very well. And they, to me, represent something new; a genuinely native literature springing from writers who have been educated in the West Indies and whose view of the world is a universal view, as is everybody's view today, but who are dominated by their conceptions of what the West Indian people are.

HILL: Do you think that this is perhaps the trend we can now expect? Do you think that West Indian writing will become more indigenous in its perspective and in its articulation?

JAMES: I don't know exactly, but I believe much will depend on the social and political developments in the West Indies. That tendency has been fairly clear already in the West Indies in the writings of Samuel Selvon. There is this homespun native quality in it. You haven't any ideas of Hemingway or George Eliot or Dickens or Thackeray or D.H. Lawrence, etc., when you read them. You felt that this had come, so to speak, it had grown up in the West Indian territory. And I believe that if the West Indies acquires some sort of social integrity, social certainty, and is not dominated so much in their economic and social life by foreign elements, one could reasonably expect that the kind of work that Earl Lovelace and this other man from *The Games Are Coming* and *A Year in San Fernando*, I believe one can expect the work to develop along those lines because that is, if anything, a very native product.

HILL: One of the very noticeable features about West Indian literature since the Second World War is a very important body of fiction writers in the English language, but somehow there has been a general lack of a corresponding poetry and a corresponding drama. Do you think there is any reason for this?

JAMES: I think there is a reason and I am encouraged to say it by the writing of the man who is perhaps the finest poet the British Caribbean has produced, Derek Walcott. Derek Walcott has written along these lines and I would like to say what I think; that poetry is, so to speak, the language of the tribe. Poetry comes from deep down in the social consciousness and attitudes of the population. The writer may not write about those things but the language that he uses expresses those attitudes and finds them.

The trouble of the West Indian poet is this: the poetry that he learns, the verse forms that he uses are the verse forms and poetry based upon what you may call the English tribe. And it becomes tremendously difficult to translate that into a form suitable for the West Indian tribe. The novelist hasn't got that difficulty but the poet has, and it is an extremely difficult problem. And I speak with such confidence because Walcott has actually written, and I quoted him in the book, that that is the problem that he and West Indian poets face.

HILL: Well, thank you very much Mr. James and good luck in the future with your three books.

JAMES: Thank you very much. I have a problem before me but, as in all these matters, one never knows. You do the best you can and hope for the best. As Napoleon used to say, "*on s'engage et puis s'en voit*"—you engage and then you see. Thank you very much, Mr. Hill.

You Don't Play with Revolution

REPORTER: I've noticed that, although this is a Congress of Black Writers, many of the writers that have come and some of the ones scheduled to speak seem to be writers only incidentally to their work in the Black liberation movement.*

JAMES: For instance, who?

REPORTER: I was thinking of Stokely Carmichael, and I was thinking of Eldridge Cleaver and H. Rap Brown. They are writers, but they seem to have been selected because of their importance in the movement.

JAMES: I think that was precisely why they should have been selected.

REPORTER: Yes, I agree with that. The question that I wanted to pose to you is, what do you think is the role of the artist, or the writer in the Black liberation movement?

JAMES: I can't say what the role of the artist should be because the artist is always a PARTICULAR artist. He does his work in terms of his own ability and his responses to the world around him. He may not write about politics at all. But he may be giving a picture of the situation as it is. He may be on one side or the other. One of the finest West Indian writers I know (I don't know what his politics are, except that by and large, he is on the correct side!) is a man called Wilson Harris. I call him an existentialist

*   C.L.R. James was interviewed by Michael Smith for the *McGill Reporter* during the Congress of Black Writers in Montreal, October 11–14, 1968. The interview was published on November 4, 1968.

writer, but his existentialism is based upon a firm grasp of the local situation in Guyana. Well, I think he is an artist who is contributing to the situation. He is making our minds clearer on the issue.

REPORTER: Do you think it is possible for an artist to remove himself from the struggle, to do art for arts sake, to write a novel for the sake of writing a novel? Or must he be continually immersed in the movement?

JAMES: He may not necessarily be immersed in the movement. An artist is immersed in what makes him an artist: his needs, his interests, his desire to express himself—and today, however you write is an expression of the stage in which you are. If you manage to write something which is not connected with the struggles that are going on, you are then stating quite clearly in your writing that you are not interested in them. So, whatever the artist does today, it is part of the world in which we live. He cannot escape that.

REPORTER: I would like to read a small section of Ralph Ellison's book *The Invisible Man*...

JAMES: Yes. I know that book well.

REPORTER: "Stephen's problem, like ours, was not actually one of creating the uncreated conscience of his race, but in creating the *uncreated features of his face*. Our task is that of making ourselves individuals. The conscience of a race is the gift of its individuals who see, evaluate, record... We create the race by creating ourselves and then to our great astonishment we have created something that is far more important: We will have created a culture."[1] Would you agree with that?

JAMES: I believe that an artist, a first-class artist, who creates an individual—it will be himself or another individual—cannot be abstracted from the social environment in which he works. And the greater the artist, the more of the social environment he embraces. So a number of artists expressing individual responses in that way ultimately result in a broad and total view of the society being expressed, I think.

He is quite right and particularly right in telling the artist to do what he wants to do to create this individual. He cannot settle to create a culture; he probably will not be successful. But if he does this, an artist will reflect, in one way or another, the life that is being lived around him.

REPORTER: I have noticed that the Black delegates at the Congress come from an extremely wide range of backgrounds—generally, perhaps, from three broad areas: from Africa, from the West Indies, and from the United States and Canada. I wonder if you would comment on the links which hold these various groups of delegates together at a conference like this?

JAMES: The link is very obvious and very simple. We are Black people. And therefore, in our various ways, we are conscious of being subjected to all sorts of degradation and humiliation. I think it is less in Canada than elsewhere—very strong in the United States. We are all conscious of our past, because we are students, and our present can only be understood by our past. All that links us together, however different the individual experiences in the particular country may be.

REPORTER: In one of your first talks you mentioned something about West Indians who were looking for their cultural heritage in Africa, and at the same time rejecting their cultural heritage from the West Indies or from the Americas. And you said that in some instances these individuals have a tendency to ignore the best of their own culture and to take the worst from the African culture. I wonder if you could explain.

JAMES: Let me express myself. I was saying that they were not opposed to the West Indian culture. What they were opposed to was the domination of European culture. And they were rejecting that by going toward Africa. But, unfortunately, the grasping and understanding of African culture is not a simple business to a man brought up in Western civilization. And they put on some jacket and all sorts of African robes and that was the end of their getting hold of African culture. So, they were rejecting European culture, which they were objecting to because it dominated them, but they weren't making any serious attempt to penetrate into the African culture. They were losing both sides.

REPORTER: In your book *Party Politics in the West Indies* you made a comment that I would like to read a small section of. You made this comment when you went to Ghana and were there during the independence celebrations: "Day in and day out, Nkrumah sings on the need for developing the 'African personality'. It is a grand phrase." The important part is the next section. You say, "He has here the inestimable advantage of an African background, language, religion, law, institutions, culture. We have to make our own way, dominated by language, institutions, culture, which are in essence similar to Britain and the still more powerful United States."[2] What I would like to know is, when someone does make a serious effort to get into the African culture, what are the valuable aspects of it which he might bring to the West Indies or to America?

JAMES: I don't know that people should go into African culture with the idea of bringing elements of the African culture to the West Indies and America. First of all, the West Indies and America are two very different places. America has a culture of its own. It has an attitude to the world— social, political, and otherwise. To bring African culture to that is quite a problem. I don't see it as something realistic.

But you go to study the African culture because, first of all, there is an immense number of people who are very sick of the state of European culture. They feel that it has reached a stage of degradation. And the man of African descent can go toward Africa, looking for African culture in the sense that he can find something to which he is organically connected, but which is offering him something which European culture is not offering anymore. That he can do. But I don't know that he is going there to bring something back to affect the American culture. That is not the view that I have of why these people act.

Maybe a social group may do something of the kind. (I can say here that Picasso and Braque used the African mask for their work, and Picasso has always objected to a period of his work being called "the African period." And I think I know why he has objected to it. He objected because he was working on some things. The African mask gave him a certain concreteness and method of finding out what he was already working at. That you can do.) But what I think one can learn is a sense of nationalist politics. The West Indian is very backward in regard to that, and the African has no trouble in being an African nationalist. That, I believe, he can learn. But I don't know that that is a part of culture in the sense in which we are using the term.

REPORTER: Isn't Negritude something that West Indians and Black Americans already have in common with Africa?

JAMES: My concept of Negritude is essentially a concept put forward by Aimé Césaire. A lot of other people have different views about what Negritude is. Aimé Césaire looks upon Negritude as an essential contribution to human civilization of something which the African environment has developed and which is valuable. I insist that it is a poetic sentiment. I don't think that Césaire is telling Europeans, "go and do that."

But he is aware of the breakdown of European civilization. And he is pointing out the fact that the African has something which, if you look at it, you will see is a valid contribution to what he calls "the rendez-vous of victory"—where all of us are meeting. And he is not merely a despised, degraded person. His ideals and the things that he thinks have a natural and important validity. That's what Césaire, the poet, is saying. I don't think it is correct for *me* to go further. I know many other people take it and make it a sort of demonstration of the validity of the African culture against European domination. That, I think, is quite justified. But I take it more as a poem that Césaire wrote. Other people can make use of it.

I have seen where Nkrumah has launched a ferocious attack on it, and *he* has been talking a great deal about African personality. I begin and insist that what Césaire wrote is something that is a poetic contribution to the concept of race. And I think it has validity. When you think about what he says about what is real to the African, you can then see African civilization and the civilization of people of underdeveloped countries in a different way than you did before you saw Césaire's poetic work. I hope that means something to you.

REPORTER: It does. I would like to quote once more from your book *Party Politics in the West Indies*. You say here that "Political power, a dynamic population which knows its political power, a backward economy. That is a potentially explosive situation...." And you have a footnote here which says, "Marxism equals 'communist' equals r-r-revolution. That is the fashionable logic. I am a Marxist, I have studied revolution for many years, and among other thing you learn not to play with it."[3] Could you elaborate this?

JAMES: I am saying that in the West Indies today—I say it now still more than then—you have a situation which is potentially revolutionary. The economic basis and social structure of those islands are in a certain situation where most of the wealth is owned and controlled by people abroad; you have a small concentrated population. It is an explosive situation. And therefore we must look out and be prepared for a revolutionary development. At the same time, I was talking to people who, when you ask for some simple human democratic right, they immediately call you "communist." So I say, you don't play with it.

But I am aware of the important revolutionary character of the situation, and at the same time I am not calling everybody who asks for a human democratic right, or protests against some autocratic act by the government—neither is he a communist nor does he claim to be. Immediately when you call him "communist," you are playing with it. I use the term "revolutionary situation" in a very serious way. That is why I put that in the footnote. The moment you demand something: "We need the sugar estates, we are working on the sugar estates to get so and so and so and so," they shout "Communist!"

REPORTER: Then you believe that there is an alternative to a revolution, to a revolutionary situation.

JAMES: In the Caribbean? I believe there is an alternative. A desperate authoritarian regime, essentially fascist as far as they can impose it—that, I have written, is what the Caribbean faces. The particular situation which they have at the present time cannot continue. And either the governments move forward with a revolution essentially social in content, or they are going to be struck down and made to submit to a very autocratic regime.

By the way, let me say that I do not believe it will be easy for any autocratic regime to impose autocracy on the Caribbean population. I say those are the two alternatives and I would like to say the domination, the forced domination and submission of West Indians by an autocratic government would be very difficult. It would be wrong for me to go further, speculating as to what will happen... but I pose the two alternatives.

REPORTER: This morning Stokely Carmichael made a differentiation between two types of oppression—exploitation which was essentially economic in character—and colonization, where one race subjugated another, completely stripping the colonized race of its culture and dehumanizing it. Would you make the same distinction?

JAMES: The distinction that he makes can be a valid distinction. The only thing is, when colonialism is carried down to its roots, it is a form of economic exploitation, as well as racial, because it is the mass of the population that is being exploited economically under the colonialist's regimes. If he wishes to insist that the colonialist regime is a little bit different because it always has racial overtones, he is entitled to.

But his idea that poor people (he talks about poor people; I speak about the proletariat), the mass of the population in an advanced country has got the same culture and values and so forth as those people who are exploiting them, I don't accept that. I don't believe that the culture and the values of De Gaulle are the culture and values of the mass of the population in France. I don't believe that the culture and values of Franco are the culture and values of the mass of the population in Spain.

So, his unification and consolidation of culture in an advanced country as being the same values and culture of all people there, while in the colonial regime it is different, I don't accept that completely at all. There is a difference, but it isn't as great a difference as he seems to make it out to be.

REPORTER: Do you think the battle that must go on in the United States, for example, is essentially one of restructuring the system, or one of restructuring mental attitudes toward people in the system?

JAMES: You cannot reconstruct a system without restructuring mental attitudes. And I was extremely pleased today to hear the talk of Harry Edwards, and then James Forman. Those fellows have a firm grasp of the way that racism could seriously be removed from the United States by a total revolutionary change in the social system.

REPORTER: One of the dilemmas I find myself in...

JAMES: You are an American citizen?

REPORTER: I am a Canadian citizen, but I have very close ties with the United States and I find it is becoming increasingly difficult not to take sides. As Stokely Carmichael said, the job today for him and his people is to *make* it increasingly difficult not to be committed: that is, not to pick up a gun and go into the streets.

JAMES: If a man talks about picking up a gun and going into the streets, I am not going to oppose him, because that is the revolution, and we may come to that. But I don't think that in 1968 in the United States it is correct to talk about the revolutionary struggle in terms of picking up a gun and going into the streets. I don't quite see that people in Harlem should pick up guns and go into the streets. There *are* times when you have to use violence and many of the American Negroes have been using violence under certain circumstances. I don't oppose anybody doing that. That means he is on the correct side. But there is a lot more to the social revolution than merely picking up a gun and going into the streets.

REPORTER: Could you elaborate on that perhaps?

JAMES: The social revolution means that the great mass of the population have come to the conclusion that the life that they are living cannot continue and they want to change it. That happened in Britain in the 17th century, and that was the basis of the support of Oliver Cromwell and the rest of them. They broke up the old regime. It is true that what they thought they would substitute for it didn't come exactly, but the thing you must remember is that, as Mr. Hilaire Belloc says, "Royalty returned when Charles II came back; the monarchy did not." The Cromwellians had finished the old monarchical regime, and that can only be broken up when the mass of the population feels the time has come to finish up with it. What may take its place depends on what the mass of the population feels that it requires.

People talk about leaders, but leaders can only lead a developed people who have an instinct in a certain direction, and that is a thing that takes time. A great revolution took place in the United States in 1776. They wanted to finish up with the imperialist regime of Britain, and they wanted to substitute something new. That they did, and were highly successful in doing so because, by and large, the population either was sympathetic to them or it was neutral: it didn't see any cause to fight for the British, although it might not have plunged into the revolutionary struggle.

The finest example I know of social revolution today is what took place in Hungary, where a mass of the population rose up and broke the Stalinist regime. And the only way that regime could be restored was by Russian tanks coming in and physically destroying it. But that was a social revolution in which the population wanted to finish with what there was and to create something new.

There is one in Cuba. They are creating something new in Cuba. There were immense difficulties, but they finished with Batista and found that in order to finish completely with what Batista represents, they had to make certain new creative social and political forces. And that they are doing, and doing, in my opinion, extremely well, despite immense difficulties.

And I should say that a socialist revolution in the United States—nobody will be in any doubt as to what it really is. That will be something that will write itself across the sky. No, there's no problem.

REPORTER: What do you think is the significance of the events that have taken place in Africa over the last eleven years, since Ghana became independent, for people in the West Indies and in the Americas?

JAMES: The significance of those events is this: I was in Ghana in 1957 talking at times to Nkrumah and Padmore. We had been very much involved in the struggle for political emancipation of the African people, and Ghana was the first of them. And if we had heard anybody preaching to people saying, "In ten years there will be thirty new African states; there will be over a hundred million Africans who will gain political independence," we would have got together and said, "We have got to attack that fellow and expose him as an adventurer; a man who is ready to carry the African people into all sorts of dangerous policies, putsches, and so forth. Because that is *nonsense*." We couldn't believe that in ten years there would be over thirty new African states and over one million people free, politically free. Because that is all that political emancipation means: politically free.

What that means to us is this: there is enormous revolutionary potential contained even in all sorts of elements in the population where you didn't expect it. We didn't expect that there would have been such a terrific force that would have swept over Africa with the tremendous rage with which it has done. What it means to me and what I say it would mean to other people is this: those people are on the move. They have moved in ten years in a manner that *nobody* expected. And over the next few years we must expect them to move in the way that the Black people, and particularly those in the Americas have moved, in harmony with tremendous social and political developments that are taking place in Western civilization itself. The slave revolt in San Domingo was an inextricable part of the French Revolution and the change from feudalism to modern bourgeois society.

And what is taking place in Africa today and what the people in other parts Western civilization—the Africans—must know, is that the struggle they are carrying on is part of an immense change in the whole social structure that exists in the world at the present time. It may be Black Power here, another thing there, independence here, freedom, democratic rights there. But it is part of this tremendous change that is taking place in the whole social structure that exists in the world at the present time.

And the African revolt is part of that. And we, Black people in America and in the Caribbean, must look upon the African revolt as a symbol of what is likely to take place everywhere and to which we are very closely allied.

PART IV
CORRESPONDENCE

ALFIE ROBERTS & MERVYN SOLOMON to C.L.R. JAMES

2873 Bedford
Montreal, Quebec
March 28, 1964

Mr. C.L.R. James
C/O Caribbean Affairs Section
British Broadcasting Corporation
LONDON, England.

Dear Mr. James,

It is in virtue of your record of undoubted loyalty to the West Indies that we are taking the liberty of addressing this letter to you, on the following questions:

West Indian politics, and West Indian cricket.

WEST INDIAN POLITICS:

We are West Indian students of Sir George Williams University studying for a degree in Economics and Political Science. Our special interest is in political developments in the West Indies, in so far as they are affected by influences of the world outside.

As a first step, we believe that it will be to our advantage to study the writings of all outstanding West Indian thinkers. We shall, therefore, be pleased to if you will let us have a list of all the published works of which you are the author. You may wish, in particular, to note our vain efforts to

locate either of your works—*World Revolution*,[1] or your Marxist disserta-
tion on the Negro Problem in the U.S.A.[2]

It will also be appreciated if you will advise us as regards relevant works
of other important writers on West Indian problems.

WEST INDIAN CRICKET:

We must necessarily limit our observations to what we consider the
most urgent problems of West Indian cricket. Today our cricket thrives; in
spite of the journalistic abyss which exists throughout the islands. And this
abyss, we believe, is the first cause of our predicament.

We note with relief your recent efforts to "push" us "Beyond a Boundary." It is our profound wish that you will be able to use your influence to
cause an early start to the tackling of the under-mentioned problems (some
of which you have already brought to the notice of the public):

(i) A statistical report of Inter-Regional Tournaments (formerly Inter-
colonial)

(ii) Individual biographies, or some appropriate work which will recall
the era from George Headley to the "Terrible W's."[3]

(iii) Compilation of data on the lives and achievements of Sobers, Kanhai, Hall[7] and other leaders of the present generation.

(iv) A History of West Indian Captaincy; *with special reference to the
influences of Queen's Park Cricket Club.*

Meanwhile, we are anxiously awaiting the visit of Australia to the West
Indies in 1965. If it is at all possible for you to visit the West Indies for the
tour, we can, for the first time, look forward to adequate coverage of the
series by an eminently qualified West Indian.

We trust that your recent visit to Africa was a success and look forward
to your kind reply,

Yours sincerely,
Alfie Roberts
(ST. VINCENT)
Mervyn Solomon
(TRINIDAD AND TOBAGO)
c.c. Sir Frank Worrell

MARTIN GLABERMAN to C.L.R. JAMES July 12, 1965

Dear Nello,

I was glad to hear from you, especially that your health is satisfactory. I imagine that the familiar food and climate compensate for the strain, etc.

I have been reading the clippings and the issues of the paper[8] and I must say straight out that I found your deep involvement in Trinidad politics very disturbing. I have not been able to write before and it is difficult to for me to write now because I believe that we here have failed in the major responsibility to make it possible for you to do with ease and with security the work that it is necessary for you to do—and that only you can do. We are approaching that point, but in a crucial period in our history you are very distant so that consultation and discussion are very difficult.

Le me mention two things in particular, which fit in very closely with the perspectives we had agreed upon. Our young friend in Germany, Jim Evrard,[9] has been writing voluminously about Sartre, Existentialism and many other things. I have sent copies to London. W[illia]m[10] could write to him but will not—he seems to be hostile to the ideas Evrard puts forward, but even more, he says he is not interested. But moving the work forward so that it can be published in the reasonably near future in *Modern Politics* and the Nevada[11] depends overwhelmingly on you. I do not know that Evrard is right (he himself is prepared to modify his views) but I am certain he can make a contribution. He can make a fruitful collaborator and be brought along in the process.

The second is our own development here, slow as it has been. We have now reached the point where we could set September as the date on which I go on full time. George [Rawick] is still working on publishers, but we have decided for ourselves that we will not permit the question of publishing the

Ghana book[12] to go on indefinitely: we will publish it ourselves and win our market. More than that, the head of George's department at Michigan State University has raised the possibility of having you come there for semester, paid, as a sort of scholar in residence. That may involve insuperable barriers that we might not be able to overcome, although I would not dismiss it.

However, there is now something much more concrete open to us. On the same day I received your letter we received two separate letters from West Indians in Canada. One was from Robert A. Hill, a Jamaican in Ottawa. He ordered a mass of books and pamphlets, is organizing discussions among West Indians (one of them will be on "C.L.R. James: The Man and His work"). He will move to the University of Toronto in the fall where he will organize a C.L.R. James Study Circle.

The second letter came from Alfie Roberts, from St. Vincent, who is at the University of Montreal.[13] They have a wide circle around them. From that, and the fact that your BBC Shakespeare tapes were broadcast all over Canada, it would be a very simple matter to arrange a lecture tour in Canada and possibly (with all the limitations understood) in the States. By the end of such a trip we will be certain of having a fund raised to take care of an extended period thereafter.

The work on philosophy and the dialectic (and the publication of the Nevada), the Ghana book and the African revolution, the preparation for a conference and the necessary collaboration with people around the world—it cannot be done without you. I have written about the need to answer Cardan.[14] I feel perfectly qualified to do it—but I hesitate to attack an old friend and collaborator without consultation with you (that may be an introduction to SC&WR[State Capitalism and World Revolution][15]).

Compared to this work for which we have trained for so many years and which only we can do, and which will leave a profound and permanent imprint on the history of mankind, the involvement in West Indian politics seems to me to be an entirely unwarranted drain on your resources. You have told us so many times: he who does something is not doing something else. Your involvement inevitably involves us—what business have we there?

We had a long discussion on the London tapes.[16] We have an expanding circle around us with whom we have discussed our perspectives. What can I say to them and to the organization? With the Civil War book, *Modern*

Politics, etc. on the agenda, how can I go to people for money for a Trinidad paper? How does it fit into the building and training of a Marxist group? What perspective can I say we have in Trinidad? What organization, what theory are we building there?

Nello, I just don't see it. *You* need to come north and *we* need you to come north. Please tell me what is involved. A perspective of indefinite (if not permanent) residence in Trinidad must involve more than [the fact] that Trinidad is in difficulty. Isn't there an alternative?

With warmest wishes,
Marty

ROBERT A. HILL to MARTIN GLABERMAN

127 Crichton St.
Ottawa 2, Ontario
August 7, 1965

Dear Mr. Glaberman,

Greetings.

Thank you for the first batch of C.L.R. James publications ("Marxism for the Sixties") which arrived about a fortnight ago. I suspect that the postal strike here in Canada has probably delayed the rest.

Enclosed are the transcripts of the two lectures which Nello recently gave at the University of the West Indies in Kingston.[17] I have also received the tapes, and so far we have had some very successful listening sessions. I am [at] present making arrangements with the Canadian Broadcasting Corporation with a view to broadcast [them], the rights of which I have been granted. I am also arranging a tour for the tapes to Washington, New York, Montreal and Toronto.

I have recently come across an announcement of a "Socialist Scholars Conference" at Rutgers University on September 11–12, with Isaac Deutscher, Connor Cruise O'Brian, Staughton Lynd, etc. Have you any plans for attending? I am trying to attend, so it might be a good opportunity for us to meet. I hope to hear from you on this.

In reading H. Marcuse's *One Dimensional Man*, I came across a reference to *Correspondence* and *News and Letters* in Detroit. Could you let me know about the value of these publications, as well as the subscription arrangements?

As Secretary of the forthcoming "Conference on West Indian Affairs: Facing the Future," I would like to take this opportunity to invite you and your associates. The Conference will be held in Montreal on Oct. 8–9, and represents the joint effort of West Indian Associations in North America. We are awaiting word from George Lamming as to whether he will be able to attend as Guest Speaker.

This seems to be all for now.

Fraternally,
Robert A. Hill

MARTIN GLABERMAN to ROBERT A. HILL

August 22, 1965

Dear Mr. Hill,

Again apologies for my delay, both in the books and in my letter. The person who is usually in charge of our book service was away and it seems I made the bundles too large and they were returned by the post office. By the time I had them wrapped again in smaller bundles the mail strike intervened. I also made an error in crediting you with $9.30 (assuming your check was in Canadian dollars, on which there is a 7% discount). You are credited with the full $10. We have no copies of the Federation pamphlet[18] and so cannot send any. We were short of copies of *Black Jacobins*—the remainder of your order will be sent shortly.

Correspondence was a paper which our group put out from 1955 to 1962. We could not sustain it, however, in part because of internal weakness in the paper itself, and it is no longer being published. We hope eventually to publish a weekly paper again. *News and Letters* is published by a group that split off from *Correspondence*. Both papers were based essentially on the ideas of C.L.R. James although it is my belief that *News and Letters* has remained stagnant since the time they split and their paper embodies some of the good points, and most of the defects, of the old *Correspondence*. I do not think that *News and Letters* would be especially valuable although if you are interested you might write to them at 8751 Grand River Ave., Detroit, Mich.

I was very happy to receive the transcripts of Nello's lectures in Kingston. I purchased some time ago the tapes of some lectures he gave on the

BBC Caribbean Service on Shakespeare. They were heard rather widely in Canada and the United States. If you are interested in them you might be able to borrow them for a while. We also have a number of other tapes of Nello's (four of them made in London, when we were there a year and a half ago) dealing with broad political questions that are of concern to our organization. Unfortunately, they were made at his home and are of poor quality and cannot be played for a large audience. Two or three people, however, who are familiar with his ideas, should have no difficulty in following them. Perhaps some time, if you are able to visit Detroit or I can come up to Toronto, we might work something out with regard to them.

I have been in touch with Nello in Trinidad and we here are also very worried about how all this activity will affect his poor health.[19] We are also worried in another connection—how this will limit the most important philosophical and political work on a world scale that only he can do. As an example of what is involved, we have a number of works of his that we are trying to get published. One is a book on Ghana, a superb work on the development of African independence.[20] Several editors of major publishers have given it unstinted praise. However, whenever it comes to the final decision on whether to publish, it seems to always be vetoed. They seem to find it too hot too handle politically. We are continuing our efforts, but we have decided that if a commercial publisher cannot be found in the reasonably near future, we will attempt to publish it ourselves and will try to raise the money.

There is also a book on Shakespeare and modern politics which is in rough draft and which is in a similar situation. In addition there is a book called *Modern Politics*.[21] It consists of six lectures that Nello delivered at the Public Library in Trinidad and was printed there as a book. They are, in my mind, the finest popular statement of the Marxist view of history and its importance for our time that I have ever seen anywhere. The book was suppressed in Trinidad but two copies were smuggled out. We have one that we intend to print—but that is a matter of $2000–$3000. There is also a draft that Nello wrote in 1948 on dialectics and the modern world.[22] It had been handed around for years in typed copies until all were lost—or almost all. We recently found one copy and are in the process of typing a new set (7 copies). We hope that he can edit this and bring it up to date and then we can publish it. It is a remarkable document which, among things, forecasts the general form of the Hungarian Revolution some eight years before the event.

We are now also out of print of *Mariners, Renegades and Castaways*. The same is true of *State Capitalism and World Revolution*, of which Nello is the author and which we hope to reprint with a new introduction.

What is involved in this, among other things, is our estimate of the man and his work. In each generation or two some major figure has arisen who has had a world-wide and historical grasp of society and has given Marxism a new form and a new life. Lenin was such a man. Trotsky could have been such a man but did not make it. In our view, James is such a man. So, you can see our concern at his being confined narrowly to the politics of a single country. This concern is compounded by our awareness of our own failure to provide the means for him to support himself and his family, and his having constantly to do a lot of work just to make a living (his trip to the West Indies to report on cricket is just such a job, forced on him by the need to make a living).

We had been hoping that it might become possible to arrange a lecture tour in Canada (in the United States, there are difficulties with the immigration authorities which we may not be able to overcome) which would give Nello a respite from W[est] I[ndian] politics and at the same time give him some money.

If you need biographical information about Nello, the best source is *Beyond a Boundary*. I understand that the book has been sold out by the publisher, but single copies may still be available from book sellers. If you are interested, you might write to Blackwell's, Broad Street, Oxford, England to see if they have some copies left. If you cannot get a copy from them or would like one sooner, I would be happy to lend you my personal copy. (Before I forget, I will mention here that we have made up extracts of *Modern Politics*—about 90 percent of the texts—and are sending you a copy.)

Spurred by your note that you may attend, we have decided to attend the conference at Rutgers in September.[23] I am also very happy to accept your invitation to the Conference on West Indian Affairs in Montreal. If, by the way, it is possible for you to come to Detroit at any time, we would be very happy to see you and to put you up for the length of your visit. Would it be feasible for you to come down to Detroit before the Rutgers Conference and drive with us?

Our group is now in the process of raising a fund with the purpose of having me go full time some time in September. One of the consequences will be that I will attempt to arrange a tour in the fall in the East (New York and Philadelphia) and in the West. Would anything be possible in Montreal and Toronto?

Since you plan to visit New York, it might be of some help to you if I gave you the address of one of our people there. She is Mrs. Constance Pearlstein at the Hotel Albert, 23 E. 10 St., New York 3, N.Y. She is Nello's former wife (his son, Robert, is there too), since remarried.

By a happy coincidence, I received a letter from Mr. Alfie Roberts at the same time that I received yours. He ordered a copy of *Negro Americans Take the Lead* and I wrote to him briefly. I have not yet written to Mr. Morris.

Once again, please accept my apologies for the delay in writing. I hope we meet soon and discuss some of these things at greater length. With very best wishes,

Fraternally,
Martin Glaberman

ROBERT A. HILL to MARTIN GLABERMAN

Ottawa 2, Ontario
August 30, 1965

Dear Martin,

Greetings.

Thanks very much for your over-generous letter of August 22. Believe me, there is no reason for you to apologize for the delay, as I shudder to think of the heavy burden of work you must carry from day to day. Whenever I write I know for certain that you will reply when you can, and that is all that matters.

First of all, I warmly accept your invitation to Detroit—you can expect me there on Tuesday, September 7, the exact time of my arrival I shall telegraph you. There is a lot of important business to discuss about yourself, Nello, myself, and Facing Reality. At present, I am working on a fairly short memorandum on everything that has so far been discussed as well as some other possibilities which still remain to be developed between us. Thanks again for your kind invitation.

Last week, I sent Nello's five tapes to John H. Clarke, associate editor of *Freedomways*, the quarterly review (very influential in the right circles) of the Negro freedom movement. Mr. Clarke's letter of August 19 says *inter alia*: "We will make very good use of the C.L.R. James tapes. There are several writers from the Caribbean area now living New York City who will assist me…. C.L.R.J. has several passionate admirers in the U.S.A. Mrs. Paul Marshall, one of the best woman writers, will help me plan a reception for you when you are in town…. Both Mrs. Marshall and I will try to raise some money for C.L.R.J. while you are here." I have asked him to arrange to have the tapes sent to other established groups affiliated with the journal. Sept. 10th has been suggested for the reception in New York, so we should plan to be there for that date.

I heard from my uncle in Trinidad today,[24] and he sends this information: "Maragh and C.L.R.J. and others have now formed the Workers and Farmers Party, and have launched it in the teeth of the President of the Oil Workers Trade Union, George Weekes' campaign against [the] Industrial Stabilization Act. Both the OWTU and the WFP have weekly newspapers now. WFP's is *We the People*, edited by C.L.R.J. They also hold separate public campaigns against the Act. Weekes supports the WFP, so does the OWTU"

Reading the Trinidad newspapers, it seems that Williams might be in serious political trouble. Weekes has called for a poll among the sugar cane workers to challenge the government-backed trade union for representation rights—and everything points to his success. What we must always keep in mind is that Nello is first and last a Trinidadian, and the political decadence there must have been truly enormous for him to jeopardize his very health.

I was very happy to learn of Nello's still unpublished works. Without a doubt, this will have to be my major responsibility in anything I do. It can be done, it will have to be done. I have recently initiated the establishment of a C.L.R.J. Study Circle in Montreal, and by the end of September Toronto's should be organized. If I can help it, they will not remain an academic pastime. I shall fight to make them a contributory element in anything that you do or find that needs to be done.

I think it will be an excellent opportunity for us to discuss the Ghana book with John H. Clarke when we are in New York. The late W.E.B. Du Bois's widow, Shirley Graham, who now lives permanently in Ghana, is one of the founders of *Freedomways* and still remains one of the Contributing Editors.

We have had a lot of success with Nello's tapes here in Ottawa and Montreal. There were two sessions each in Ottawa and Montreal, and there is still an enormous audience still left untapped. By the way, instead of my presenting the paper on Nello for the Conference Seminar, I thought it would be best to use the tapes. The Ibo Society in Toronto, a group of West Indian intellectuals and students, has requested the tapes for the end of September.

The question of a lecture tour for you in Montreal and Toronto is certainly feasible. The Study Circles in both cities would make it a major promotion. However, I am still unfamiliar with Toronto, so it would have to be thoroughly looked into. I shall be in Montreal on Thursday for a meeting with the Conference Committee, so I shall alert our people there from now.

Thanks very much for the books which arrived safely. I shall be bringing the balance of them to Detroit as the money is still being collected. I hope you received the order for Sangsters Bookstore in Kingston, [Jamaica]. Last weekend, I was in Toronto and, just walking on the street, I sold two sets of books—that place can be organized to great advantage.

Once again, thanks for you kind letter. Please expect my telegram. With best wishes for our future united.

Fraternally,
Robert

MARTIN GLABERMAN to C.L.R. JAMES

October 13, 1965

Dear Nello,

I had a most extraordinary weekend in Montreal at the Conference on West Indian Affairs. We picked up the Hills in Toronto and got there in time for George Lamming's opening address Friday night. It was a tremendous speech to an audience of over three hundred. The audience was moved by his statement that this was his first speech to a West Indian audience. His speech will be published in the Conference proceedings (which I believe will be done by the University of Montreal), but an effort will also be made to issue George's speech as a long playing record and, possibly, as a pamphlet.

Jessie and I finally had the chance to meet George and we spoke to him on Friday night and a few times on Saturday. He is quite a wonderful person and we hit it off very well. He will attempt to spend a few days in Detroit with us either at the tend of October or the beginning of November. Meetings have been arranged for him at NYU, Harlem Writers Guild, and one other in NY. Fisk University (the annual student convocation); Toronto U., Carleton U. (Ottawa), Queens U. (Kingston, Canada), and possibly U. of Indiana (through Mervyn Alleyne), and possibly Detroit.

On Saturday there were three sessions: Race and Culture (Alleyne and Dr. Frances Henry of McGill); Economic Change (Dr. Hugh Walker and Bernard Yankey); Politics and Change (Locksley Edmonson and Alvin Johnson). They were all rather academic and unsatisfactory to the delegates, with the economic panel being the worst and Dr. Kari Levitt of McGill and a fellow Carrington launching biting attacks on the panel as glossing over the real problems of the West Indies.

I followed the last session with my speech, which is enclosed. It was well delivered and very well received. Dr. Frances Henry immediately proposed that you be the invited guest at the next conference. And Dr. Levitt and Carrington came up to me to propose that I send my speech to New World in Jamaica for publication in their next issue, which I will do. It will also be printed in the conference proceedings.

Although the reports tended to be much like the reports at scholarly conferences, the conference as a whole was quite impressive. It was organized by a small group of West Indian students [in] Ottawa and Montreal and they raised a considerable amount of money and got the support of Montreal U. and McGill. Most of the West Indies was represented and the sentiment was overwhelmingly for Federation and for revolutionary change.

We had a literature table at the conference and sold about $55 worth of publications. We also made extensive contacts, both among West Indians and the Canadian academic community. There should be up to five C.L.R. James Study Circles set up: Toronto, Montreal, Ottawa, Nova Scotia, N.Y., with Hill as the guiding spirit. There are tentative plans for the Circles to meet in the spring (April or May). The Hills will spend Christmas week with us in Detroit and Bobby wants to spend at least one month next summer working with us.

Hill has been showing *Modern Politics* around in Toronto and several faculty members and others are interested (including McPherson[25]). He thinks the money can be raised and the book can be printed here.

Everyone is concerned (including George [Lamming]) that you do not write. Even if just a word that you are well… Take care of yourself.

With best wishes,
Marty

ROBERT A. HILL to ALFIE ROBERTS

319 Beech Ave.
Toronto 13, Ontario
November 6, 1965

Dear Alfie,

Greetings,

Thanks very much for your short note with the enclosed information. You must forgive me for not replying before this, but I have been up to my ears in work of every description.

Mervyn[26] was supposed to send you the material that you asked for. I hope that it reached you in time. It should be a most interesting paper when it is finished—you ought to think about making copies of it so that our people can get to read it.

Enclosed is your copy of the Proposal for a C.L.R. James Study Circle. I don't think that there is any other West Indian student that knows more about the man and his work than you do. So, I think that you will be a great loss to the group in Montreal—I don't know if we still have a group there. You can try your best to pull together a few of our people in Ottawa—get in touch with CLAUDE ROBINSON[27]—but I don't know how successful you'll be.

I think that it might be a nice gesture if you wrote C.L.R. in Trinidad and asked him to put you on the paper's[28] mailing list as well as for the Party's[29] pamphlets. His address is: 22 Ariapata Ave., Port of Spain. You could also tell him about our Study Circle.[30]

Could you get in touch with Professor Johnson in the English Department (he's a good friend of mine and a wonderful person). Show him your copy *Mariners, Renegades, and Castaways* by C.L.R. and tell him that we can fill any order by the Department if it is put on the reading list. You can also give him my address.

Here are two references that you should locate immediately:

George Shepperson, Notes on Negro American Influences on the Emergence of African Nationalism, *Journal of African History*, Vol. 1960, No. 2.

Bennett, Norman Robert. Christian and Negro Slavery in Eighteenth-Century North Africa. (Same Journal), 1960, No. 1

Their conclusions are there for you to find, they don't seem to appreciate what they are.

The Autobiography of Malcolm X has just come out—you must read it immediately! If you can't afford to buy it right now and the Library hasn't got it, let me know and I will send you my copy as soon as I am through with it.

Enclosed is the thing you wanted from Italy. It's all in Italian, so it isn't much help unless you can get it translated.

This seems to be all for now. I wait to hear from you about the Proposal.

Fraternally,
Bobby

P.S. I shall be attending the McGill Conference in Montreal from Nov. 10–15. If you can come down to Montreal, it might be very helpful to our work. You can get in touch with me through ROSIE.[31]

C.L.R. JAMES to ROBERT A. HILL

20 Staverton Rd.,

N.W. 2

December 31, 1965

My Dear Robert,

Your correspondence has run me to earth in London where I will be for a few days, to be quite precise until January 8, when I will return to Trinidad. I can only say that I trust to the goodwill with which your correspondence overflows and to your consciousness of the way in which I am being knocked by fate from pillar to post and back to pillar again to account for my dilatoriness in correspondence. However, after I return to Trinidad that deficiency will be repaired.

Meanwhile, I want to say not only from your correspondence but also from the detailed reports I have got from George Lamming that I am not only delighted but stimulated by the response which my work seems to have awakened in the West Indians in Canada. I am very much accustomed over the years to interest expressed and concern projected and even organizations begun in relation to matters of this kind. But it is a long time that I have seen one in which the ideas stated and the scope and precision of the organization to correspond have reached the pitch that I have seen in what you all are doing and of which you seem to be the center. I can assure you that it means a great deal to me at this time. Let me get down at once to a statement of what I shall call first principles.

(1) I am prepared to do all that is needed to make the conference on "The Making of the West Indian Peoples" a success. As you will have detected I have been working on that for some years now. I believe that already and as time goes on I will have a lot to say. But I am hoping that the title that you have given to this conference originated in a magnificent book called *The Making of the British Working Class* by an Englishman E.P. Thompson. The English publisher is Gollancz. It is an expensive book, but I met Thompson over a year ago in England. He is a very fine fellow and he told me, at that time, that there was a probability of a paperback edition being published in the United States. That is something worth inquiry. If there is such an edition, I would be glad to know. The other books I would recommend as a preliminary are *Black Reconstruction* by W.E.B. Du Bois, *The Masters and the Slaves* by Gilberto Freyre, and of course the works of Karl Marx.

I regret to say I have to recommend (apart from the West Indian Novels) my own political and sociological writings and Lamming's *The Pleasures of Exile*. I may say that I have some fifty or sixty thousand words of a manuscript on the development of the West Indian people. I ought to be able within some weeks to send you a copy of it for private circulation. I also have and can put my hand in the West Indies, on some writings which will supplement your very full list. I will bear that in mind and shall do my best to draw your attention and even to send you manuscripts which are missing from your list; there are quite a few. I shall also make notes on them as I send them to you.

I shall also send you copies of the paper from the very first issue and, when I return to Trinidad, shall send you two copies of everything that we publish, including of course the weekly.

(2) Let me at once inform you of what my future plans are:

(a) I am going back to Trinidad on January 8 to devote myself to establishing a political party and victory in the forthcoming elections. You will review all the material of our recent convention, where you will see that we intend to carry out a policy such as will ignite the whole of the Caribbean if it is successful. I think I will leave it to you, from the material I shall send you and future issues of our paper and literature, to decide what we are likely to do. I believe that that will not only occupy me but will prove the occasion for the development of many of my ideas upon the West Indies and its people.

(b) I have in mind and am quite set to do another book which will attempt to do for the Western world what has been done in the book on Melville[32] and the book on cricket.[33] I have it on my fingertips and I know how valuable it will be. It is a book on Shakespeare's *King Lear*. I am quite certain that what I shall say in this book, in fact what I have briefly said already has never been said before and will startle even acknowledged scholars of Shakespeare, in much the same way that the thesis of *The Black Jacobins*, although not exactly new, in England at any rate, startled students of slavery. As a supplement to this book, I intend to add notes on two frescoes by Michelangelo in the Cappelle Paolina in the Vatican, the last quartets, the last piano sonatas and the Ninth symphony of Beethoven with probably furthers notes on Leonardo da Vinci, Tolstoy, and a re-statement, to be more precise, a development of my views on Melville. This would seem to be a very tall order, but I have been at it for many years and the greater part of the book will be a statement showing that *King Lear* represents a summation and stage of Shakespeare's work. That being established, I can then more easily show the same process and development at work in the great figures that I have mentioned. It will not take me very long to do this book, but I want to see some time and some ease of mind.

Dr. Augier's[34] sympathy for undue pressure upon me on account of my age can best be mediated by this fact: that having these books inside of me and being unable to write them takes far more out of me than actually doing them.

(c) I am committed to doing some work on the Existentialist philosophy in relation to Marxism and in particular the collapse of Jean-Paul Sartre. I am steadily doing the work but I find it somewhat difficult because I have not got near to me nor am I in correspondence with anyone familiar with this work. Although I know the roads that I have to travel, strict philosophy is a very technical business and I need someone who is trained in the field to exchange ideas and to do some of the work that I require. I have to repeat, however, that I know quite well what I have to do.

I think that that is what I see in front of me during the next year. For the moment, I will add only two things. The first is that the fund that has been opened for me makes me look at this work with far more confidence that it can be done as it ought to be done than I have previously and, secondly, I keep my eye open to the currents of world politics. But I am certain both in theory and in practice that there is never any substitute for practical activity in the analysis of any kind of politics and, while true in general, it is particularly true of the West Indies which, as I have written in my article in *Freedomways*, seems to be a slice of the modern world cut away for the scientific investigations of universal problems.[35]

For the time being, my dear Robert, that is all I have to say but from now on our correspondence will be, I hope, not only regular, but ample. Allow me to say once that this recognition of my work and of all of it by a group of West Indians centered in Canada seems to me to have political implications of far more than a merely national significance.

Ever yours,
C.L.R.

TIM HECTOR to ROBERT A. HILL

Wolfville, Nova Scotia
March 29, 1966

Comrade along the same road,

I greet you.

I cannot relate the enthusiasm which your letter, or rather the relay letter form C.L.R., brought to me.

I do not know if H[arvey] told you that since January I have been down with pneumonia and am now nearly over it, though still confined to bed. Before I go any further, please excuse the atrocious handwriting.

I believe too that my failure to write may have given you reason to hold that our interest had waned. On that score there need be no doubt. C.L.R.'s work is sufficient to ensure the sustained interest of any person.

I know of course that it is unreasonable of me to ask if there is anything available on C.L.R., such as "Dialectics and the Fate of Humanity." However, is *Beyond a Boundary* available in Canada?

Now, to my work in the Study Circle;

(a) I have attempted a study of James's view of Revolutionary Socialism in the 1960s. This is based on work done on *The Black Jacobins* and a comparison with Boissonade's history of San Domingo.[36] Besides, C.L.R.'s analysis of revolution and revolutionary activity in the San Domingo Revolution has led me on to a study of Lefebvre, De Tocqueville, etc. The work is rewarding, particularly with the unequalled guidance of C.L.R.'s work. But there are my limitations. First, an inadequate grasp of Marxism, since I have not as yet completed Vol. II of *Capital*, nor do I believe my grasp of much of Marx and Lenin's work to be sufficient to undertake this task. Yet the work proceeds apace and my illness has enabled me to be away from the thrall of academic pursuits, made worse by the cramping circumstances of Nova Scotia.

(b) Having read *Mariners*[37] it was obvious to me that I had merely acquired the academic tools of literary criticism, that is, the approach relative to style, structure, symbolism, etc., but not the essence of literary criticism as to meaning and vision in the particular work. This deficiency James on Melville has somewhat corrected, and so I re-read all the available West Indian novels and will put together some preliminary views on the subject.

(c) It is of course elementary that to understand James (though his inimitable style makes this easy) a fundamental grasp of the Marxist theory of society is an inescapable pre-requisite. To be sure, like nearly every representative West Indian bourgeois-student, I have declared myself a Socialist. Of course with only the Welfare State and its attendant shams and volte-faces in mind. Added to this my education had been and *is* consciously or unconsciously anti-Marxist. However, something tells me that I have overcome these growing pains (terrible they were) and I am proceeding nicely.

(d) H[arvey] and I have been corresponding on the subject, "The View of the Party" in C.L.R.J. and Frantz Fanon, using *The Wretched of The Earth* and *Party Politics in the West Indies* as the levers for discussion and argument. To my mind, Fanon envisages the Vanguard One Party state whereas James deals thoroughly with the Party as the key instrument towards shaping and making the "national" community. I use the word "national" here, not in the perverted sense of unrestrained nationalism, but in the sense of a people in relation to the world. This too has been going quite well.

(e) At Christmas in Montreal, I continued my efforts to get Trinidadians interested in the significance of the WFP [Workers' and Farmers' Party]. To me, this is the most significant event in the West Indies and Caribbean history since the uprisings in the Fyzabad,[38] and comparable only (but only comparable) to Fidel Castro's struggle and Cuba's struggle with the ever-grasping tentacles of colonialism and its bed-fellow, neo-colonialism. Now, with the WFP, *a Caribbean* is a distinct possibility.

By some odd twist, I wrote to get *We the People*[39] but apparently my letter and subscription did not get there. To date, I have not seen a copy of the paper. By the way have you seen C.L.R.'s articles in the Trinidad *Daily Mirror*, "The Rise and Fall of Kwame Nkrumah"?[40] If there are any spare copies, please send them along.

The above is not exactly a comprehensive account of our activities in this area, but I hope for now that it will suffice. Are any meetings of the Study Circle planned for this summer?[41] If so, when?

Now, to a more personal note. Do you get *New Left Review*, an English pseudo-Marxist publication of good, though distinctly intellectual, quality. The January–February issue has an essay in reply to E.P. Thompson's essay in the 1965 edition of *Socialist Register*.[42] The argument itself is valuable for the student of Marxism.

Well B., on to the meat of this letter. Obviously the WFP provides for us an excellent, nay unsurpassable, source of knowledge. Please give me a detailed account of its activities, success, and difficulties, and if possible send me a few of the back issues of *We the People*. If this is not possible, do not hesitate to say so, for I am always requesting something and giving so little, if anything. I shall make amends.

But B., I have something to say which is burning to be said. Could you on behalf of the C.L.R.J. Study Circle send a protest letter to the press and the P.M. of Trinidad, protesting the searching of C.L.R. at the airport on his return from England, and the rifling and humiliating search of George Weekes and George Bowrin[43] after their return from Cuba? There can be no question that these events, taken together, bid fair and augur the worst developments for the West Indies. What is most striking is the refusal of anyone to come forward and call public attention to this gross political persecution. I would be only too anxious to sign such a protest, and if you do so, please have no fear in attaching my name. I believe that this would be an excellent first practical step for the C.L.R.J.S.C.

And now what else? This copy of C.L.R.'s letter to you, I shall always keep. For those of us stricken with doubt about our future activities on the West Indian scene, C.L.R.'s words, strength of conviction, his absolute earnestness, and his undying vision of a Caribbean and a New World, make this letter an eternal keep-sake, and a well-spring of courage.

Truly B., my membership of the C.L.R.J.S.C. has been the greatest step forward for me. I shall always remember meeting you in Toronto. I hope too that you will not excuse my negligence in writing, but only accept it, in so far as you expect to see work that can justify it.

Now I must return to Babylon's work.

Peace and Love,
T.

ROBERT A. HILL to TIM HECTOR

319 Birchview Ave.
Toronto, Ontario
April 1, 1966

Dear Tim,

Greetings.

First of all, let me say how sorry I was to hear of your protracted illness. This certainly is not the side of the sea you want to get sick on. I hope that you are almost over it now and "up and down" once more.

It was a great pleasure to receive your deeply encouraging letter. I have made several copies and sent them out to our various centers—Montreal, Ottawa, New York, Detroit, and Britain. I have also sent C.L.R. a copy and expect that if he has time, we shall be receiving some reply.

Very *confidentially*, I don't think that C.L.R. James is having an easy time with his colleagues. I received a note from him saying that the political situation was more favorable than ever, but the party is having its growing pains. If you like, you can write him under the address (for security reasons) of Mr. Dalip Gopee Singh, Lyndon Street, Curepe, T[rini]dad. However, I would advise you against mentioning what I have told you, again for the same reasons.

I am currently preparing a limited mimeographed publication of C.L.R.'s *Notes on the Hegelian Dialectic*, which was written in 194[8] and which runs to well over 200 pages. Nothing comparable exists in any language, not just today but for the last fifty years. The cost of publication is

$80 plus and whatever you can do to help will be gladly appreciated. This will be a joint Study Circle effort.

Please let me know what your plans are for the summer. I have some very important lectures by C.L.R. James on tape which you might think of using for a West Indian group during the summer.[44]

Let me know if you are subscribing to *New World Quarterly*. George Lamming is editing a special Guyana Independence issue and has written desperately requesting our help.[45]

This is all for now. Thanks again.

Robert

C.L.R. JAMES to
MARTIN GLABERMAN & ROBERT A. HILL

D. Gopeesingh
63 Lyndon St.
Curepe, Trinidad
June 24, 1966

Dear M[artin] G[laberman] & R[obert] H[ill],

A most painful letter. I am not a complainer but it would be wrong not to…. we *can* win the election. The immediate consequences will be the political electrification of the whole Caribbean.

(2) The public and the disinterested intellectuals are depending heavily on me, on C.L.R. James, or as all point me out in the street, on C.L.R. With $10,000 in my hand I feel sure we can win, but that is not a political point I can make.

(3) My own colleagues take me for granted. Since my return, they have missed four weeks at $50.00 a week. Even when they pay me, I pay my own chauffer, private secretary, personal servant, gas, etc. I live by the charity of the Gopeesinghs. I make some money by writing. I spend every morning at it.

(4) I owe here $480.00 that I borrowed for the Party. Selma bears a burden too heavy for her. Not a single soul asks me a single word about her.

(5) I am sick of the whole business. I need $1000. Useless to try here, useless, ruinous. Not only do I see the immense possibilities for the whole Caribbean, but every day I feel more and more that if I left, the government and many would feel "that is that".

On the other hand, while I act on my own premises (and do not take a political step because of what others fail to do), I am scared stiff at falling ill again. I am living on the edge. Sometimes to leave the house I borrow

$1.00 from the maid to get gas. For the first time in a long life, I feel I can't take it.

If I get a stenotypist ($15.00 a day), I will send a political report and a copy of the play that I have finished.[46] It is a good play.

It is no use talking to the people I work with. It would only annoy them (they are the result of centuries of slavery and colonialism and ten years of [Eric] Williams). It would not only humiliate me, but [it would also] destroy my moral authority. My report will deal with all this but [I want] to give you an idea.

For Selma to accept the invitation (and leave her job), I had to borrow $200.00 which I have promised to repay, and the WFP did not pay me for the week I was away. I must either get some money and be free, or just clear out. I don't like the way I'm feeling at all. My health is not what it was and I don't think I should continue to submit myself to this unceasing strain.

I cannot help remembering that this transference from living in Britain and the United States to the political atmosphere of an undeveloped country has had some dreadful consequences.

Yours,
C.L.R. James

P.S. There are people here I can ask for money. But that will discredit the Party. I will do it only to leave.

Note from Robert A. Hill:

This letter from James makes a number of things obvious. First of all, what is involved here is not merely the success or failure of the political opposition to the most advanced form of neo-colonialism in the Caribbean. Involved is the survival of the man by whose ideas we profess to live and work. Sooner or later, most of us had to grow into this stage of struggle—it awaits all of us. For us in particular it begins with James. Those of us who wish to carry on from this early stage will know their duty to James and the Caribbean people now. It is as simple as that.

ROBERT A. HILL to MARTIN & JESSIE GLABERMAN

July 7, 1966

Dearest Marty and Jess,

Greetings.

Thanks to you for your letter and the copy of Nello's.

There is still no baby as yet from Diane but her parents have arrived and are staying with us. It rather brightens things up.

I have been badly shaken by the letter from Nello. Since I returned to Toronto, I have written him two full letters and there is still so much left to write about. But now I just don't know how to write. I have made copes of the letter and sent it out to the colleagues with a note attached. Who knows, perhaps they can do something to help. However, when I do write, I shall know what exactly to say: C.L.R. is not going to be any martyr to such worthlessness! Hence, *get out* and go back to London. It is not easy for one West Indian to say that to another, particularly for me. But at this stage it is not political possibilities that detain me—the very survival of the man hinges on what we do, or do not do. I don't wish to alarm anyone, but my reading of the letter implies far more than political impasse. I feel that he is quickly losing his strength.

The letter has convinced me further of sending the $600 (BWI). It will be $600 worth of freedom, not what he asked for but at least something he can support himself with. It is a horrible thought that, to even live, he has to look outside for help. Middleton[47] was here with me a couple of days ago and I made a statement that quite astonished him: from now on, anything that we do, we do on our own, *finally* and *completely*. We have to make a start somewhere, to bear responsibility for ourselves—*self-nourishment*. Funnily enough, I see the Afro-American movement learning the same lesson.

I received a letter from my uncle this week from Trinidad. He now wants to get his book written and wanted me to tell him when I would be heading home. Well, I had to tell him that the book on Garvey *stands*.[48] He will be glad, but I know that it will disappoint him. The letter ended with the question: "Please try and give me the answer to the vital question— what is to be done to depart from the traditional political path[?]"

You want to know what I did? I sent him the introduction to the 1844 Manuscripts in *Speak Out*.[49] There is no other answer. That man was one of the founders of the nationalist movement in the Caribbean, he lived through its most glorious moments, and today he writes to ask me: "what is to be done to depart from the traditional political path?" When *he* asks that question, I *know* that it is now not a question but profoundly a part of the consciousness of the Caribbean people. And only Marxism can explain it in its specific Caribbean context, exactly as Marx explained the past, present, and future in the unexciting days of 1844, of industrial man. Consider what I have said well and *see the position that you hold in the coming epoch of Caribbean revolution.*

I cleared the shipment of *New World*[50] today from the customs and will be sending you a couple of copies in the mail tomorrow. It is a magnificent achievement!

No luck with a job yet but still trying.

Give our love to all and write soon.

Love,
Robert

MARTIN GLABERMAN to FRANK MONICO

October 13, 1966

Dear Frank,[51]

We have just gotten through a fabulous week here—and in Montreal. First Montreal:

Jimmy was in Montreal from early Friday morning (2:30) to about 5:00pm Sat. afternoon. His main speech was Friday night, a beautiful job (the chairman, in the introduction, quoted at length from my speech on James at last year's conference on West Indian Affairs). He also participated on a panel on Saturday morning. Bobby Hill participated in another panel. There were quite a few West Indian Johnsonites[52] around. Jimmy also held three other meetings, more or less informal. Two on Friday afternoon with people around us and others, and a special one Saturday midday at which he taped a talk on Existentialism and Marxism. It was great to be able to represent the principal guest of the Conference.

We sold $200 worth of literature! We also have some pretty solid contacts: Hill in Toronto (who finished the Nevada[53]), Roberts in Montreal, Hector in Nova Scotia, plus others in Canada and in the W[est] I[ndies] who will be raising money, doing typing, etc. On Sunday, I had a meeting with some of these and reported on our Conference and we discussed problems of relations between us and joint work. Besides me, George, Diane, April, and Ross came from Detroit [and] William, for whom this was very important.[54] The old man was very glad to see him and gave him a tremendous boost—he will be developing the work on Existentialism.[55]

C.L.R., by the way, made it pretty clear that he wanted to come back to Canada for a lecture tour after his election is over (November 7) and stay for about two weeks. That will bring him much closer to home—Toronto, Windsor. I think the James Study Circle will arrange it. We will send you a copy of the Nevada. As to SC&WR [*State Capitalism and World Revolution*], I will have to hunt up a copy that we can spare. That Cuban edition of *Black Jacobins*: the problem is not copyright but paper shortage—they have to work out priorities—and it will be for Cuba, not for export. Still, it would be great if it comes off.[56]

With best regards,
Marty

MARTIN GLABERMAN to C.L.R. JAMES

November 14, 1966

Dear Nello,

I was shocked and surprised at the total defeat.[57] I did not expect a great victory (mostly, in the absence of any information about what was happening in Trinidad, because of the failure of the WFP to support a press, no matter how meager), but it did not seem unlikely that such a party, with support from people like Weekes, etc., would win a some seats. Was their overt intimidation? I would suspect, under the circumstances, that there was an undercurrent of feeling that—WFP would be fine, but with all this shouting Marxist, to elect WFP would be to invite the U.S. Marines. Not that crude, but nevertheless a factor in the election.[58]

Am I right in assuming that under the British parliamentary system the WFP, with no seats, has no legal status and is, for all practical purposes, dissolved, at least for five years? Does that put an end to your obligations to them (if not theirs to you)? What are your plans? I have not heard as yet from Robert, although I assume there will be no great difficulty in arranging lectures for you in Canada. We can arrange at least one meeting in Windsor (across the river from Detroit) either at the University or in the city, or both.

William has finished transcribing the Existentialism talk.[59] I have to check it over and then I will send it on to you. I finally made the breakthrough to getting paid for lectures to student groups at two universities. The Hungary lectures are just about over although there are two more to give, at Toronto and Ohio State U.[60] Next I begin to work on the introduction to SC&WR [*State Capitalism and World Revolution*]. Any suggestions you may have on subject, direction, etc. would be very welcome.

The contact with Kaufmann[61] on dialectic[s] will be made. William gave a wonderful talk introducing the Nevada and now he is leading a discussion group on it. I should note, by the way, that the air letter before the last from Trinidad had no message whatever on the inside.

I hope all is well with you personally. Please take care.

With very best wishes,

Marty

ALFIE ROBERTS to MARTIN GLABERMAN

2873 Bedford Rd.
Montreal 26
Canada
January 27, 1967

Dear Marty,

I regret not having been able to attend the conference,[62] but am hoping to pay a visit sometime in the summer.

The November issue of *Flambeau* is out, and among other things, it carried your eulogy of C.LR. at the University of Montreal Conference in 1965.[63] For the material and resources available, *Flambeau* is doing a fair job. As a matter of fact, the fellows are even thinking in terms of starting a newspaper in St. Vincent.

I sent them that last chapter of *Nkrumah Then and Now*—"Lenin and the Problem"[64]—and they are thinking of publishing it in the next issue— February. I also asked them to look into the possibility of publishing it as a pamphlet—getting an estimated cost for 500 or so copies and then communicating with you directly as to what can work out. The ball is on their lap, but [I] will keep at them.

C.L.R. did after all get to Detroit.[65] It must have been somewhat of a personal triumph for him over the State Department, and further, it must have been delightful to have been reunited with old colleagues on old but familiar soil.

I also have a copy of "Education, Agitation and Propaganda" to send.[66] I missed Franklyn[67] when he left for Detroit, and since then, I subsequently misplaced it at someone's house. But I have it to send now. Tell me whether one is sufficient!

You had also to check to see if you had an extra copy of *Hungary 56*;[68] I will be grateful to know if it can be obtained. Further, will it be possible to even obtain or borrow a copy of "The Americanization of Bolshevism."[69] I will be grateful to have one.

Lenin was truly an incredible person. I have been reading Vol. 7 & 8.[70]

Regards to all, including your family.
Alfie

ALFIE ROBERTS to C.L.R. JAMES

2873 Bedford Road
Montreal 26,
Canada
December 8, 1967

Dear C.L.R.,

I regret the long delay in replying, but do so now.

I must say at the outset, that I have *not* received the material you were supposed to have sent me.

The conference and its convention has come and gone, and I assume that you have been accurately apprised of its proceedings.

Things are rather dull around here at the moment, and I am still holding on at that job.

Guevara has passed on. A truly exemplary human being. Jagan[71] was here recently. Was proclaiming among other things the virtues of Peaceful Coexistence à la Russia. He is probably a decent and honest man but he did not give one much hope.

Williams has now more than ever bared his face. Yet there is absolutely no reason to despair.

Hope you are in best of health. Speak me fair to your dear wife.

Alfie

ALFIE ROBERTS to C.L.R. JAMES

2873 Bedford Road
Montreal 26
Canada
May 3, 1968

Dear C.L.R.,

We were very glad that you enjoyed your trip to Cuba. We would be very glad to hear your views on what you saw; what you thought of the Party and the principle of "Every Cook Can Govern,"[72] and whether this principle is being applied or projected in theory.

One or two of us are attempting to bring out a magazine called *Caribbean International Review*,[73] and I want to request your permission to reprint in part or in toto your article from *Nkrumah Then and Now* dealing with "The Revolution in Theory".[74] We want to reprint speeches or lectures like "A New View of W[est] I[ndian] History," "The W.I. Personality," and others. Further, I wonder if you would find it convenient to write an article or two on "The Law of Value, Economic Calculus, and Marxism," dealing with such questions as what is the law value? Did it operate in primitive society? Its (the law of value) operation during feudal times through the different stages of capitalism; whether it operates in a society in transition to socialism and communism; and also whether it will operate during or after the construction of socialism and communism: Could you differentiate between a commodity and a product; the relation between a commodity and a product; the relation between the operation of the law of value and economic calculation in a socialist generated economy? Then, tie in all this with a review of Part I of *Capital*, Vol. I and any other relevant section in the writings of Marx, Engels and Lenin, and especially Part IV of *Capital* Vol. III, CONVERSION OF COMMODITY-CAPITAL AND MONEY-CAPITAL INTO COMMERCIAL CAPITAL AND MONEY-DEALING CAPITAL (MERCHANT'S CAPITAL); Part V (Chapters XVI–XXIII), *Capital*, FLPH Moscow.[75]

Thanking you in anticipation of your co-operation. Please speak me fair to your dear wife and best of health to you.

Respectfully yours,
Alphonso Roberts

P.S. The book "Speeches &Writing of Guevara," ed. by Gerassi, seems quite good.[76]

ROSIE DOUGLASS to C.L.R. JAMES

2052 Closse, Suite 10
Montreal, Quebec
June 9, 1968

Dear Mr. James,

The Congress of Black Writers Committee was formed in Montreal by a group of West Indians (English and French-speaking) for the specific purpose of organizing a Conference of Black writers, scholars, and politicians in the coming October, in which an attempt will be made to trace the whole history of the Black liberation struggle in a series of popular lectures. One of the crying necessities at the present stage of the struggle, we feel, is the need for the Black masses to develop a sense of their own history, of the role which their own people have played in the whole history of Black-White confrontation. Such a total conception of the development of the Black struggle seems to us absolutely vital as a means of giving moral strength to the concrete political struggle now being waged. Black people must begin to see themselves as the subjects, rather than the objects, of history—the active creators, rather than the passive sufferers, of historical events.

The Conference will be held on the weekend of 11th to 14th, and the program, which we hope to publish and make available to a wider audience eventually, will be as follows:

Theme: TOWARDS THE SECOND EMANCIPATION – The Dynamics of Black Liberation.

Topics:

A. The Origin and Consequences of the Black-White Confrontation:

1) The History and Economics of Slavery in the New World.

2) The Psychology of Subjection – Race Relations in the U.S.A.

B. The Germs of Modern Black Awareness

3. The Haitian Revolution and the History of Slave Revolt

4. The Fathers of the Modern Revolt: Garvey, Du Bois, etc.

C. The Revaluation of the Past:

5. The Origins and Significance of Negritude

6. The Civilizations of Ancient Africa.

7. The Contributions of the Afro-American to American History and Civilization.

D. Perspectives for the Future:

8. Racial Discrimination in Britain and the Way Out.

9. Black Power in the U.S.A.

10. The Black Revolution, the Third World, and Capitalism

On behalf of the Congress Committee, I would like to take this opportunity to invite you to be one of our guest speakers at the Conference, and to address us on the first and third topics of the program: "The History and Economics of Slavery..." and "The Haitian Revolution and the History of Slave Revolt". We hope that you will be able to accept our invitation, and we shall be grateful for any advice, suggestions, or opinions that you may have to give us on the program. Looking forward to hearing from you as early as possible.

Yours sincerely,
Rosie Douglas, Chairman.

P.S. We would like to invite a prominent member of the Black community in England to address us on the eighth topic, but we would like your advice as to who you think would be best in a position to satisfy our requirements. Ideally, he should be actively involved in some organization or union. Could you let us have an early answer on this?

C.LR. JAMES to ROSIE DOUGLASS

20 Staverton Road
London NW2
June 27, 1968

Miss [sic] Rosie Douglas
Chairman
Congress of Black Writers
2052 Close – Suite 10
Montreal, Quebec
Canada

Dear Miss [sic] Douglas,

I believe your proposal to be one of extreme importan[ce] and timeliness, and I will be glad to take part in it.

First of all, however, I want to be absolutely certain not only that the Congress will take place, but that arrangements would be made without difficulty for my transport there and journey back home. I say this because on the last occasion that I came to Canada, I had no personal trouble but was told that BOAC or some company had promised a free passage for someone like myself, but when they heard that the person involved was C.L.R. James, they hastily said that they would not be able to give the passage and some money had to be found. I mention this to prevent any misunderstanding or embarrassment on either side. That being in order, I will be glad to come and wish the conference every success.

May I suggest that the subject on which I am to speak be phrased a little differently; for example, A1) Slavery in the New World, and B3) The

Haitian Revolution and Slave Revolt in the New World. I hope that your committee will approve of this suggestion for their consideration.

Hoping to hear from you soon so that I can rearrange my affairs and have everything in order.

Very truly yours,
C.L.R. James

APPENDIX

APPENDIX I
C.L.R. James: The Man and His Work

Mr. Hill, delegates to this West Indian Conference, friends.*

I am deeply grateful to the Conference for this opportunity to present this report. I first saw C.L.R. James in 1938 when he came to the United States on a lecture tour. I saw him keep the rapt attention of an audience of several hundred people in New York City as he lectured for three hours on the British Empire. I last saw James about a year and a half ago at his flat in London. We had several days of intense discussion on the Negro question in the United States. My wife and I had just returned from a trip to continental Europe and one of the most delightful evenings I have ever spent in my life was spent listening to James discuss the long list of statues and other works of art that the traveler in Europe is supposed to see. He brought to life Michelangelo and the days of the Medici in Florence, and he not only brought them to life, but made them most relevant to our day.

Between these two occasions, I have seen James lecture on the work of Herman Melville to an academic audience in New York and to an audience of workers in Detroit, and keep them equally enthralled. But what I associate most in my own mind with C.L.R. James is not so much his ability to give to others of his own store of knowledge and wisdom, but rather his ability to draw out others' knowledge of themselves and to develop the talents and abilities that are in them. In his writings, in his lectures, in his conversations with individuals, the outstanding characteristic is the development of the reader or listener.

There are people in many parts of the world who are familiar with the work of C.L.R. James. Apart from the West Indies, there are sharecrop-

* This speech was delivered Université de Montréal by Martin Glaberman during the First Annual Meeting of the Caribbean Conference Committee, "The Shaping of the Future of the West Indies," October 9, 1965

pers in southeast Missouri in the United States whom James worked to organize in the 1940s. This was twenty years before Martin Luther King and the Student Non-violent Coordinating Committee began their work in the South. There are South Africans who secretly used *The Black Jacobins* as an underground textbook in the struggle for freedom. There are cricket-lovers in England who found their experience of that sport deepened and enriched, whose experience of modern industrial society was recorded and their understanding made more profound by the writing of C.L.R. James. In many countries, there are thinkers, writers, teachers, and politicians whose education and training came in part from James personally, and from his works.

Yet, despite all this, the significance of James and of his work is little known and hardly understood. In part, this is because much of James's work is unpublished and out or print. But more important than this is the tremendous range of his interests and his accomplishments. Many people have seen the trees which he has planted, but few have seen the forest.

James has written a novel, a play which was produced in London, and a number of short stories. He has written a history of the rise and fall of the Communist International. He was the first to write on the case of West Indian independence. His *The Black Jacobins*, the story of the first successful slave revolt, was written in the cause of African independence. He was one of that small band in England, the African Bureau, who fought and educated for the freedom of Africa when to most men it was only a dream. George Padmore was the head of the African Bureau, James was the editor of its paper, Jomo Kenyatta was a member, Kwame Nkrumah became a member.

But his interests and his talents were universal, not to be limited by a nation, a continent, or a race. His translation of Souvarine's biography of Stalin[1] and his studies of the Soviet Union and of economics led to the development of a theoretical point of view which made possible a serious understanding and critique of the Russian dictatorship, a point of view which is fully in the revolutionary socialist tradition and retains for that tradition its democratic essence. His study of, and writings on, modern industrial society have illuminated the social process for many who would otherwise have been lost in the confusion so characteristic of those who think about the problems of the modern world. And his work is characterized, not by the dullness of the scholar's ivory tower, but by the fire of the participant; not by the supposed impartiality of the academic, not by the pessimism of the small in heart and mind, but by the optimism of one who can see the broad historical process and can see, above all, the life, the talents, the contribution to freedom and to history of the millions of ordinary people who inhabit our planet.

James wrote a study of Melville, the American author, which provided a unique interpretation both of Melville and his works and of modern American society. This book, *Mariners, Renegades, and Castaways* is now one of the standard texts of Melville criticism. He has used his knowledge of Shakespeare to illuminate the modern political personality, and to rekindle interest in Shakespeare himself, in broadcasts for the BBC and an unpublished manuscript on Shakespeare and Lenin. In *Beyond a Boundary*, through his understanding of cricket, he has helped both West Indians and Englishmen to better understand themselves and their cultures. It has been called by English reviewers the finest book on sports ever written.

In his writings on and participation in the struggles of Negro Americans, James has put forward conceptions of that struggle which cut away narrow ideological and group interests and place the Negro American at the center of the historical stage in the United States, as the most revolutionary of America.

It is easy to believe that this tremendous range of work and thought reflects an individual genius who has simply exercised his talents in many fields. That would be only a half-truth and therefore wrong, because the many and various questions that have occupied James during most of this century are not separate and unrelated, but are parts of a unified totality. The unity comes from a fundamental philosophical point of view which can be described as dialectical; that the world is torn by contradictions, the contradictions are the struggles between men, and that men, knowingly or unknowingly, make their own history; and that the fundamental thread that runs through and illuminates the history of mankind is the continuing struggle of the great masses of ordinary people for liberty.

We want to mention two books. One, unpublished, is called *Notes on the Dialectic*. It was written in 1948 as an effort to apply the Hegelian and Marxian dialectic to the understanding of our own time. It is both philosophical and concrete, and so perceptive was this philosophical tool that eight years before the Hungarian Revolution, James was able to indicate, in abstract and theoretical form, what the Hungarians demonstrated in life; that the domination of the traditional political party over the masses of the industrial countries had come to an end and men would, for the first time, take their fate directly into their own hands.

The second book is *Modern Politics*.[2] It was the result of six lectures delivered at the Public Library in Port of Spain, Trinidad. It was published as a book in Trinidad and immediately suppressed, so that only two or three copies are now in the possession of the author and his friends. The book presents the panoramic history of the Western world in a way that is understandable to anyone. It shows the struggle for human freedom continuing in all ages and on all continents. And it offers to the reader the means to understand his own history and, what is more important, the means to make his own history. It is small wonder that the book was suppressed—but it will be republished.

It should be clear that it is my opinion that C.L.R. James is a world figure of the greatest importance. He is, in a very real sense, a citizen of the world. But he is, because of that, very much a West Indian. It is not an accident that such a man was born in Trinidad. It is part of the contribution of the West Indies to the modern world. The West Indies has what is essentially a European culture. And this is embodied in C.L.R. James to a degree that would be difficult to match. But unlike Europe, the West Indian intellectual has not experienced the unparalleled catastrophes and defeats that have been the fate of Europe in this century. Two world wars, the defeat of revolutions in the major countries of Europe, the barbarism of Nazism and fascism and Stalinist totalitarianism, all this has made of the European intellectual a cynic and a pessimist. As a result, to many Europeans, the narrow view has seemed more rewarding than the broad view.

In C.L.R. James is embodied both the totality of Western culture and the optimism and fire of a people who have not been defeated by history, who have still to make their own history. He is not the least that the West Indies has contributed to the world.

APPENDIX II
C.L.R. James: Beyond the Mournful Silence

Mr. Chairman, comrades.*

Today, at this conference of your organization, I represent a scattered group of West Indians who have found in your work and perspectives something that corresponds to the necessities of our age. Together we are struggling for some perspective on the historical development of the New World, the civilization which brought us jointly into existence and which faces today its most crucial test under the impact of the Negro struggle and the emancipation of the Caribbean. This stage of our common history I choose to call "beyond the mournful silence."

At another level, I represent the new generation of Caribbean men and women who have commenced the struggle to extend the experience and the vision of a free, united Caribbean people. I emphasize "the experience and vision" so that you might find a new dimension of meaning in the man who founded this organization, and under whose name we carry out our work, C.L.R. James. The world of circumstance for James was the United States, but it was a Caribbean necessity that drove his work forward, the necessity for the Caribbean man to universalize himself in the struggle of man everywhere. That is the necessity that continues to drive my generation forward, and today it comes back to you. Facing Reality and the James Study Circle meet therefore not merely on the common ground of precedence; our joint efforts might be termed the "undying vision" of the New World civilization.

So that you may better understand yourselves and grasp the significance of your place in this historical development, something which you need

---

*   This speech was delivered by Robert A. Hill at Facing Reality's Annual Conference in Detroit, Michigan, September 17, 1966.

continually to deepen and extend, I shall tell you how the James Study Circle came into existence. On the basis of a profound study of your work and many long hours of reflection, it became clear that not only were the ideas of James the only hope of Caribbean transformation, but what also was even clearer was your exemplification of method as the only certain basis on which we could drive ourselves into the antagonism of Caribbean society. As "a small group of people acting together in the midst of the vast confusion that the world is in at the present time," we have found something that corresponds *in general* to the great tasks that lay before us. I know that you all would be greatly surprised at the height to which many of us have reached in the last year. On the other hand, while we continue to learn more from you, it is not inconceivable that you here in America will in the future be able to learn from our work when it is transferred to its Caribbean home.

It would be only proper for you to ask, what do these people *concretely* represent in their own countries? In his "Vision of Caribbean Society Tomorrow and Today," James has said: "I expect to see such parties as I have described coming into existence, or groups establishing in principle the necessity for such parties."[1] The latter is the reality of our work in the present: to establish in principle the new stage of Caribbean history inside the body of the old. And that, if I am correct, is precisely how you have been able to make the impact on American society that you have since 1941.

In the same article James goes on to say: "Some West Indians love the mess and acquire remarkable competence in sweeping up not only the crumbs on the table, but those on the floor. But they have no independent future."[2] Elsewhere in *Marxism for the Sixties*, James affirms that "it is necessary for a Marxist to have some criterion of judgment, and that criterion is the inevitability of socialism. That is the result of the Marxist application of Hegelian dialectic."[3] I leave it to you to judge where you stand in the movement of history today. The people I represent here today know where they stand.

The work of the Study Group, apart from its continuing probing of the past degeneration into the present, is now focused on the preparation of a book, *Manifesto for Change in the Caribbean*.[4] In addition to that, we are also at the center of the work on the Second Annual "Conference on West Indian Affairs," to be held in Montreal on October 7–9 at McGill University. We are also participating in the promotion of the Caribbean journal of criticism, *New World*, which I recommend to you as an invaluable guide to the direction in which Caribbean thought and experience are moving.

There are other associates who would have liked being here today but who, unfortunately, could not be. From them, I bring you greetings and best wishes for your important deliberations. What you do, not only at this conference, but in the future, is an inescapable part of their development. Be not afraid that your voice will not be heard.

Thank you.

APPENDIX III
On the Banning of Walter Rodney from Jamaica

You will allow me to be somewhat individualistic in the approach that I take to this question.* Most of all, I want to speak of Walter Rodney, not only as a person persecuted but also as the subject, the necessary subject, for a protest. I want to let you know that in West Africa, in East Africa recently, and in London among circles interested in Africa, Mr. Walter Rodney is already noted as a distinguished scholar in African affairs. He has not written much, but what he has done shows an invasion of a field that has either been neglected or spoken about without sufficient knowledge—the state of Africa before the slave trade began.[1] This has been recognized as of tremendous importance to us who are concerned with our own origins and the impact of the African race upon ancient and modern civilizations.

Already he has made his impact in that sphere and, as I say, on two sides of the African continent. And in London, I hear his work spoken about by people who understand it and its importance. It is a scandal that the University of the West Indies has seen fit to carry out this political activity against him. That is the first point I want to make.

The second point I want to make is a negative point. I hear people speaking about things in the Caribbean and elsewhere and I repeatedly hear the remarkable initials, C.I.A. Now it is not for me to say what the C.I.A. has done or what it will do. What I want to say here tonight is that I do not see the slightest reason for detaching the full responsibility of what has taken place in the Caribbean as a whole and passing it on to the United

---

* This Speech was delivered by C.L.R. James at a Montreal Rally against the banning of Walter Rodney from Jamaica where he taught at the University of the West Indies. Rodney was expelled following his participation in the Congress of Black Writers in Montreal. The rally took place at Sir George Williams University (now Concordia), October 18, 1968. Another rally was held in Ottawa a few days later.

States.[2] The persons responsible for this are the political rulers of the Caribbean territories. And what I want to do this evening is to show you that what has taken place has been anticipated.

I have here a book, *Party politics in the West Indies*. (This is not an advertisement because I don't think that they are still for sale.) I will read certain passages from it to show you the reasons why I left the Caribbean. I knew what was going to happen and this was no surprise. It is not the erratic behavior of some individual. It is characteristic of a whole tribe and race of people who are now misgoverning the West Indies. Now, I will read this passage:

> Politics is not an activity. Not merely to support something or somebody. It is to discuss and plan and to carry out some program and perspective of our own and then to judge how far you have succeeded or failed, and why. It does not limit a government. The more of this the people do, the bolder and more comprehensive the plans of a Government can be, the more it can defy its enemies. Otherwise as sure as day you find you have to shoot them down.[3]

In other words, this shooting down of the population is not an accident. It is not some method of government of the present rulers of the Caribbean countries. Here it is: "Otherwise," if you don't govern properly, if you do not develop a democratic government of the people, if you do not let a new people, formerly slaves, realize that independence must mean something to them then, "as sure as day you find you have to shoot them down."[4]

I am going to read another passage:

> Some readers may remember seeing the movie of the night of the independence of Ghana, and hearing Nkrumah choose at that moment to talk about the African Personality. This was to be the aim of the Ghanaian people with independence. Is there a West Indian personality? Is there a West Indian nation? What is it? What does it lack? What must it have? The West Indian middle classes keep far from these questions. The job, the car, the fridge, the trip abroad, preferably under government auspices and at government expense, these seem to be the beginning and end of their preoccupations. What foreign forces, social classes, ideas, do they feel themselves allied with or attached to? Nothing. What in their own history do they look back to as a beginning of which they are the continuation? I listen to them, I read their speeches and their writings. "Massa Day Done" seems to be the extreme limit of their imaginative concepts

of West Indian nationalism [*James: Massa day done and they have become 'massa'*]. Today nationalism is under fire and every people has to consider to what extent its nationalism has to be mitigated by international considerations. Of this as of so much else the West Indian middle class is innocent. What happens after independence? For all you can hear from them, independence is a dead end. Apart from the extended opportunities of jobs with the government, independence is as great an abstraction as was Federation. We achieve independence and they continue to govern.[5]

But it is not going to stop there—they continue to misgovern the country and already we see in Jamaica—and I am saying this is going to happen all over the Caribbean—a violent confrontation between the backward reactionary government that still is living in the 17th century with a population that is part of the 20th century. That is the problem that is going to explode all over the Caribbean. We must be ready for it.

Before I sit down I want to bring one more point before you, and this is something that I was told by a man for whom I have the greatest personal respect and affection—George Lamming. He told me this story, and he told it to me with a significant purpose in mind. George was in Barbados, his home country, and [Frank] Walcott,[6] head of the trade union movement, asked him to speak to trade unionists. So all the trade unionists heard Mr. Lamming, a great writer, was going to speak. There were thousands of them and they had to put loud speakers outside.

And George spoke. He spoke about the Conference in Berlin. He was speaking about Black people and how in Berlin, Bismarck beat them back and European governments divided up Africa—"That is for me and that is for you, and you take that." And he, Lamming, drew the development from these days up to 1958 when there took place the first Conference of the Independent African states. George spoke about the development of the Negro people, of the Barbadian people, of African Independence, etc. There was tremendous applause, a great deal of excitement and enthusiasm. George went back home.

George never made any sort of reference to any Barbadian politicians. He did not say he wished to stay in Barbados to make politics. But after that speech—the next day—the question from Barbadian politicians and their friends was "George, when are you leaving?" They did not want anybody to tell Barbadians that they had an important history. The mere fact that

George had spoken to them about the history of Black people and the strife that we had met during the previous seventy or eighty years was enough to get them frightened and ask, "George, when are you leaving Barbados?"

So, Rodney is in difficulties because he is telling the people something about the history of Africa, history that has been much neglected. I think that it is not only important, but also highly significant that we not only say what we think but also, by resolutions and in other ways, register our disapproval, not only of what has happened to Rodney, but also the way that the educated classes in the Caribbean are misgoverning our poor countrymen.

Thank you very much.

Notes

INTRODUCTION

1   David Scott, "The Sovereignty of the Imagination: An Interview with George Lamming," *Small Axe: A Journal of Criticism*, 6 (2), September 2002, 164.

2   Selma James, interviewed by David Austin, audio recording, London, England, 11 March 2004.

3   Antonio Gramsci, *Selections from the Prison Notebooks* (New York: International Publishers, 1980), 5–6.

4   Edward Said, *Representations of the Intellectual* (New York: Vintage Books, 1996), 62.

5   Dave Renton mentions the comparison between James and Hegel in his *C.L.R. James: Cricket's Philosopher King* (London: Haus Books, 2007), 7. See C.L.R. James, *Notes on Dialectics: Hegel-Marx-Lenin* (London: Allison & Busby Ltd., 1980). For an assessment of Hegel and Aristotle in James's 1963 revised edition of *The Black Jacobins* see David Scott, *Conscripts of Modernity: The Tragedy of Colonial Enlightenment* (Durham: Duke University Press, 2004). The comparisons between James and Plato appear in numerous places but was perhaps first mentioned in a review blurb on the jacket of *The Black Jacobins* in which James is described as a Black Plato by *The Times*, but the "Black Plato" comparison was also raised in a 1984 interview to which James responded that "when people call me a 'Black Plato' they mean to say that I have touched various subjects with a certain effect. But I am very aware of the vast distance that lies between the original, seminal work of Plato and Aristotle and what I have been able to do at the present time." When asked whether he liked the label he initially replied, "Of course not," but then went on to say, "I don't *like* it, I don't *dislike* it. I just pay no attention to it." (Anon., "An Audience with C.L.R. James," *Third World Book Review*, 1(2) 1984.)

6   See C.L.R. James, *Notes on Dialectics: Hegel-Marx-Lenin* (London: Allison & Busby Ltd., 1980), John H. McClendon III, *C.L.R. James Notes on Dialectics: Left Hegelianism or Marxism Leninism* (Lanham, MD: Lexington Books, 2005), and David Scott, *Conscripts of Modernity.*

7   Thomas R. Martin, *Ancient Greece: From Prehistoric to Hellenistic Times* (New Haven & London: Yale Nota Bene 2000), 185.

8   For an extract of *Preface to Criticism* see C.L.R. James, "Preface to Criticism," in *The C.L.R. James Reader* (Oxford, UK: Blackwell Publishers, 1995).

9   Cornelius Castoriadis, James's former collaborator and founder of the French political group Civilization or Barbarism says that, although he is Greek, it was James who first pointed out to him the significance of Ancient Greece for contemporary problems. See Cornelius Castoriadis, "C.L.R.

James and the Fate of Marxism," in *C.L.R. James: His Intellectual Legacies*, eds. Selwyn R. Cudjoe and William E. Cain, (Amherst: University of Massachusetts Press, 1995), 277.

10   C.L.R. James, *Every Cook Can Govern: A Study of Democracy in Ancient Greece: Its Meaning for Today* (Detroit: Bewick Editions, 1992 [1956]), 18. Anon., "An Audience with C.L.R. James," *Third World Book Review*, 1(2) 1984.

11   According to James, "In the early days, Greek slavery did not occupy a very prominent place in the social life and economy of Greece. The slave was for the most part a household slave. Later, the slaves grew in number until they were at least as many as the number of citizens. In later years," he continues, "slavery developed to such a degree, with the development of commerce, industry, etc., that it degraded free labor. And it is to this extraordinary growth of slavery and the consequent degradation of free labor that Engels attributes to the decline of the great Greek democracy." As for women, James states that recent writers have challenged the idea that women in Ancient Greece were mere child-bearers and housekeepers and that "we believe that before long, the world will have a more balanced view of how women lived in the Greek Democracy." (James, *Every Cook Can Govern*, 15–17.)

12   Ibid., 19, and Matthew Quest, "Legislating the Caribbean General Will: The Late Political Thought of Tim Hector, 1929–2002," *The C.L.R. James Journal*, 13(1), Spring 2007, 220–221.

13   Hannah Arendt, *The Promise of Politics* (New York: Schocken Books, 2005), 76.

14   C.L.R. James, "The Artist in the Caribbean," *C.L.R. James: The Future in the Present* (London: Allison & Busby, 1977), 187 and C.L.R. James, "Tomorrow and Today: A Vision," *New World: Guyana Independence Issue*, 2(3), 1966, 86–87.

15   Ibid., 189.

16   C.L.R. James, "Kanhai: A Study in Confidence," *New World: Guyana Independence Issue*, 2(3), 1966, 14–15.

17   For an analysis of how Caribbean intellectuals have engaged Ancient Greece see Emily Greenwood, "Classics and the Atlantic Triangle: Caribbean Readings of Greece and Rome Via Africa," *Forum of Modern Language Studies*, 1(4), 2004, 365–376.

18   Robert A. Hill and Barbara Blair, "Introduction," *Marcus Garvey: Life and Lessons* (Berkley: University of California Press, 1987), xxxiv.

19   Ibid., xli.

20   Eric Williams, "Trinidad and Tobago: International Perspectives," *Freedomways*, 4(3), Summer 1964, 331. See also Eric Williams, "The Case for Party Politics in the Trinidad and Tobago," in, *Eric E. Williams Speaks: Essays on Colonialism and Independence*, ed. Selwyn R. Cudjoe (Wellesley, Mass: Calaloux Publications, 1993), 204–205.

21   Ibid., 339.

22   Ibid., 340. In the same Caribbean special issue of *Freedomways* in which Williams's article appeared, James also contributed an article which presented an entirely different image of Trinidad and the entire Caribbean. James noted the indirection and the lack of vision of Eric Williams and other Caribbean governments; that "Caribbean politics consists essentially of the capacity to administer the old colonial system either by means of the brutality of Trujillo or the democratic forms of Trinidad and Tobago or Jamaica." See C.L.R. James, "Parties, Politics and Economics in the Caribbean," *Freedomways*, 4(3), Summer 1964, 315.

23   Robert Brown and Cheryl Johnson, "An interview with Derek Walcott," 216–17 in Robert D. Hammer, *Epic of the Dispossessed: Derek Walcott's Omeros* (Columbia, Missouri: University of Missouri Press, 1997), 1.

24   See Louis James, "The Necessity of Poetry," *New World: Guyana Independence Issue*, 2(3), 1966, 113–114.

25   Anon., "An Audience with C.L.R. James," *Third World Book Review*, 1(2) 1984.

26   Paget Henry, *Caliban's Reason: Introducing Afro-Caribbean Philosophy* (New York: Routledge, 2000), 50.

27   Ibid., 53.

28   Ibid., 61.

29   Nicosia Shakes, "Legitimizing Africa in Jamaica," in *After Man, Towards Human: Critical Essays on Sylvia Wynter*, ed. Anthony Bogues (Kingston, JA and Miami: Ian Randle Publishers, 2006), 301.

30   C.L.R. James, "Appendix: From Toussaint L'Ouverture to Fidel Castro," in *The Black Jacobins: Toussaint L'Ouverture and the San Domingo Revolution* (London: Allison & Busby, 1980 [1963]), 399.

31   Ibid., 394.

32   Angus Calder, "A Place for All at the Rendezvous of Victory," *Third World Book Review*, 1(2) 1984.

33   Ibid.

34   James Millette, "Doctrines of Imperial Responsibility," *New World: Guyana Independence Issue*, 2(3), 1966, 84.

35   Kenneth John, Baldwin King and Cheryl L.A. King (eds.), *Quest for Caribbean Unity: Beyond Colonialism* (Madison, NJ: Kings-SVG, 2006), ix.

36   See Alphonso Roberts, "On Constitutional Proposals," *Flambeau* no. 4, April 1966; "Why We Must Think for Ourselves," *Flambeau* no. 6, November 1966, and "The Rights of the People Must Remain Inviolate," *Flambeau* no. 7, March 1967.

37   David Scott, "The Archaeology of Black Memory: An Interview with Robert A. Hill," *Small Axe: A Journal of Criticism* 3(1), 1999, 94–95. For a detailed account of the rise and fall of the West Indian Federation see F.A. Hoyos, *Grantley Adams and the Social Revolution* (London and Basingstoke: Macmillan, 1974) and C.L.R. James, *Federation: "We Failed Miserably", How and Why* (San Juan: Vedic Enterprises Ltd., 1962).

38   Scott, "The Archaeology of Black Memory: An Interview with Robert A. Hill," 96.

39   Ibid and Robert Hill and Alfie Roberts, discussion, audio recording, August 24, 1995. Alfie Roberts Institute. See also Obika Gray, *Radicalism and Social Change in Jamaica, 1960–1972* (Knoxville: University of Tennessee Press, 1991), 87–114.

40   Robert Hill and Alfie Roberts both studied political science, Hill eventually at the University of Toronto and Roberts at Sir George Williams University before pursuing graduate studies at Carleton University in Ottawa, Ontario. Franklyn Harvey already had a degree in engineering from the University of the West Indies and was pursuing a graduate degree in urban planning at McGill University when he joined the group, and Anne Cools studied social sciences at McGill. Tim Hector was "the lone wolf" at Acadia University in Wolfville, Nova Scotia where he pursued a degree in philosophy.

41   Ibid., 67.

42   See David Austin, "All Roads Led to Montreal: Black Power, the Caribbean, and the Black Radical Tradition in Canada," *The Journal of African American History*, vol. 92, 2007.

43   Robin Winks, *The Blacks in Canada* (Montreal: McGill-Queens Press, 1997 [1971]), 438. See also Dorothy A. Williams, *The Road to Now: A History of Blacks in Canada* (Montreal: Véhicule Press, 1997), 105. The population estimates for Montreal vary between 7, 000 Black residents in 1961 and 50, 000 Blacks in 1968, though the latter figure is believed to be a serious overestimation (Williams, *Blacks in Montreal*, 65).

44   Pierre Vallières, "Quebec: Nationalism and the Working Class," *Monthly Review*, vol. 16, no. 10, February 1965, 597. For an account of this unique period in Quebec history and the impact of anti-colonial thinkers, particularly Frantz Fanon, on the Montreal left see Malcolm Reid, *The*

Shouting Singpainters: A Literary and Political Account of Quebec Revolutionary Nationalism (New York, 1972).

45   Denis Forsythe, "By Way of Introduction: The Sir George Williams Affair," in *Let the Niggers Burn: The Sir George Williams Affair and its Caribbean Aftermath*, ed. Denis Forsythe (Montreal: Black Rose Books-Our Generation Press, 1971), 10.

46   Walter Rodney, *Walter Rodney Speaks: The Making of an African Intellectual* (Trenton: Africa World Press, 1990), 27.

47   Alfie Roberts, *A View for Freedom: Alfie Roberts Speaks on the Caribbean, Cricket, Montreal, and C.L.R. James* (Montreal: The Alfie Roberts Institute, 2005), 71.

48   Ibid., 72.

49   Anne Walmsley, *The Caribbean Artists Movement, 1966–1972: A Literary and Cultural History* (London: New Beacon Books Ltd., 1992).

50   See Roberts, *A View for Freedom*, 62. For a general account of New World's activities see Denis Benn, *The Caribbean: An Intellectual History, 1774–2003* (Kingston and Miami: Ian Randle Publishers, 2004), 122–151.

51   Roberts, *A View for Freedom*, 76. Guests included George Lamming, C.L.R. James, Jan Carew, Norman Girvan, Austin Clarke, Orlando Patterson, Lloyd Best, Richard B. Moore, M.G. Smith, and calypso singer The Mighty Sparrow.

52   See "Introduction: Recovering the Radical Black Female Subject: Anti-Imperialism, Feminism, and Activism" in Carole Boyce Davies, *Left of Marx: The Political Life of Black Communist Claudia Jones* (Durham and London: Duke University Press, 2008). See also Rhoda Reddock, *Elma Francois: Negro Welfare Cultural and Social Association and the Workers' Struggle for Change in the Caribbean in the 1930's* (London: New Beacon Books, 1988), and Michelle Ann Stephens, *Black Empire: The Masculine Global Imaginary of Caribbean Intellectuals in the United States, 1914–1962* (Durham and London: Duke University Press, 2005).

53   Anne Cools, "Womanhood," in Black Spark Edition of the *McGill Free Press*, February 1971, 8. See also David Austin, "An Embarrassment of Omissions, or Rewriting the Sixties: The Case of the Caribbean Conference Committee," in *New World Coming: The Sixties and the Shaping of Global Consciousness* (Toronto: Between the Lines, 2009).

54   George Lamming, "West Indian People," *New World*, vol. II, no. 2, 1966, 63. This edition of *New World* also includes a resume of the October 1965 conference.

55   Martin Glaberman to Alfie Roberts, August 22, 1965, Robert Hill to Martin Glaberman, July 6, 1965, and Martin Glaberman to C.L.R. James July 12, 1965. See Antillean [Alfie Roberts], "On Guevara's Message to the People of the World," *Speak Out*, November 1967 and James Abeng [Robert Hill], "Marcus Garvey—Yesterday and Today," *Speak Out*, January 1967. We know Antillean is Alfie Roberts because of a letter from Roberts to Glaberman dated September 27, 1967 in which he mentions the article. Robert Hill's essay on Garvey also appears under his name in a CCC bulletin under the title "Marcus Garvey: Yesterday and Today," *Caribbean Symposium: West Indian Nation in Exile*, October 6–8, 1967.

56   Robert Hill to Alfie Roberts, 21 June 1966, Alfie Roberts Institute.

57   See David Austin, "An Embarrassment of Omissions, or Rewriting the Sixties: The Case of the Caribbean Conference Committee" and Robert A. Hill's "Rejoinder" (unpublished, 1969) in response to A.W. Singham, "C.L.R. James on The Black Jacobin Revolution in San Domingo: Notes Toward a Theory of Black Polities," *Savacou* 1(1) 1970.

58   When asked to describe what had been his greatest contribution, James proposed that his "contributions have been, number one, to clarify and extend the heritage of Marx and Lenin. And number two, to explain and expand the idea of what constitutes the new society." Asked what he considered to be his "most important work," he replied that, in light of the Solidarity movement

in Poland that was dismantling Stalinism, *Notes on Dialectics* was his unequivocal choice. C.L.R. James, "Interview," in *C.L.R. James: His Life and Work*, ed. Paul Bhule (London: Allison and Busby, 1986), 164.

59   Martin Glaberman to Selma James, October 16, 1966, [Glaberman, WSU Box 8-5].

60   Martin Glaberman to Selma James, October 16, 1966, [Glaberman, WSU Box 8-5].

61   Derek Walcott, "A Tribute to C.L.R. James," in eds. Selwyn R. Cudjoe and William E. Cain, *C.L.R. James: His Intellectual Legacies* (Amherst: University of Massachusetts Press, 1995), 34.

62   Hector is referring to the June 1937 strike by oilfield workers in Fyzabad, Trinidad. The sit-in quickly evolved into widespread unrest and rioting across the island when police repression was used to break up what was initially a peaceful protest. This period marked the birth of the trade union movement in Trinidad. For details on this and other labor rebellions in the region in the 1930s see O. Nigel Bolland, *On the March: Labour Rebellions in the British Caribbean, 1934–39* (Kingston, JA: Ian Randle Publishers/London, U.K.: James Currey Publishers, 1995).

63   Alfie Roberts, *A View for Freedom*, 70–71.

64   Scott, "The Sovereignty of the Imagination: An Interview with George Lamming," 140.

65   Selma James to Martin Glaberman, circ. July 1965, [Glaberman, WSU Box 7-12].

66   Martin Glaberman to C.L.R. James, 12 July 1965, [Glaberman, WSU Box 7-12].

67   Selma James to Martin Glaberman, July 1965, [Glaberman, WSU Box 7-12]. Again in fairness to Glaberman, Hill's "caution" was written a month after Glaberman expressed his concerns about James's involvement in Trinidad politics.

68   Lloyd Best, interviewed by David Austin, audio recording, Tunapuna, Trinidad October 14, 2003, Walton Look Lai, interviewed by David Austin, audio recording, Port of Spain, Trinidad, October 6, 2003, and Norman Girvan, interviewed by David Austin, audio recording, Port of Spain, Trinidad, October 8, 2003.

69   C.L.R. James to Selma James, July 5, 1965, [Glaberman, WSU Box 7-12].

70   Selma James to Martin Glaberman, August 13, 1965, [Glaberman, WSU Box 7-12].

71   C.L.R. James to Martin Glaberman, February 4, 1966, [Glaberman, WSU, Box 8-2] and C.L.R. James to Martin Glaberman, April 24, 1966 [Glaberman, WSU Box 8-3].

72   C.L.R. James to Robert A. Hill and Martin Glaberman, November 1966 and C.L.R. James to Martin Glaberman, November 11, 1966 [Glaberman, WSU Box 8-6]. James repeated the claim in Montreal during an undated and untitled presentation about the WFP and the election, likely delivered early in December 1966 when James returned to Montreal.

73   C.L.R. James to Robert A. Hill and Martin Glaberman, November 1966 [Glaberman, WSU Box 8-6] and C.L.R. James, "To Whom it May Concern," circ. September 2 and 3, 1966 [Glaberman, WSU Box 8-5].

74   Paul Buhle, *Tim Hector: A Caribbean Radical's Story* (Jackson: The Press of University of Mississippi, 2006), 137.

75   Ibid.

76   Roberts, *A View for Freedom*, 70. According to Franklyn Harvey, James also delivered a lecture on Marxism and Christianity, but it appears to have not survived.

77   Kent Worcester, "The Question of the Canon: C.LR. James and Modern Politics," in, *C.L.R. James's Caribbean*, eds. Paget Henry and Paul Buhle (Durham, NC: Duke University Press, 1992), 216–217.

78   C.L.R. James, "Parties, Politics and Economics in the Caribbean," 313, 315.

79   C.L.R. James, *Party Politics in the West Indies* (San Juan, Trinidad: Vedic Enterprises Ltd., 1962), 89.

80   Michael Smith, "You Don't Play with Revolution," interview with C.L.R. James, *McGill Reporter* November 4, 1968.

81   See Kevin B. Anderson, "The Rediscovery and Persistence of the Dialectic in Philosophy and in World Politics," in *Lenin Reloaded: Towards a Politics of Truth*, ed. Sebastian Budgen, Stathis Kouvelakis, and Slavoj Slavoj Žižek (Durham and London: Duke University Press, 2007), 121–147.

82   Arendt, *The Promise of Politics*, 77.

83   See Sylvia Wynter, "Beyond the Categories of the Master Conception: The Counterdoctrine of Jamesian Poiesis," in *C.L.R. James's Caribbean*, ed. Paget Henry and Paul Buhle (Durham: Duke University Press, 1992), 78, 80, 81, 85, 87.

84   C.L.R. James to Martin Glaberman, September 1 and 28, 1966 [Glaberman, WSU Box 8–5].

85   C.L.R. James, "Wilson Harris and the Existentialist Doctrine," *Spheres of Existence: Selected Writings* (London: Allison & Busby, 1980), 157–168.

86   C.L.R. James, "Introduction to 'Tradition and the West Indian Novel,'" *Spheres of Existence: Selected Writings* (London: Allison & Busby, 1980), 171.

87   Robert Hill returned to Jamaica in 1967 where he continued his studies and became ensconced in the country's political struggles. His work was primarily centered around the group Abeng, which emerged on the heels of Walter Rodney being banned from Jamaica by the Shearer government in October 1968. Hill served as the editor of Abeng's weekly organ of the same name. Out of Abeng emerged the Worker's Liberation League which became the Worker's Party of Jamaica, the country's communist party. Tim Hector returned to his native Antigua and Barbuda where he became a leading figure in the country's labor movement and editor of *Trumpet* before establishing the Antigua Caribbean Liberation Movement. He sat in the Antiguan senate and was the publisher of the leading opposition paper, the *Outlet*, in which he penned his sweeping "Fan the Flame" essays. He also played an important role in linking Cuba to the Anglophone Caribbean left. Franklyn Harvey left Montreal for Trinidad and was one of the founding members of the popular-based, bottom up, New Beginning Movement. He was later one of the founders of the Movement for Assemblies of People (MAP) in Grenada, a grouping that eventually merged with JEWEL to form the New Jewel Movement which ushered in the Grenada Revolution.

Anne Cools was active in the 1969 Sir George Williams University Affair, a Black student protest against racism that helped spark the Black Power protests in Trinidad in 1970. She later became very active in Canada's women's movement in the 1960s and 1970s and is credited with founding one of the first women's shelters in Canada. Today she is a senator, Canada's first Black woman in that position. Although not actively involved in the CLRJSC, Rosie Douglas, a co-founder of the CCC, was one of the key organizers of the historic 1968 Congress of Black Writers and one of the central figures in the Sir George Williams Affair. Before becoming prime minister of Dominica, Douglas was well known for his active involvement in African and Caribbean affairs and has been credited for playing a role in galvanizing support for the African National Congress under apartheid.

Alfie Roberts remained in Montreal. He was a founder of the St. Vincent and the Grenadines Association, the International Caribbean Service Bureau, and numerous other organizations and was renowned for his keen sense of history and his acute political instincts. A number of students from Grenada, St. Vincent, and other parts of the Caribbean, who later became active political figures in their respective countries, came under his influence and he served as an informal advisor to many, both locally and internationally.

88   Deryck R. Brown, "The Coup that Failed: The Jamesian Connection," in *The Black Power Revolution, 1970: A Retrospective*, eds. Selwyn Ryan and Taimoon Steward, with the assistance of Roy Mc Cree (St. Augustine, Trinidad: ISER, The University of the West Indies, 1995).

89   C.L.R. James, *Perspectives and Proposals* (Detroit: Facing Reality, 1966).

90   Robert Hill to Franklyn Harvey, January 11, 1970, Alfie Roberts Institute.

91   Robert Hill, interviewed by David Austin, audio recording, Los Angeles, California, May 15, 2004. During and after the Second World War, James was actively involved in the Johnson-Forest Tendency, a Marxist organization that he co-founded and that was alternately involved in the Workers Party and Socialist Workers Party before establishing itself as an independent organization.

92   Fanon Che Wilkins's *"In the Belly of the Beast"* is one of the few studies that connects the Caribbean Conference Committee to political developments in the Caribbean. Wilkins refers to Robert Hill's political activity in Jamaica, including his collaboration with Walter Rodney. (Fanon Che Wilkins, *"'In the Belly of the Beast': Black Power, Anti-imperialism, and the African Liberation Solidarity Movement, 1968–1975"* [Ph.D. diss., N.Y. University May 2001], 19–21.) See also C. L. R. James, "Black Power," ed. Anna Grimshaw the *C. L. R. James Reader* (Oxford, UK: Blackwell Publishing, 1992), 363 and Stokely Carmicahel with Ekwueme Michael Thelwell, *Ready for Revolution: The Life and Struggles of Stokely Carmichael (Kwame Toure)* (New York: Scribner, 2003), 544.

93   Aaron Kamugisha, "The Coloniality of Citizenship in the Contemporary Anglophone Caribbean," *Race and Class*, 49(2), October–December 2007, 21.

94   Ibid., 36.

95   Ibid.

96   See Susan Buck-Morss, "Hegel and Haiti" *Critical Inquiry* 26 (Summer 2000): 821–65 as well as her forthcoming book *Hegel, Haiti, and Universal History*.

THE MAKING OF THE CARIBBEAN PEOPLE

1   England. West India Royal Commission, *West India Royal Commission Report*, House of Commons Sessional Papers, Vol. 6, Cmd. 6607 (London, 1945). The commission was chaired by Walter Edward Guinness, first Baron Moyne (1880–1944), English politician and traveler.

2   *Study Conference of Economic Development in Underdeveloped Countries*, August 5–15, 1957, University College of the West Indies, Jamaica, W. I.

3   Richard Ligon, *A True & Exact History of the Island of Barbadoes* (1673).

4   Gilberto Freyre, *The Mansions and the Shanties: the Making of Modern Brazil*, trans. and ed. By Harriet de Onis, with an introd. by Frank Tannenbaum (New York: Alfred Knopf, 1963).

5   C. L. R. James, *The Black Jacobins: Toussaint L'Ouverture and the San Domingo Revolution*, 2d ed., rev. (New York: Vintage Books, 1963). The original edition was published in 1938 in England.

6   Richard Pares, *Merchants and Planters*, The Economic History Review, Supplements, 4 (Cambridge, U.K.: Published for the Economic History Review at the University Press, 1960).

7   Sir John Fortescue, *A History of the British Army*, 13 vols. (London: Macmillan, 1910–1930).

8   G. M. Craig, ed., *Lord Durham's Report: An Abridgement of the Report on the Affairs of British North America* (Toronto: McClelland and Stewart, 1963).

9   Captain Arthur Andrew Cipriani (1875–1945), a French Creole of Corsican descent, was one of the founders of Trinidad and Tobago's nationalist movement. For a more detailed account of his life and work see *The Case for West Indian Self-Government* (1933), written by C.L.R James and republished in *The C.L.R. James Reader*. This is a shortened version of James's biography of Cipriani, *The Life of Captain Cipriani*, published in 1932. See also James's 1963 appendix to *The Black Jacobins: Toussaint L'Ouverture and the San Domingo Revolution* (1938; New York: Vintage Books, 1989) entitled "From Toussaint L'Ouverture to Fidel Castro."

10   George Lamming, *Season of Adventure* (London: Michael Joseph, 1960), 18.

THE HAITIAN REVOLUTION IN THE MAKING OF THE MODERN WORLD

1   See Hilaire Belloc and Cecil Chesterton, *The Party System* (London: Stephen Swift, 1911).

2   James is referring to the speech he delivered at the Congress on the morning of October 12 entitled, "The History and Economics of Slavery in the New World." No record of the speech has been located.

3   The French Revolutionary Wars.

4   James in referring to Robert A. Hill, who made a presentation at the Congress of Black Writers, which, according to the conference program, was entitled "The Fathers of the Modern Revolt: Garvey, etc."

5   James, *The Black Jacobins*, 265.

6   The person credited with originating the Pan-African movement was Henry Sylvester Williams of Trinidad.

7   James, *The Black Jacobins* 265.

8   Ibid., 265.

9   Ibid., 343.

10   Ibid., 346.

11   Ibid., 350.

12   Ibid., 353.

13   Ibid., 368–369.

14   W.E.B. Du Bois, *Black Reconstruction* (1935; New York: Touchstone, 1992), 100.

15   The exact speech reads:

Four score and seven years ago our fathers brought forth on this continent a new nation, conceived in liberty and dedicated to the proposition that all men are created equal. Now we are engaged in a great civil war, testing whether that nation or any nation so conceived and so dedicated can long endure. We are met on a great battlefield of that war. We have come to dedicate a portion of that field as a final resting-place for those who here gave their lives that that nation might live. It is altogether fitting and proper that we should do this. But in a larger sense, we cannot dedicate, we cannot consecrate, we cannot hallow this ground. The brave men, living and dead who struggled here have consecrated it far above our poor power to add or detract. The world will little note nor long remember what we say here, but it can never forget what they did here. It is for us the living rather to be dedicated here to the unfinished work which they who fought here have thus far so nobly advanced. It is rather for us to be here dedicated to the great task remaining before us—that from these honored dead we take increased devotion to that cause for which they gave the last full measure of devotion—that we here highly resolve that these dead shall not have died in vain, that this nation under God shall have a new birth of freedom, and that government of the people, by the people, for the people shall not perish from the earth.

16   *Les jacobins noirs: Toussaint L'Ouverture et la révolution de Saint Domingue* (1949; Paris: Editions Caribéennes, 1983).

17   In a fragment of James's other speech that has survived from the Congress of Black Writers, he also had the following to say about Haiti:

I know very well that Black Power can be, today, a very oppressive power. So that the slogan Black Power is a general slogan against colonialism, neo-colonialism, and against what Frantz Fanon was so clear about, native local governments that are merely continuators of the imperialist government that has been overthrown. We must be quite clear about that. So that Stokely used to say, for him, Tshombe was not a Black man [*Applause*]. He says Tshombe served the interests of imperialism. And we are very clear about that—I from personal experience. A Black government does not necessarily mean a government which does not feel the power that we mean when we say Black Power. So that Doc Duvalier is Black, that does not matter at all. I myself am waiting, and a lot of other people are waiting, for the day when the Haitian people are going to overthrow him. That is certain to come [*Applause*]. Maybe not as quickly as some of you Haitians might like but you must understand and take it for certain, he cannot continue indefinitely. Many of them have tried and he is certain to go. The population everywhere is aware of that. The other day I saw in the paper that he said he was going away. He was ill and he wanted to go to the United States for medical attention. And some of his friends told him no, you don't go to the United States for medical attention. All the medical attention you need, we will give you here [*Laughter*]. So, he's still there. But he had reached the stage where he wanted to get out. I read that in the French paper *Le Monde* which tells less lies than the other bourgeois papers [*Laughter and applause*]. So that, a few months ago, Duvalier thought it was best to seek medical advice abroad. We don't know when he will need to go abroad for medical advice again but we can hope for the best...

SHAKESPEARE'S *KING LEAR*

1   The critic J. C. Maxwell wrote that *Lear* was "a Christian play about a pagan world" ("The Technique of Invocation in 'King Lear,'" *Modern Language Review*, 45, 2 [April 1950], 142–147).

2   George Wilson Knight, *The Wheel of Fire: Interpretations of Shakespearian Tragedy with three new essays,* 4th rev. and enl. ed. (London: Methuen, 1949), "The Lear Universe".

3   Edmund Burke, *Reflections on the Revolution in France* (1790):

The age of chivalry is gone.—That of sophisters, economists, and calculators, has succeeded; and the glory of Europe is extinguished forever. Never, never more, shall we behold a generous loyalty to rank and sex, that proud submission, that dignified obedience, that subordination of the heart, which kept alive, even in servitude itself, the spirit of an exalted freedom. The unbought grace of life, achieved defensive nations, the nurse of the manly sentiment and heroic enterprise is gone! It is gone, that sensibility of principle, that chastity of honor, which felt a stain like a wound, which inspired courage while it mitigated ferocity, which ennobled whatever it touched, and under which vice itself lost half its evil, by losing all its grossness....

4   John Gielgud played the lead role and was co-director of a production of *King Lear* at the Palace Theatre in London, in July 1955 (Richard Findlater, *These Our Actors: A Celebration of the Theatre Acting of Peggy Ashcroft, John Gielgud, Laurence Olivier, Ralph Richardson* (London: Elm Tree Books, 1983), 159.

5   Edward Hyde, Earl of Clarendon, *The History of the Rebellion and Civil Wars in England begun in the year 1641,* 6 vols. (Oxford: Clarendon Press 1992).

EXISTENTIALISM AND MARXISM

1   In his draft appendix to *Modern Politics,* James argues that the "origin of existentialism is in itself a remarkable example of the Hegelian method." As Heidegger acknowledged in *Being and Time*, his work "represented a certain stage of social development and a new approach to the theory of knowledge." According to James:

Heidegger aimed at the foundation of a new vision of human society which rejected the behavior and thought of men in the mass. Men in the mass had submitted themselves to the violence and inhumanity of World War One and what had followed it. This, for Heidegger, was the inauthentic existence which was lived by the majority of men. He coined a superb phrase, "everydayness" for the fact that we all more or less live the same kind of life, eat the same kind of food, read the same newspapers, the same kinds of books—the elements of an essentially inauthentic existence.

James continues:

There is no doubt whatever that this excessive emphasis on the role and value of the individual gained strength not only from the mass submission and hysteria of World War One, but from the mechanical analysis and dictatorial brutality which Stalinism had made of Marxism. Existentialism has undoubtedly brought elements of correction into the Marxism corrupted by Stalin." See C.L.R. James, "Appendix to Modern Politics: Notes on Philosophy," [Glaberman, WSU Box 22–3].

2   According to Lenin:

Human knowledge is not (or does not follow) a straight line, but a curve, which endlessly approximates a series of circles, a spiral. Any fragment, segment, section of this curve can be transformed (transformed one-sidedly) into an independent, complete, straight line, which then (if one does not see the wood for the trees) leads into the quagmire, into clerical obscurantism (where it is anchored by the class interests of the ruling classes). Rectilinearity and one-sidedness, woodenness and petrification, subjectivism and subjective blindness—voilà the epistemological roots of idealism. And clerical obscurantism (= philosophical idealism), of course, has epistemological roots, it is not groundless; it is a sterile flower undoubtedly, but a sterile flower that grows on the living tree of living, fertile, genuine, powerful, omnipotent, objective, absolute human knowledge. (V.I. Lenin, "On the Question of Dialectics," *Lenin's Collected Works*, 4th Edition, Vol. 38 [1915; Moscow: Progress Publishers, 1976]. http://www.marxists.org/archive/lenin/works/1915/misc/x02.htm)

In a charge that is perhaps reminiscent of the old dogmatism that plagued Marxist and communist circles throughout the 20th century up until the collapse of the former Soviet Union when such arguments were seemingly rendered futile, John H. McClendon III "accuses" James of Hegelian idealism. According to McClendon, in *Notes on Dialectics* (1948), which many decades later James described as perhaps his most important book,

James makes, in my estimation, some serious and fundamental blunders with regard to his conception of Marxist philosophy and more specifically his treatment of dialectics. The method James advances, in his *Notes*, consists of identifying the Hegelian method of categorical (philosophical) motion with the concrete (empirically grounded) historical movement of the international proletariat, that is, its political practice. This dual mode of inquiry, James thinks, is the correct means of concretizing a dialectically formulated philosophical mode of cognition and, in turn, providing the proletarian class struggle with a philosophically grounded political theory. James, in adopting such a method, I contend, falls prey to Hegelian idealism. (John H. McClendon III, *C.L.R. James's Notes on Dialectics: Left Hegelianism or Marxism-Leninism* [Lanham, MD: Lexington Books, 2005], 23). Unlike Lenin, according to McClendon, James is hypnotized by Hegel's [idealistic] fog as well as the dialectic" in what McClendon describes as "the hiatus between James's abstract idealist reading [of Hegel's *Logic*] and Lenin's materialist reading of Hegel." (Ibid., 278).

3   R.D. Laing and Ronald David, *Reason and Violence: A Decade of Sartre's Philosophy, 1950–1960* (London: Tavistock Publications, 1964).

4   See Walter Kaufmann, "Existentialism from Dostoyevsky to Sartre," in *Existentialism from Dostoyevsky to Sartre*, ed. Walter Kaufmann (1956; New York: Meridian, 1989), 48.

5   In *Words*, Sartre writes the following:

> I have changed. I shall speak later on about the acids that corroded the distorting transparencies which enveloped me; I shall tell when and how I served my apprenticeship to violence and discovered by ugliness—which for a long time was my negative principle, the quicklime in which the wonderful child is dissolved; I shall also explain the reason why I came to think systematically against myself to the extent of measuring the obvious truth of an idea by the displeasure it caused me.

Sartre adds:

> I've given up the office but not the frock; I still write. What else can I do?
>
> Nulla dies sine linea.
>
> It's a habit, and besides, it's my profession. For a long time, I took my pen for a sword; I now know we're powerless. No matter. I write and will keep writing books; they're needed; all the same, they do serve some purpose. Culture doesn't save anything or anyone, it doesn't justify. But it's a product of man: he projects himself into it, he recognizes himself in it; that critical mirror alone offers him his image. Moreover, that old, crumbling structure, my imposture, is also my character: one gets rid of a neurosis, one doesn't get cured of one's self. Though they are worn out, blurred, humiliated, thrust aside, ignored, all of the child's traits are still to be found in the quinquagenarian. Most of the time they lie low, they bide their time; at the first moment of inattention, they rise up and emerge, disguised; I claim sincerely to be writing only for my time, but my present notoriety annoys me; it's not glory, since I'm alive, and yet that's enough to belie my old dreams; could it be that I still harbor them secretly? I have, I think, adapted them. since I've lost the chance of dying unknown, I sometimes flatter myself that I'm being understood in my lifetime. (Jean-Paul Sartre, *Words* [1964; Grenwich, Conn.: Fawcett Publication, 1969], 158–159).

6   Martin "Marty" Glaberman and William Gorman of Facing Reality.

7   James is referring to the interest in his *Notes on Dialectics* which was reproduced from his original manuscript by Robert A. Hill and delivered to James during his appearance at the Caribbean Conference Committee's second annual conference, "The Making of the Caribbean People" in October 1966.

8   Martin Heidegger, *Being and Time*, trans. John Macquarrie and Edward Robinson (New York: Harper and Row, 1962), 27, translators' footnote.

9   Heidegger, *Being and Time*, 31.

10   Ibid.

11   Ibid.

12   Ibid.

13   Ibid, translators' footnote.

14   William Barrett, *Irrational Man: A Study in Existential Philosophy* (New York: Doubleday Anchor Books, 1958), 192.

15   Ibid, 193.

16   Ibid.

17   Kaufmann, "Existentialism from Dostoyevsky to Sartre," 39.

18   Ontical thinking bears resemblance to Hegel's notions of common sense and vulgar empiricism, and understanding. According to James, there are three categories of cognition in Hegel's system of logic: 1) Simple, everyday, common sense, vulgar empiricism, or ordinary perception 2) Understanding and 3) Dialectic (C.L.R. James, *Notes on Dialectics: Hegel-Marx-Lenin* [London:

Allison & Busby Ltd., 1980], 18). Understanding is Hegel's philosophical term for thinking in finite categories, whereas the dialectic or reason involves recognizing that seemingly finite categories are not static but shift and move (Ibid., 16). As James writes: "And, holy heaven help us, *if* you do not get out to Dialectic and stay in Understanding too long, you tumble right back into empiricism and common sense" (Ibid., 18).

19   Ibid.

20   Heidegger, *Being and Time*, 376.

21   Ironically, Heidegger was an early and active supporter of the Nazis in his native Germany. As Walter Kaufmann has written: "Heidegger disdains the openly hortatory tone—so much so that some of his readers fail to notice altogether that he, too, appeals to us to change our lives." But "Heidegger's enthusiastic exhortations, immediately after Hitler came to power, that the students and professors at the German universities must now think in the service of the Nazi State...are a very noteworthy exception" (Kaufmann, "Existentialism from Dostoyevsky to Sartre," 34). See also Heidegger, *German Existentialism* (New York: The Philosophical Library Inc., 1965).

22   Heidegger, *Being and Time*, 394.

23   Ibid.

24   Ibid., 398.

25   Speaking on Wilson Harris in 1965 at the University of the West Indies in Trinidad, James remarked that although Sartre writes philosophical works such as *Being and Nothingness*, "he also writes novels and plays, and [he seeks to portray] his existentialist philosophy in [his] novels and plays. I have never known a philosophy so closely reported in fiction and drama." And then referring to Harris's novel *Palace of the Peacock*, James continues:

> But Harris has done more than that. Within the covers of one small book of ninety or one hundred pages Harris gives you a big slab of actual everyday existence, the inauthentic life we all lead, and then, within that same novel, he takes you to an extreme situation right away in the interior of British Guiana with men pulling a canoe or raft up some waterfall or descending it with all sorts of dangers around them. And then he does what Sartre does not do, within the covers of the same volume he proceeds to give you pages of philosophical exploration. There is no other novelist that I know of doing the same things today... Harris is a remarkable novelist whether he writes about everydayness, or of the life [of] men and women living in the boundary situation out in the wilds of British Guiana...and then he proceeds to write philosophical views of the world in general. I think it is most remarkable that this West Indian, uneducated in German, uneducated in European universities, should have found out these things practically for himself and should be writing the kind of book that he does. (C.L.R. James, "Wilson Harris and the Existentialist Doctrine," *Spheres of Existence: Selected Writings* [London: Allison & Busby Ltd., 1980], 165.)

26   Heidegger, *Being and Time*, 400.

27   Ibid., 401.

28   Ibid., 422.

29   Ibid., 437.

30   Herman Melville, *Pierre, or the Ambiguities* (1852; New York: HarperCollins, 1995). For James's analysis of Melville's work see C.L.R. James, *Mariners, Renegades, and Castaways: The Story of Herman Melville and the World We Live In* (1953; Dartmouth: University Press of New England, 2001).

31   Heidegger, *Being and Time*, 437.

32   Ibid.

33   Ibid., 442.

34   Ibid., 449.

35   Jean-Francois Lyotard, *La Phénoménologie* (1954)/*Phenomenology*, trans. B. Beakley (New York: SUNY Press, 1991).

36   Jean-Francois Lyotard joined Pierre Chaulieu, née Cornelius Castoriadis, in the political group Socialism or Barbarism and was involved in Worker Power when Socialism or Barbarism split in 1964. Castoriadis founded Socialism or Barbarism in Paris and worked closely with C.L.R. James in the late 1940s and in the 1950s, collaborating on the book, *Facing Reality* (1958). For an analysis of this relationship and James's work see Cornelius Castoriadis, "C.L.R. James and the Fate of Humanity," in *C.L.R. James: His Intellectual Legacies*, eds. Selwyn R. Cudjoe and William E. Cain (Amherst, Mass: University of Massachusetts Press, 1985), 277–297.

37   William Gorman, a phenomenologist by instinct, was charged with transcribing and editing James's lecture on existentialism and Marxism as well as developing his own analysis of Heidegger for Facing Reality. Gorman was one of James's most important collaborators. Despite his abilities, Gorman was often unproductive and James was one of the few people, perhaps the only one, who could motivate him to exercise his intellectual talents. In a note to Martin Glaberman, James expresses his pleasure that Gorman appears to be getting down to work.

ROUSSEAU AND THE IDEA OF THE GENERAL WILL

1   Writing in 1946, according to Bertrand Russell, Modern Europe and America have been divided into three camps: the Liberals who follow Bentham and Locke; the Marxists embodied in Russia; and the third camp, "represented politically by Nazis and Fascists...It is anti-rational and anti-scientific. Its political progenitors are Rousseau, Fichte, and Nietzsche. It emphasizes will, especially will to power; this it believes to be mainly concentrated in certain races and individuals, who therefore have a right to rule (*A History of Western Philosophy* [1946; London: Unwin Paperbacks, 1984], 744–755). Elsewhere Russell writes: "the dictatorships of Russia and Germany (especially the latter) are in part an outcome of Rousseau's teaching. What further triumphs the future has to offer to his ghost I do not venture to predict." (Ibid, 674)

2   Paul Hazard, *European Thought in the Eighteenth Century* (Cleveland: World Publishing Co., 1963).

3   Historian Edward Gibbon makes numerous references to folly and vice in his towering history of Rome including the following: "Antoninus diffused order and tranquility over the greatest part of the earth. His reign is marked by the rare advantage of furnishing very few materials for history, which is, indeed, little more than the register of the crimes, follies, and misfortunes of mankind." (Edward Gibbon, *The Portable Gibbon: The Decline and Fall of the Roman Empire* [1776, 1781, 1788; New York: Penguin Books, 1978], 108.)

4   The Dijon Academy.

5   Fredrick Engels, *Anti-Dühring: Herr Eugen Dühring's Revolution in Science* (1878; New York: International Publishers, 1966).

6   *Julie: or, The New Eloise* (*Julie: ou, la nouvelle Héloïse* [1761]).

7   *Du Contrat social* (1762)

8   Stokely Carmichael (1941–1998), later known as Kwame Toure, was the former leader of the Student Non-violent Coordinating Committee (SNCC) and once a prominent figure in the Black Panther Party. Carmichael popularized the phrase "Black Power." James first met Carmichael when James delivered a talk in Windsor in January 1967 and later heard Carmichael speak publicly in Montreal at Sir George Williams University (now Concordia University) in 1967 (C.L.R. James, "Black Power," in ed. Grimshaw *The C.L.R. James Reader*. The two began corresponding with one another and Carmichael later joined James at the October 1968 Congress of Black Writers in Montreal.

9   The People's National Movement (PNM) was the political party founded in 1956 by the late Dr. Eric Williams, Trinidad and Tobago's first prime minister.

10   Chaguaramas, a deep-water harbor in Trinidad, was the site of a U.S. military base. The U.S. obtained a ninety-nine year lease on Chaguaramas, as well as several other military bases throughout the West Indies, from the British in exchange for several dozen antiquated warships in 1940. The base became a strong point of contention between the PNM and the U.S. government once Williams's PNM came into office in 1956 and demanded that the base be returned to the West Indies for use as the capital for the West Indian Federation. The issues surrounding this debate were described weekly by James, then editor of the PNM newspaper, *The Nation.*

11   *Les Confessions* (1782–89).

12   Ernest Cassirer, "Rousseau and Kant," in *Rousseau, Kant, Goethe: Two Essays,* trans. James Gutmann, Paul Oskar Kristeller, and John Herman Randall, Jr. (New York: Harper & Row, 1963).

13   Albert Soboul, *Les Sans-culottes: parisiens en l'an II; mouvement populaire et gouvernement revolutionnaire, 2 juin 1793–9 Thermidor an II* (Paris: Clavereuil, 1958). The abridged English edition was published as *The Sans-Culottes: The Popular Movement and Revolutionary Government, 1793–1794* (Oxford: Clarendon Press, 1964).

14   James is referring to Georges Lefebvre (1874–1959), the renowned French historian and author of numerous books on the French Revolution including *The Coming of the French Revolution* and *The Thermidors.*

15   Jean Guehenno, *Jean-Jacques Rousseau* (Paris: Gallimard,1962).

16   Lévi-Strauss argues that Rousseau's insight into ethnographic knowledge was astonishing because "it forestalls by a number of years the very first ideas about totemism." Furthermore, "Rousseau…sees the 'specific' character of the animal and vegetable world as the source of the first logical operations, and subsequently of a social differentiation which could be lived out only if it were conceptualized." Claude Lévi-Strauss, *Totemism* (Boston: Beacon Press, 1963), 99.

17   According to Engels, "Rousseau…regards the rise of inequality as progress. But this progress contained an antagonism; it was at the same time retrogression." Engels continues:

> Already in Rousseau, therefore, we find not only a sequence of ideas which correspond exactly with the sequence developed in Marx's *Capital,* but that correspondence extends also to details, Rousseau using a whole series of the same dialectical developments as Marx used: processes which in their nature are antagonistic, contain a contradiction, are the transformation of one extreme into its opposite; and finally, as the kernel of the whole process, the negation, And though in 1754 Rousseau was not yet able to use the Hegelian jargon, he was certainly, twenty-three years before Hegel was born, deeply bitten with the Hegelian pestilence, dialectics of contradiction, Logos doctrine, theology and so forth. (Engels, *Anti-Dühring,* 153–154)

MARX'S EIGHTEENTH BRUMAIRE OF LOUIS BONAPARTE AND THE CARIBBEAN

1   Karl Marx, *The Eighteenth Brumaire of Louis Bonaparte.* (1852; New York: International Publishers, 1991), 7. Hereafter, the title will be abbreviated by the acronym *EBLB.*

2   Victor Hugo, *The Destroyer of the Second Republic; being Napoleon the Little* (1852; New York: Sheldon, 1870).

3   Marx's actual text reads: "Victor Hugo confines himself to bitter and witty invective against the responsible publisher of the *coup d'état*" (*EBLB,* 8).

4   The late Dr. Eric Williams was the founder and leader of the People's National Movement political party in Trinidad and Tobago. He was Trinidad and Tobago's first premier (1956–62)

and later became the first prime minister (1962–1981). A renowned historian, he is the author of several books including *Capitalism and Slavery* (1944) and *From Columbus to Castro: The History of the Caribbean, 1492–1969* (1970). James was a former teacher and mentor of Williams and he collaborated with Williams and his government between 1958 and 1960 after which they went their separate ways due to political differences. See footnote below.

5   James is referring to an essay by Ivar Oxaal entitled "C.L.R. James Versus Eric Williams" which was published in the *Trinidad and Tobago Index*. The opening paragraph of the essay was reprinted in the September 24, 1965 issue of *We the People*, a weekly newspaper that was edited by James in Trinidad when he was a member of the Worker's and Farmer's Party. The essay reads:

> Perhaps the most significant single event in the contemporary history of Trinidad and Tobago occurred early in 1960 when C.L.R. James resigned as editor of the PNM *Nation*, broke-off his already alienated relationship with Dr. Eric Williams and entered the political wilderness. During the past five years James has been a lone voice crying in that wilderness: A voice often muted by illness, exile and indifference, but recently resurgent. As a prophet of West Indian nationalism, James has not been altogether without honor in his own land, but [that] general neglect, indifference and even persecution has been his lot in Trinidad is difficult to understand.... He has therefore been subjected to crude, if not malicious, misrepresentation, the most common charge being the furthest from the truth: that he is a communist.

See also Ivar Oxaal's *Black Intellectuals Come to Power* (Cambridge, Mass.: Schenkman Publishing, Inc., 1968) in which Oxaal compares and contrasts Eric Williams's *Capitalism and Slavery* with James's *Black Jacobins* as a prelude to his discussion of the eventual political split between James and Williams in 1960.

6   "In 1833, therefore, the alternatives were clear: emancipation from above, or emancipation from below. But EMANCIPATION. Economic change, the decline of the monopolists, the development of capitalism, the humanitarian agitation in British churches, the contending perorations in the halls of Parliament, had now reached their completion in the determination of the slaves themselves to be free. The Negroes had been stimulated to freedom by the development of the very wealth which their labour had created." (Eric Williams, *Capitalism and Slavery* [1944; London: André Deutsch Limited, 1990], 208).

7   James is referring to his lecture, "The Making of the People of the Caribbean," delivered in Montreal in October 1966 at the Second Annual Conference on West Indian Affairs and reproduced in this volume.

8   Slavery was legally abolished in Britain in 1833 and in France in 1848.

9   Elsa V. Goveia, *Slave Society in the British Leeward Islands at the End of the Eighteenth Century* (New Haven and London: Yale University Press, 1965).

10   James is referring to Orlando Patterson and his book, *The Sociology of Slavery: An Analysis of the Origin, Development, and Structure of Negro Slave Society in Jamaica* (Rutherford, N.J.: Farleigh Dickerson University Press, 1969). At the time, Patterson was both a promising novelist and sociologist and in 1967 Patterson was invited as the main guest speaker at the Caribbean Conference Committee's annual meeting.

11   Elsewhere James states that slavery was abolished in 1833, not 1834. Both dates are correct for Britain. The Abolition Act was passed by British Parliament in 1833 and on August 1, 1834 slavery was officially abolished in all British territories.

12   Ebenezer Joshua was the former chief minister of St. Vincent and the Grenadines. In 1952, he founded the People's Political Party, advocating independence and the improvement of working conditions for the poor. Joshua became the first chief minister, a position he held between 1956 and 1967. The fortunes of the PPP declined and the PPP was dissolved in 1984.

13   C.L.R. James, *Party Politics in the West Indies* (San Juan, Trinidad: Vedic Enterprises Ltd., 1962), 134. Hereafter, this book will be referenced by the acronym *PPWI*.

14   James is referring to Robert Milton Cato, a lawyer by training and St. Vincent's first prime minister (1979–1984). The principal founder of the St. Vincent Labour Party in 1954, he was chief minister and prime minister prior to independence (1979).

15   Vere Cornwall Bird became Antigua and Barbuda's first prime minister when the former colony gained independence in 1981. Prior to that he served as the colony's first premier when it was granted Associated Statehood by Britain in 1967.

16   Julius Nyerere, the first president of independent Tanzania (1961), is the co-author, along with other members of the Tanganyika African National Union's (TANU) Executive Committee, of the 1967 Arusha Declaration which outlines TANU's program for socialist development in Tanzania. James spoke highly of the Declaration and Nyerere's approach to socialism and devoted a section to it in *A History of Pan-African Revolt* (Washington: Drum and Spear Press, 1969), a revised edition of his 1938 *A History of Negro Revolt*. James's thoughts on the Arusha Declaration, entitled "...Always out of Africa," are reproduced in his *Nkrumah and the Ghana Revolution* (Westport, CT: Lawrence Hill and Co., 1977). To quote James, "The [TANU] government aims at creating a new type of society, based not on Western theories but on the concrete circumstances of African life and its historic past," and later adds, "'Marxism is a humanism' is the exact reverse of the truth. The African builders of a humanist society show that today all humanism finds itself in close harmony with the original conceptions and aims of marxism." See also Julius K. Nyerere, *Uhuru na Ujamaa/Freedom and Socialism* (Dar es Salaam: Oxford University Press, 1968).

17   Kwame Nkrumah, Ghana's first prime minister, was the leader of the Convention People's Party that brought the Gold Coast to independence in 1957. Nkrumah's efforts served as an inspiration for other African countries which eventually followed suit. He was overthrown by the military in 1966 as support for his government waned. For James's account of the rise and fall of Kwame Nkrumah see *Nkrumah and the Ghana Revolution*.

18   Norman Washington Manley was the founder of the People's National Party (PNP), Jamaica's first national party. His long-time rival was his cousin, William Alexander Bustamante, founder and head of the Jamaica Labour Party (JLP). Manley was one of the key figures in the development of the West Indian Federation which was inaugurated in 1958, only to witness its demise when the Jamaican electorate voted to opt out of the federation, followed by the withdrawal of Trinidad and Tobago under the leadership of Dr. Eric Williams.

19   This is a reference to Williams's famous "Massa Day Done" speech that was delivered on March 22, 1961. Using firm, witty, and unequivocal language as well as his command of Caribbean history, Williams declared an end to the reign of colonial economic and political policies in Trinidad and Tobago and the inauguration of a new day under his leadership. See "Massa Day Done," in *Eric Williams Speaks: Essays on Colonialism and Independence*, ed. Selwyn R. Cudjoe (Wellesley, Mass., Callaloux Publications, 1993), 237–264.

20   George Beckford was a celebrated Jamaican economist and a prominent member of the New World Group. In July–August 1965, Professor Beckford spent three weeks in Cuba studying the country's agrarian reform. Shortly after his return, his passport was seized by Jamaican authorities. See George Beckford, "A Public Statement on the Deprivation of My Freedom to Travel," January 10, 1965 in *New World: Journal of Caribbean Opinion*, n.d.

21   James is of course referring to former Cuban president Fidel Castro who led the overthrow of the Fulgencio Batista dictatorship and ushered in an new era in Cuban history on January 1, 1959. Batista was deposed after two years of guerilla warfare which began when a yacht named Granma, carrying Castro and others, landed in the Oriente province in December 1956.

22   Sir William Alexander Bustamante was Jamaica's first prime minister and founder of the Bustamante Industrial Trade Union. Bustamante founded the Jamaica Labour Party in 1943. In a

1961 referendum on federation, the Jamaican electorate opted for independence, precipitating the break-up of the West Indian Federation. Bustamante became prime minister in 1962.

23   James is referring to Hitler's hand-picked personal Brown Shirt guards and Mussolini's Black Shirts. These armed guards swore allegiance to their respective leaders and used terror and violence to destroy the opposition or force them into submission.

24   Errol Walton Barrow was Barbados's first prime minister and the driving force behind that country's independence movement. Independence was granted to Barbados in 1966.

25   Cheddi Jagan was the leader of government in 1953 when his political party, the People's Progressive Party (PPP), won the first elections in Guyana under universal adult suffrage. Fearing that it would not be able to control Jagan and his socialist politics, the British government dissolved his government only 133 days after it was formed. Jagan was later re-elected and served as chief minister and premier from 1957 to 1964, when the People's National Congress, under the leadership of Linden Forbes Sampson Burnham, came to power. For three decades, Jagan and the PPP remained in opposition to the PNC until it came to power in 1992.

26   Linden Forbes Sampson Burnham was premier of Guyana between 1964 and 1966, after which he became prime minister when the country became independent in 1966. Prior to forming the People's National Congress in 1958, Burnham was one of the leading figures in the People's Progressive Party.

27   Referring to Alfie Roberts, a member of the Caribbean Conference Committee and the C.L.R. James Study Circle, who was present for James's lecture.

28   See C.L.R. James, "Discussion with Trotsky," in C.L.R James, *At the Rendezvous of Victory* (London: Allison & Busby Ltd., 1984), 61 for the text of the 1939 discussion between James and Trotsky in Coyoacan, Mexico where Trotsky was then living in exile. Part of this same discussion is also reproduced in *Leon Trotsky on Black Nationalism and Self-Determination*, ed. George Breitman (New York: Pathfinder Press, 1980).

29   Ibid., p. 75.

30   *Maquereaus* = Procurers.

31   Referring to Franklyn Harvey, another member of the Caribbean Conference Committee and the C.L.R. James Study Circle, who was present for James's lecture.

32   The Industrial Stabilization Act was rushed through Trinidad parliament by the government of Eric Williams in 1965 during a period of worker unrest in the country. During a visit to Trinidad in this period, James was placed under house arrest by the government. It was in the aftermath of this period that the he co-founded Workers' and Farmers' Party in Trinidad and Tobago.

33   See C.L.R. James, "The Rise and Fall of Nkrumah," *At the Rendezvous of Victory* (1966; London: Allison & Busby Ltd., 1984), 172–180.

34   Born Slinger Francisco, The Mighty Sparrow, the Grenadian-born singer, nurtured the art of calypso singing in Trinidad. In the 1960s he emerged as one the Caribbean's most important cultural and political voices with his often satirical takes on current events in the Caribbean. He also performed as a guest of the Caribbean Conference Committee at their third annual conference in 1967. For James's assessment of Sparrow's influence, see *Party Politics in the West Indies*, 164–175.

35   The Vendôme Column was a monument erected by Napoleon Bonaparte and which he dedicated to himself shortly after seizing power.

MARX'S *CAPITAL*, THE WORKING DAY, AND CAPITALIST PRODUCTION

1   Karl Marx, *Capital: A Critique of Political Economy*, Vol. I (New York: International Publishers, 1967), 233. References hereafter to this book will be indicated by the page number.

2   Referring to Franklyn Harvey, a member of the Caribbean Conference Committee and the
C.L.R. James Study Circle.

3   Referring to Alfie Roberts, also a member of the Caribbean Conference Committee and the
C.L.R. James Study Circle.

4   In the summer of 1963, Alfie Roberts worked in a factory for Admiralty Plastics in New
York City.

5   James is likely referring to Marx's analysis in *The Eighteenth Brumaire of Louis Bonaparte*
where he describes the contingency and uncertainty involved in politics.

6   Bobby is Robert A. Hill, co-founder of the Caribbean Conference Committee and founder of
the C.L.R. James Study Circle and who, at the time, was a student at the University of Toronto.

LENIN AND THE TRADE UNION DEBATE IN RUSSIA, PART ONE

1   V. I. Lenin, *Selected Works*, Vol. IX: New Economic Policy—Socialist Construction (New
York: International Publishers, 1937).

2   Henry Ireton (1611–1651), son-in-law of Oliver Cromwell and a general in the Parliamentary army during the English Civil War (Ian J. Gentles, "Ireton, Henry," *Oxford Dictionary of
National Biography*, Oxford University Press, 2004 [http://www.oxforddnb.com/view/article/14452,
accessed 8 June 2008]; see also David Farr, *Henry Ireton and the English Revolution* [Rochester, NY:
Boydell, 2006]).

3   A reference to the debates of 1647 between radical members of Cromwell's New Model
Army and the Levellers who challenged Cromwell and Ireton and the army grandees regarding a
new constitution for England. The debates, which began on October 28, 1647, took place inside
a church, in Putney, Surrey (now South West London), the location of the headquarters of the
New Model Army. The debates continued until November 11, 1647 (see William Lamont, "The
English Civil War and Putney Debates," in *Democracy: The Long Revolution*, ed. David Powell and
Tom Hickey [London; New York: Continuum, 2007]; Phillip Baker, ed., *The Putney Debates: The
Levellers* [London; New York: Verso, 2007]; Trevor Royle, "The Levellers and the Putney Debates,"
in Trevor Royle, *The British Civil War: The Wars of the Three Kingdoms* [New York: Palgrave Mac-
millan, 2004]; Michael Mendle, ed., *The Putney Debates of 1647: The Army, the Levellers, and the
English State* [Cambridge; New York: Cambridge University Press, 2001]; A. S. P. Woodhouse, ed.,
Puritanism and Liberty, being the Army Debates (1647–9) [London: Dent, 1951]).

4   "The Trade Unions, the Present Situation and the Mistakes of Comrade Trotsky," Speech
delivered at a Joint Meeting of Delegates to the Eighth Congress of Soviets, Members of the All-
Russian Central Council of Trade Unions and of the Moscow Gubernia [City] Council of Trade
Unions, December 30, 1920, Lenin, *Selected Works*, Vol. IX, 7; also found in V. I. Lenin, *Collected
Works*, 1st English ed., Vol. 32, (Moscow: Progress Publishers, 1965), 22.

5   Ibid., 7–8.

6   Ibid., 8.

7   Ibid., 8–9.

8   N. Bukharin and E. Preobrazhensky, *The ABC of Communism* (various editions).

9   "The Trade Unions, the Present Situation and the Mistakes of Comrade Trotsky," 9–10.

10   Ibid., 15.

11   Ibid.

12   Ibid., 16.

13   Yan Ernestovich Rudzutak (1887–1938) was the Latvian secretary general of All-Russia
Central Council of Labor Unions from 1920 to 1921. His trade union theses were adopted by the
Fifth All-Russia Trade Union Conference on November 2–6, 1920, and developed in the resolu-

tion, "The Role and Tasks of the Trade Unions," adopted at the Tenth Party Congress. According to Lenin, "The serious mistake they (and I above all) made was that we 'overlooked' Rudzutak's theses, *The Tasks of the Trade Unions in Production*, adopted by the Fifth Conference. That is the *most* important document in the whole of the controversy" (speech delivered January 19, 1921, on "The Party Crisis" (Lenin, *Collected Works*, Vol. XXXII, 43–53). He also stated, "If anyone is to be taken thoroughly to task and 'shaken up,' it is not the A.C.C.T.U. [All-Russian Central Council of Trade Unions] but the Central Committee of the R.C.P. [Russian Communist Party] for having 'overlooked' Rudzutak's thesis, and, owing to this mistake, allowed a useless discussion to flare up." (Lenin, *Selected Works*, Vol. IX, 32) Lenin shortly afterward referred to them as "Rudzutak's *practical* theses, with their concrete, vital and urgent tasks (develop production propaganda; learn proper distribution of bonuses in kind and correct use of coercion through disciplinary comrades' courts)," and referring to Trotsky compared them "to the highbrow, abstract, 'empty' and theoretically incorrect general *theses* which *ignore* all that is most practical and business-like" (Lenin, "Once Again on the Trade Unions, The Present Situation and the Mistakes of Trotsky and Bukharin," *Selected Works*, Vol. IX, 40–80). According to the memoirs of one Bolshevik leader, Anastas Mikoyan, before his death in 1924, Lenin proposed that Rudzutak replace Joseph Stalin as the secretary general of the Communist Party (Anastas Ivanovich Mikoian, *Memoirs of Anastas Mikoyan*, trans. Katherine T. O'Connor and Diana L. Burgin [Madison, CT: Sphinx Press, 1988]). On May 24, 1937, Rudzutak—a member of the Central Committee of the All-Russia Communist Party from 1920 until 1937, a candidate member of the Politburo from 1923 to 1926 and from 1934 to 1937, and a full member of the Politburo from 1926 to 1932—was arrested and accused of Trotskyism as well as espionage for Nazi Germany. He was found guilty, sentenced to death, and subsequently executed (Simon Sebag Montefiore, *Stalin: The Court of the Red Tsar* [New York: Knopf, 2004], 223–4, 239–41, 246).

14   "The Tasks of the Trade Unions in Production—*Theses of Comrade Rudzutak's Report*," quoted in Lenin, *Selected Works*, Vol. IX, 23–26.

15   In one of Lenin's last works, the essay entitled "On Cooperation," written in January 1923, Lenin addressed the question of state capitalism and its role in the revolutionary transformation of Russia:

> Whenever I wrote about the New Economic Policy I always quoted the article on state capitalism which I wrote in 1918 ["Left-Wing" Childishness and the Petty-Bourgeois Mentality; part III]. This has more than once aroused doubts in the minds of certain young comrades but their doubts were mainly on abstract political points.
>
> It seemed to them that the term "state capitalism" could not be applied to a system under which the means of production were owned by the working-class, a working-class that held political power. They did not notice, however, that I use the term "state capitalism", firstly, to connect historically our present position with the position adopted in my controversy with the so-called Left Communists; also, I argued at the time that state capitalism would be superior to our existing economy. It was important for me to show the continuity between ordinary state capitalism and the unusual, even very unusual, state capitalism to which I referred in introducing the reader to the New Economic Policy. Secondly, the practical purpose was always important to me. And the practical purpose of our New Economic Policy was to lease out concessions. In the prevailing circumstances, concessions in our country would unquestionably have been a pure type of state capitalism. That is how I argued about state capitalism.
>
> But there is another aspect of the matter for which we may need state capitalism, or at least a comparison with it. It is a question of cooperatives.
>
> In the capitalist state, cooperatives are no doubt collective capitalist institutions. Nor is there any doubt that under our present economic conditions, when we combine

private capitalist enterprises—but in no other way than nationalized land and in no other way than under the control of the working-class state—with enterprises of the consistently socialist type (the means of production, the land on which the enterprises are situated, and the enterprises as a whole belonging to the state), the question arises about a third type of enterprise, the cooperatives, which were not formally regarded as an independent type differing fundamentally from the others. Under private capitalism, cooperative enterprises differ from capitalist enterprises as collective enterprises differ from private enterprises. Under state capitalism, cooperative enterprises differ from state capitalist enterprises, firstly, because they are private enterprises, and, secondly, because they are collective enterprises. Under our present system, cooperative enterprises differ from private capitalist enterprises because they are collective enterprises, but do not differ from socialist enterprises if the land on which they are situated and means of production belong to the state, i.e., the working-class ("On Cooperation," V. I. Lenin, *Collected Works*, 2nd English Edition [Moscow: Progress Publishers, 1965], Vol. 33, 467–75).

16   The document that James is referring to was *Oktyabr'skaya Revolyutsiya i fabzavkomy* [The October Revolution and the Factory Committees]. Published in 1927, the original Russian text has been edited with an introduction, notes, bibliographical sources, and indexes by S. A. Smith (Publications of the Study Group on the Russian Revolution: No. 6 [Millwood, NY: Kraus International Publications, 1983]).

17   There has been no English translation of *Oktyabr'skaya Revolyutsiya i fabzavkomy* published to date.

18   A flood of documents about the revolution in general and about workers' meetings, factory committees, trade unions, red guards, and district soviets were released in the late 1950s and in the 1960s. According to historian Rex Wade, one of the leading authorities on the Russian Revolution, in a statement to the editor:

> Generalizations here are difficult, but in general, the trade unions were more Menshevik oriented and led, while the factory committees became more radical and more Bolshevik or Left SR as 1917 and the revolution wore on. (I'm assuming that factory committees is what he [James] means by "workers' councils"—there isn't an institution that would fit with the Russian equivalent by strict translation and thus the latter term isn't normally used in English for any Russian institution of the time, although I think that it may have been popular among Western radicals in the 1920s and onwards, in an imprecise way, to include any worker organization in Russia of the revolutionary era). Then, after the Bolsheviks took power, bringing the factory committees and worker self-assertiveness under control was a major problem for the Bolshevik regime. They used the trade unions to do that, as I recall. It was a very complex process... There also was a resurgence of factory-based worker organizations in early 1918, and then and periodically down to 1921, in opposition to the centralizing and authoritarian practices of the Bolsheviks as the latter worked to bring worker spontaneity and self-organization (and self-definition of their interests) under Party control. The Kronstadt rebellion in 1921 started, of course, in significant part out of the sailors' support for Petrograd workers' demands vis-à-vis the regime (Rex Wade to David Austin, April 8, 2006).

19   "The Tasks of the Trade Unions in Production," quoted in Lenin, *Selected Works*, Vol. IX, 23.

20   At the time that James made this statement, in the 1960s, it was certainly correct. Since that time, however, the situation has markedly changed, with the publication of a good deal of in-depth scholarly investigation of the factory committees and of the Petrograd factory committees in particular. See A. Andryev, *The Soviets of Workers' and Soldiers' Deputies on the Eve of the October Revolution, March–October 1917* (Moscow: Progress Publishers, 1971); (William G. Rosenberg, "Russian

Labor and Bolshevik Power: Social Dimensions of Protest in Petrograd After October," in *The Russian Revolution: The Essential Readings*, ed. Martin Miller (Malden, MA: Blackwell Publishers, 2001), 149–179; Alexander Rabinowitch, *The Bolsheviks in Power: The First Year of Soviet Rule in Petrograd* (Bloomington & Indianapolis, IN: Indiana University Press, 2007); S. A. Smith, "Editor's Introduction: The Birth of the Factory Committees," *Oktyabr'skaya Revolyutsiya i fabzavkomy (The October Revolution and the Factory Committees)* (Millwood, NY: Kraus International Publications, 1983), xi–xxxii, and *Red Petrograd: Revolution in the Factories 1917–18* (Cambridge; New York: Cambridge University Press, 1983).

21   Isaac Deutscher, *Soviet Trade Unions: Their Place in Soviet Labour Policy* (London & New York: Royal Institute of International Affairs, 1950). In the footnote that James refers to, Deutscher wrote:

At the first All-Russian conference of factory committees which opened a few days before the October revolution, Schmidt, the future Commissar for Labour in Lenin's Government, stated: 'At the moment when the factory committees were formed the Trade Unions actually did not yet exist, and the factory committees filled the vacuum.' Later on, after the trade unions gained in strength, 'control from below' was exercised by the factory committees. (See *Oktyabrskaya Revolutsiya I Fabzavkomy* [The October Revolution and the Factory Committees] Moscow, 1927, II, 188.) Another speaker stated at the conference: ' ...the growth of the influence of the factory committees has naturally occurred at the expense of centralized economic organizations of the working class such as the Trade Unions . . . . This, of course, is a highly abnormal development which has in practice led to very undesirable results . . . .' ibid., 190. Against this an anarchist speaker argued: 'The Trade Unions wish to devour the factory committees. There is no popular discontent with the factory committees, but there is discontent with the Trade Unions . . . To the workers the Trade Union is a form of organization imposed from without. The factory committee is closer to them . . . Anarchists think that they should set up and develop the cells of future society . . . The factory committees are such cells of the future . . . They, not the state, will now administer . . .' ibid., 191. The anarchist influence in the factory committees was fairly strong at that time, but the antagonism between Bolshevism and anarchism was still largely hidden. In the first half of 1917 the Mensheviks, dominating the trade unions, tried in vain to bring the factory committees under control. The Bolsheviks then juxtaposed the factory committees to the trade unions and so they had some common ground with the anarchists. Ibid., 104. The Bolshevik attitude changed later in the year when, having gained the decisive influence in the trade unions, they sought to subordinate the factory committees to the trade unions (Chap. 2, "Trade Unions and the Revolution," fn. 1, 16).

22   Karl Marx, *Economic-Philosophic Manuscripts*. The Johnson-Forest Tendency was the first to translate these manuscripts into English in 1947, though not in their entirety. The three essays it published were "Alienated Labour," "Private Property and Communism," and "Critique of the Hegelian Dialectic." Lenin was not aware of these manuscripts.

23   "The Tasks of the Trade Unions in Production," Lenin, *Selected Works*, Vol. IX, 23.

24   Ibid.

25   Ibid., 23–24.

26   Hannah Arendt, *On Revolution* (New York, Viking Press, 1963).

27   Yan Ernestovich Rudzutak, "The Tasks of the Trade Unions in Production," Lenin, *Selected Works*, Vol. IX, 24.

28   Ibid.

29   Ibid., 24–25.

30   Ibid., 25.

31   Ibid.

32   Ibid.

33   Ibid.

34   Ibid.

35   Ibid., 25–26.

36   Lenin, "The Trade Unions, the Present Situation and the Mistakes of Trotsky," *Selected Works*, Vol. IX, 26.

37   Ibid.

38   "The Party Crisis," January 19, 1921, Lenin, *Selected Works*, Vol. IX, 28.

39   Ibid., 28–29.

40   "Once Again on the Trade Unions, The Present Situation and the Mistakes of Trotsky and Bukharin," January 25, 1921, Lenin, *Selected Works*, Vol. IX, 40–80; see also Lenin, *Collected Works*, Vol. 32, 70–107.

41   Lenin, *Selected Works*, Vol. IX, 457–458.

42   James is referring to the manuscript which was eventually published as *Nkrumah and the Ghana Revolution* (Westport, CT: Lawrence Hill and Company, 1977).

43   The Workers' Opposition emerged in 1920 as a faction within the Russian Communist Party in response to the rapidly increasing bureaucratization of the party and the government. Led by Alexander Shliapnikov, the chairman of the Russian Metalworkers' Union, it was made up of a group of trade union leaders and industrial administrators who had earlier been industrial workers. The group's chief mentor and advocate was Alexandra Kollontai (1872–1952), the famous social-ist and feminist. Although the Tenth Congress of the Russian Communist Party, condemned the Workers' Opposition for factionalism, some of its proposals were nonetheless adopted (see Robert Daniels, *The Conscience of the Revolution: Communist Opposition in Soviet Russia* [Cambridge, Mass.: Harvard University Press, 1960; rev. ed. Boulder, Col., 1988]; Larry E. Holmes, *For the Revolution Redeemed: The Workers Opposition in the Bolshevik Party, 1919–1921,* The University of Pittsburgh, *Carl Beck Papers in Russian and East European Studies,* no. 802 [1990]; Alexandra Kollontai, *The Workers' Opposition* [San Pedro, CA: League for Economic Democracy, 1973]; *Selected Writings* [New York: Holt, 1980]; Cathy Porter, *Alexandra Kollontai: A Biography* [London: Virago, 1980]; Jay Sorenson, *The Life and Death of Soviet Trade Unionism: 1917–1928* [New York: 1969]).

44   Alexander Shliapnikov (1885–1937), a metalworker and Bolshevik trade union leader, in 1917 helped to organize the Petrograd and All-Russian Metalworkers' Unions, being elected the chair of both bodies. He supported the Bolshevik seizure of power in October 1917 and served as commissar of labor until Fall 1918. By the following Fall, Shliapnikov began to express misgivings and disagreements regarding the trade union policy of the Communist Party. He presented his theses proposing trade union control of industry and the "workerization" of the party's principal organs to the Ninth Party Congress in 1920. The supporters of his views came to be called the "Workers' Opposition" (see Alexander Shliapnikov, "On the relations between the Russian Com-munist Party, the soviets, and production unions," March 1920, http://www.marxists.org/archive/shiliapnikov/index.htm; see also Barbara Allen, "Alexander Shliapnikov and the Origins of the Workers' Opposition, March 1919–April 1920," *Jahrbuecher fuer Geschichte Osteuropas,* 53 [2005]: 1–24; Larry E. Holmes, "For the Revolution Redeemed: The Workers Opposition in the Bolshevik Party, 1919–1921," *The Carl Beck Papers in Russian and East European Studies,* no. 802 [1990]; and "Soviet Rewriting of 1917: The Case of A. G. Shliapnikov." *Slavic Review* 2 [1979]: 224–242.)

45   During the Russian Communist Party's Tenth Party Congress, in March 1921, Lenin sharply criticized the views of the various opposition groups within the party. Specifically, the party congress adopted Lenin's draft resolution "On the Syndicalist and Anarchist Deviation in our

Party," which was aimed at the Workers' Opposition. The congress resolution, "On Party Unity," adopted on Lenin's motion, ordered the dissolution of all party factions and groups (V. I. Lenin, "Tenth Congress of the R.C.P.[Bolshevik], Part IV," 8–16 March 1921, *Collected Works*, 1st English Edition [Moscow: Progress Publishers, 1965], Vol. 32, 165–271).

46 Boris Souvarine, *Stalin: A Critical Survey of Bolshevism* (New York: Longmans, Green, & Co., 1939). James translated this book from French to English.

47 Edward Hallett Carr (1892–1982), British historian, journalist and international relations theorist, author of *A History of Soviet Russia,* 14 volumes (London: Macmillan, 1950–1978), *1917 Before and After* (London: Macmillan, 1969; American edition: *The October Revolution Before and After* (New York: Knopf, 1969), and *The Russian Revolution: From Lenin to Stalin (1917–1929)* (London: Macmillan, 1979); see Michael Cox, ed., *E.H. Carr: A Critical Appraisal* (London: Palgrave, 2000), and Jonathan Haslam, "E.H. Carr and the History of Soviet Russia," *Historical Journal,* 26, no. 4 (1983): 1021–1027.

48 George Weekes, the militant leader of Trinidad's Oilfield Workers Trade Union was a fellow member with James of the Workers' and Farmers' Party. Weekes was a prominent critic of the government of Eric Williams and played an important role in the 1970 Black Power protests which challenged Williams's leadership.

49 The Workers' and Farmers' Party in Trinidad.

50 James is referring to Norman Girvan, the renowned Jamaican economist. Girvan was part of a study group in James's London home in the early 1960s and maintained a close relationship with James. The "they" and "the fellows" that James refers to appears to be the former British colonial authorities and the owners and administrators of major foreign-owned companies in Trinidad.

51 Alfie Roberts often stated that it was the Caribbean Conference Committee and Roberts in particular who alerted James to the significance and importance of the Cuban Revolution. James's remark here is likely in relation to discussions between James and Roberts about the Cuban Revolution. For an account of James and Robert A. Hill's 1967–1968 visit to Cuba, see Andrew Salkey's *Havana Journal* (Middlesex: Pelican Books, 1971). See also Frank Rosengarten, *Urbane Revolutionary: C.L.R. James and the Struggle for a New Society* (Jackson: University Press of Mississippi), 107–114.

Lenin and the Tade Union Debate in Russia, Part Two

1 V. I. Lenin, *Selected Works,* Vol. IX: New Economic Policy—Socialist Construction (New York: International Publishers, 1937).

2 Lenin, "Once Again on the Trade Unions, The Present Situation and the Mistakes of Trotsky and Bukharin," in Lenin, *Selected Works,* Vol. IX, 40–80; Lenin, *Collected Works,* Vol. 32, 70–107.

3 Ibid., 40.

4 Ibid.

5 Ibid.

6 Ibid.

7 Ibid., 40–41.

8 Ibid., 43.

9 Ibid., 44.

10 A reference to the Putney debates that took place in 1647 at the height of the English Civil War. The Levellers were a 17th century English political movement and rose to prominence as a faction of the New Model Army (see Blair Worden, "The Levellers in History and Memory c.1660–1960," in *The Putney Debates of 1647,* ed. Michael Mendle [Cambridge; New York: Cambridge University Press, 2001], 280–282).

11   Franklyn Harvey, who was present at the lecture had taken an active part in debating with James about various aspects of Lenin's leadership of the Russian Revolution.

12   Lenin, "Once Again on the Trade Unions, The Present Situation and the Mistakes of Trotsky and Bukharin," 53.

13   Ibid., 54.

14   Ibid.

15   Ibid., 55.

16   See Lenin's draft resolution "On the Syndicalist and Anarchist Deviation in our Party," presented at the Russian Communist Party's Tenth Party Congress, in March 1921, which was directed against the Workers' Opposition (V. I. Lenin, "Tenth Congress of the R.C.P.[Bolshevik], Part IV," March 8–16, 19 21, *Collected Works*, 1st English Edition [Moscow: Progress Publishers, 1965], Vol. 32, 165–271).

17   Edward Hallett Carr (1892–1982), British historian, journalist and international relations theorist, author of *A History of Soviet Russia*, 14 volumes (London: Macmillan, 1950–1978), *1917 Before and After* (London: Macmillan, 1969; American edition: *The October Revolution Before and After* (New York: Knopf, 1969), and *The Russian Revolution: From Lenin to Stalin (1917–1929)* (London: Macmillan, 1979); see Michael Cox, ed., *E.H. Carr: A Critical Appraisal* (London: Palgrave, 2000), and Jonathan Haslam, "E.H. Carr and the History of Soviet Russia," *Historical Journal*, 26, no. 4 (1983): 1021–1027.

18   Lenin, "Once Again on the Trade Unions, The Present Situation and the Mistakes of Trotsky and Bukharin," 68–69.

19   Ibid., 69.

20   Ibid.

21   Ibid., 70.

22   Ibid.

23   Ibid.

24   Ibid., 45–46.

25   The name given to a series of emergency measures carried out by the Bolshevik government, such as the requisitioning of surplus agricultural produce from *kulaks* or rich peasants during the desperate days of Civil War.

LENIN AND THE TADE UNION DEBATE IN RUSSIA, PART THREE

1   Lenin, "Once Again on the Trade Unions, The Present Situation and the Mistakes of Trotsky and Bukharin," *Selected Works*, Vol. IX, 73.

2   Ibid., 73.

3   Ibid., 73–74.

4   Ibid., 74.

5   Ibid., 74.

6   Written December 1922–January 1923, and first published only in 1956 (*Kommunist*, No. 9), Lenin's last testament proposed a complete reorganization of the Soviet government. The testament contained three parts, namely, increasing the size of the Central Committee, granting legislative functions to the State Planning Commission, and on the Question of Nationalities. Lenin intended that his letters be published and read at the upcoming Congress of Soviets, the Congress of the Communist party and (the Question on Nationalities) at the First Congress of Soviets of the U.S.S.R. Lenin's letters were never read, but were withheld from publication until 1956 as part of the deStalinization of the Soviet Union (Lenin, *Collected Works*, Vol. 36, 593–611).

7   James is referring to The Johnson-Forest Tendency. "Johnson" and "Forest" were pseud-onyms for C.L.R. James and Raya Dunayevskaya, respectively, the two founding members of the Tendency. Other members of the group included Grace Lee Boggs and Martin Glaberman. This small Marxist organization produced a number of original works of socialist theory and analysis. In addition to *The Invading Socialist Society* (1947; Detroit: Bewick Editions, 1972), other publi-cations that emerged out of the group's work include *Notes on Dialectics* (1948), *Mariners, Ren-egades and Castaways* (1953), *Every Cook Can Govern* (1956), and *Facing Reality* (1958). James was forced to leave the United States in 1953. Shortly after his departure, internal problems gripped the group, resulting in a split in 1955 with Dunayevskaya and a number of her supporters in the organization.

8   Lenin's actual words, dictated on December 24, 1922, were: "He [Trotsky] is personally perhaps the most capable man in the present C.C. [Central Committee], but he has displayed excessive self-assurance and shown excessive preoccupation with the purely administrative side of work" (V.I. Lenin, *Collected Works*, Vol. 36, "Letters to the Congress" (Moscow: Progress Publishers, 1971), 595.

9   Lenin's actual words regarding Stalin read:

"Comrade Stalin, having become Secretary-General, has unlimited authority concen-trated in his hands, and I am not sure whether he will always be capable of using that authority with sufficient caution." In an addition to the same letter quoted above dated 4 January 1923, Lenin says, "Stalin is too rude and this defect, although quite tolerable in our midst and in dealings among us Communists, becomes intolerable in a Secretary-General. That is why I suggest that the comrades think about a way of removing Stalin from that post and appointing another man in his stead who in all respects differs from Comrade Stalin in having only one advantage, namely, that of being more tolerant, more loyal, more polite and more considerate to the comrades, less capricious, etc. This circumstance may appear to be a negligible detail. But I think that from the standpoint of safeguards against a split and from the standpoint of what I wrote above about the relationship between Stalin and Trotsky, it is not a detail, or it is a detail, or is a detail which can assume decisive importance."

10   A reference to Alfie Roberts.

11   A. S. P. Woodhouse, *Puritanism and Liberty* (London: Dent, 1951).

12   Thomas Rainborowe [Rainbrowe] (1610–1648), also known as Thomas Rainborough, par-liamentarian army officer and Leveller. Rainborowe was a leading figure in the English Civil War. During the Putney debates of 1647, he famously declared for the Levellers: "For really I think that the poorest he that is in England have a life to live, as the greatest he: and therefore truly, sir, I think it's clear, that every man that is to live under a government ought first by his own consent to put himself under that government." Henry Ireton, for the Army 'Grandees' replied: "no man hath a right to an interest or share in the disposing of the affairs of the kingdom … that hath not a permanent fixed interest in this kingdom" (quotations from E. P. Thompson, *The Making of the English Working Class* [New York: Pantheon Books, 1964]). His brother William Rainborowe wa a major in the New Model Army, but was dismissed in 1649 for his extremely radical opini (Ian J. Gentles, 'Rainborowe , Thomas (d. 1648)', *Oxford Dictionary of National Biography*, O University Press, Sept 2004; online edn, Jan 2008 [http://www.oxforddnb.com/view/article accessed June 9, 2008]).

13   Robert A. Hill.

14   In "*On the Party Programme: Report delivered at the Eight Congress of the C-munist Party (Bolsheviks), March 19, 1919,*" Lenin states the following:

> The best of bourgeois republics, no matter how democratic they may be, have thousands of legislative hindrances which prevent the toilers from participating in the work of government. We have removed these hindrances, but so far we have not managed to get the toiling masses to participate in the work of the government. Apart from the law, there is still the level of culture, which you cannot subject to any law. The result of this low cultural level is that the Soviets, which by virtue of their programme are organs of government *by the toilers*, are in fact organs of government *for the toilers*, by means of the advanced stratum of the proletariat, but not by means of the toiling masses (emphasis is original).

See V.I. Lenin, *Selected Works*, Vol. VIII (New York: International Publishers, n.d.), 353.

15   Grantley Adams (1898–1971) was premier and first prime minister of Barbados. He was a driving force behind and former head of the short-lived West Indian Federation. The party and union that James is referring to were the Barbados Labour Party and the Barbados Worker's Union (BWU). Hugh Springer (1917 to 1994) was the BWU's first General Secretary and later served as the country's Governor General. See F.A. Hoyos, *Grantley Adams and the Social Revolution* (London; Macmillan Education Limited, 1974).

16   This is perhaps a reference to the fact that St. Lucia's dominant language is a French Creole which is closer to the Creole spoken in Haiti, Martinique, and Guadeloupe than to Creoles of Britain's other former Caribbean colonies.

17   Albert Gomes (1911–1978) was an outstanding Trinidadian legislator. He was the publisher of the literary magazine *The Beacon* in the 1930s and worked closely with James, who was also involved in the magazine during this period. In the 1950s Gomes was the leader of Party of Political Progress Groups in Trinidad and Tobago and was later actively involved in the country's opposition Democratic Labour Party before migrating to England in 1961.

18   Leon Trotsky, *Stalin: An Appraisal of the Man and His Influence* (New York: Harper & Brother Publishers, 1941).

19   When Lenin returned to Russia from exile in April 1917, he published his "April Thesis" which proposed that the Bolshevik Party oppose the provisional government of Alexander Kerensky which had come into power after the February revolution.

20   William Haller and Godfrey Davis, ed., *Leveller Tracts: 1647–53* (New York: Columbia University Press, 1944).

21   Likely referring to Alfie Roberts.

ON LITERATURE, EXILE, AND NATIONHOOD

1   Otherwise known in English as *Notebook of a Return to My Native Country*.

2   Eventually published as *Nkrumah and Ghana Revolution* (London: Allison & Busby Ltd., 1977).

3   According to Robert A. Hill, James did in fact complete his manuscript on *King Lear*, but the sole copy was lost by the publisher. James planned to rewrite the book. (Robert A. Hill, interviewed by David Austin, 15 May 2004). In his 1965 talk, "C.L.R. James: The Man and His Work," Martin Glaberman suggests that James had already completed a manuscript on Shakespeare and Lenin.

     James is referring to writer Michael Anthony.

'T PLAY WITH REVOLUTION

     Ellison, *The Invisible Man* (1952; New York: Second Vintage International Edition,

2   C.L.R. James, *Party Politics in the West Indies* (San Juan, Trinidad: Vedic Enterprises, Ltd., 1962), 100.

3   Ibid., 89.

CORRESPONDENCE

1   C.L.R. James, *World Revolution, 1917–1936: The Rise and Fall of the Communist International* (1937; Atlantic Highlands, N.J.: Humanities Press, 1993).

2   C.L.R. James, "The Revolutionary Answer to the Negro Problem in the U.S.A," in *The C.L.R. James Reader*, ed. Anna Grimshaw, 182–189.

3   Roberts is referring to Frank Worrell, Everton Weekes, and Clyde Walcott, three of the greatest West Indian and world cricketers. The three W's were central to the West Indies' rise as a cricket power in the 1950s, a phenomenon that was seen as a symbol and part and parcel of the wave of nationalism that gripped the region during this period.

4   Garfield Sobers, Rohan Kanhai, and Wesley Hall were three of the young outstanding cricketers that succeeded the three W's in West Indian cricket. Barbadian Garfield Sobers is arguably the best all-round cricket player of all time and, along with Alfie Roberts, he was identified by Everton Weekes at an early age as and outstanding cricket talent.

5   The newspaper *We the People*, the organ of the Workers' and Farmers' Party, was edited by C.L.R. James.

6   Jim Evrard is perhaps best know for his essay, "Five O'Clock World 2: Workers' Hobbies." In this essay, which appeared in *Rebel Worker*, no. 7, "Evrard writes, in confrontational language, that the supposed hobbies that many attend to in their free time away from wage labor are not actual compensation for devoting one's life to making the boss rich. Unfortunately the article suffers from the illusion that machines will liberate human beings by doing the work deemed as onerous." Anthony Leskov, "A Review of Dancin' in the Streets," in *Flying Stone: The online bulletin of the Portland Surrealist Group*, March 2, 2007 (http://pdxsurr.blogspot.com/2007_03_01_archive.html). Evrard also wrote the essay "Consciousness and Theory" which appeared in 1966 in *Revolutionary Consciousness*, a Rebel Worker pamphlet.

7   William Gorman was a student of Hegelian phenomenology and an active member of Facing Reality.

8   *Notes on Dialectics* (1948).

9   Eventually published as *Nkrumah and the Ghana Revolution* (1977).

10   Alfie Roberts actually studied at Sir George Williams University, present-day Concordia University. He then pursued graduate studies at Carleton University in Ottawa.

11 Paul Cardan is an alias of Cornelius Castoriadis. Castoriadis founded the political organization Socialism or Barbarism in Paris and worked closely with C.L.R. James in the late 1940s and in the 1950s, collaborating on the book, *Facing Reality* (1958) under the pseudonym Pierre Chaulieu. For an analysis of this relationship and James's work see Cornelius Castoriadis, "C.L.R. James and the Fate of Humanity," *C.L.R. James: His Intellectual Legacies*, ed. Selwyn R. Cudjoe and William E. Cain (Amherst, Mass: University of Massachusetts Press, 1985), 277–297.

12   C.L.R. James, in collaboration with Raya Dunayevskaya and Grace Lee, *State Capitalism and World Revolution* (1950; Chicago: Charles H. Kerr Publishing Company, 1986).

13   These were private political discussion recorded in James's home in London.

14   Nello was James's nickname and the lectures included talks on James's book *Beyond a Boundary* and "A New View of West Indian History," as well as another lecture which is not mentioned by Hill, "The West Indian Writer."

15   C.L.R. James, *Federation—"We Failed Miserably"—How and Why* (San Juan, Trinidad: Vedic Enterprises, Ltd., c. 1960). See also "On Federation," in C.L.R. James, *At the Rendezvous of Victory* (London, U.K.: Allison & Busby Ltd., 1984), 106–128.

16   Referring to James's involvement in the Workers' and Farmers' Party and his campaign in Trinidad and Tobago's forthcoming national election.

17   Eventually published as *Nkrumah and the Ghana Revolution* (1977).

18   *Modern Politics* (1960).

19   *Notes on Dialectics* (1948).

20   The first Annual Socialist Scholars Conference. Hill and Glaberman attended the conference. Participants included Connor Cruise O'Brian and Maxwell Geismar, both of whom, according to Glaberman, delivered the best talks (Martin Glaberman to C.L.R. James, September 27, 1965 (Glaberman Collection, 7–12).

21   Robert A. Hill is referring to Ken Hill, the trade unionist and nationalist who, along with Richard Hart, Arthur Henry, and Frank Hill were expelled from Jamaica's People's National Party in 1952 after being accused of being communists. At the time, Ken Hill was working as a journalist for the *Trinidad Guardian*.

22   Crawford Brough McPherson became a Professor of Political Economy at the University of Toronto. McPherson wrote several books, including *Democracy in Alberta: The Theory and Practice of a Quasi-Party System* (1953) and *The Real World of Democracy* (1966), but is perhaps best remembered for his *The Political Theory of Possessive Individuals: Hobbes to Locke* (1962).

23   Mervyn Solomon was a Trinidadian student at the University of Toronto and a poet. He is currently an educator in Miami, Florida.

24   Claude Robinson was a Jamaican student of journalism at Carleton University in Ottawa who went on to be general manager of the Jamaica Broadcasting Corporation.

25   *We the People.*

26   Workers' and Farmers' Party.

27   The C.L.R. James Study Circle.

28   Roosevelt "Rosie" Douglas was a founding member of the Caribbean Conference Committee. Douglas was one of the key organizers of the 1968 Congress of Black Writers in Montreal and one of the leading figures in the student protest at Sir George Williams University (now Concordia) the following year. Douglas was elected prime minister of Dominica in January 2000 and died in October the same year.

29   C.L.R. James, *Mariners, Renegades, Castaways: The Story of Herman Melville and the World We Live In* (1953; Hanover: University Press of New England, 2001).

30   C.L.R. James, *Beyond a Boundary* (1963; Durham: Duke University Press, 1993).

31   Fitzroy Richard Augier was from St. Lucia and the co-author, along with D.G. Hall and Shirley C. Gordon, and M. Reckford of *The Making of the West Indies* (London: Longman Caribbean, 1960) and co-compiler with Shirley C. Gordon of *Sources of West Indian History* (London: Longmans, Green & Co. Ltd., 1962).

32   See C.L.R. James, "Parties, Politics and Economics in the Caribbean," *Freedomways: The People of the Caribbean Area*, 4(3), Summer 1964.

33   *Boissonade, P.: Saint-Domingue à la Veille de la Révolution et la Question de la Représentation aux États-Généraux* (Paris-New York, 1906).

34   C.L.R. James, *Mariners, Renegades, Castaways: The Story of Herman Melville and the World We Live In.*

35   Hector is referring to the June 1937 strike by oilfield workers in Fyzabad, Trinidad. The sit-in quickly evolved into widespread unrest and rioting across the island when police repression was used to break up what was initially a peaceful protest. This period marked the birth of the

trade union movement in Trinidad. For details on this and other labor rebellions in the region in the 1930s, see O. Nigel Bolland, *On the March: Labour Rebellions in the British Caribbean, 1934–39* (Kingston, JA: Ian Randle Publishers/London, U.K.: James Currey Publishers, 1995).

36   Edited by C.L.R. James, *We the People* was the official organ of the Workers' and Farmers' Party.

37   See C.L.R. James, "The Rise and Fall of Nkrumah," in C.L.R. James, *At the Rendezvous of Victory* (London: Allison & Busby Ltd., 1984), 172–180.

38   The C.L.R. James Study Circle.

39   See Perry Anderson, Socialism and Pseudo-Empiricism," *New Left Review*, 1(35), 2–42 and E.P. Thompson, "The Peculiarities of the English," in *The Socialist Register, 1965*, ed. Ralph Miliband and John Saville (New York: Monthly Review Press, 1965), 311–362.

40   George Weekes, the militant leader of Trinidad's Oilfield Workers' Trade Union, was a fellow member with James of the Workers' and Farmers' Party. Weekes was a prominent critic of prime minister Eric Williams and played an important role in the 1970 Black Power protests which challenged Williams's leadership. George Bowrin was a prominent Trinidadian lawyer, activist, and 1st Vice Chairman of the Workers' and Farmers' Party. Weekes was attacked in the conservative Trinidad newspaper, the *Guardian*, and by the government of Eric Williams for attending the January 1966 Tricontinental Conference in Cuba. See Khafra Kambon, *For Bread, Justice, and Freedom: A Political Biography of George Weekes* (London: New Beacon Books Ltd, 1988), 168.

41   The lectures included talks on James's book *Beyond a Boundary* and "A New View of West Indian History," as well as another lecture which is not mentioned by Hill, "The West Indian Writer."

42   George Lamming and Martin Carter, ed., *New World: Guyana Independence Issue,* 2(3), 1966.

43   The play that James appears to be referring to is *The Black Jacobins*, a revision of his 1936 play *Toussaint L'Ouverture*. *The Black Jacobins* was mounted in Ibadan, Nigeria by the Arts Theatre Group in 1967.

44   Middleton Wilson was a Jamaican PhD student in economics at the University of Toronto who worked closely with Robert A. Hill while in Canada. He returned to Jamaica after completing his studies where he worked in the National Planning Unit for the government of Michael Manley.

45   This reference is to Robert A. Hill's intention to write a book on Marcus Garvey. Today Hill is the Editor in Chief of *The Marcus Garvey and the Universal Negro Improvement Association Papers*.

46   Hill is referring to James's introduction to the 1947 edition of Marx's *Economic-Philosophic Manuscripts*. James's organization, the Johnson Forest-Tendency, was the first to publish the essays "Alienated Labour," "Private Property and Communism," and "Critique of the Hegelian Dialectic" in English. See C.L.R. James, "On Marx's Essays from the Economic-Philosophic Manuscript," in C.L.R. James, *At the Rendezvous of Victory* (London: Allison & Busby Ltd., 1984), 65–72.

47   Hill is referring to George Lamming and Martin Carter (eds.), *New World: Guyana Independence Issue,* 2(3), 1966.

48   Frank Monico was an actor and active, longstanding member of Facing Reality and its predecessors. In mid-1940s he helped to set up a branch of the Johnson-Forest Tendency in Morgantown, Virginia.

49   James used the pseudonym J.R. Johnson in the 1940s and 1950s and the name of the group he co-founded was the Johnson-Forest Tendency, Forest being the alias of Raya Dunayevskaya.

50   This was the code name given to *Notes on Dialectics* which was written by James in Nevada, Las Vegas in 1948. The manuscript was edited by Hill and published in 1966.

51   George Rawick was an active member of Facing Reality and a historian of United States history who specialized in the study of slavery. His wife Diane (née Luchtan) was also associated with the group, as was her sister April and her husband, Ross Klatte. Along with Rawick and Glaberman, William Gorman was the other active Detroit-based member of Facing Reality with whom C.L.R. James closely collaborated and whose fertile mind James greatly admired. Gorman specialized in the study of the American Civil War and was an avid student of G.W.F. Hegel.

52   This in part refers to C.L.R. James's October 8, 1966 lecture on existentialism during his visit to Montreal.

53   The Cuban edition was first raised by Caribbean Conference Committee-C.L.R. James Study Circle member Anne Cools during her August 1966 visit to Cuba, but it was never published.

54   C.L.R. James's Workers' and Farmers' Party was resoundingly defeated in the November 1966 Trinidad and Tobago national elections. In an undated letter from Trinidad written to Robert A. Hill and Glaberman, James wrote: "They robbed us. Everybody agrees, everybody. The [voting] machines were rigged." James also added: "I will return here. But now I have to get out very soon. I can't go into detail, but that is what I see very clearly. I more than ever do not go a yard without a bodyguard." C.L.R. James to Robert A. Hill and Martin Glaberman, November 1966 [Glaberman, WSU box 8–6].

55   Glaberman is referring to the attempts by James's opponents to discredit him during the 1966 Trinidad election campaign by calling him a communist and Marxist.

56   Referring to Facing Reality member William Gorman, who was transcribing James's lecture on "Existentialism and Marxism" that was delivered in Montreal on October 8, 1966.

57   Glaberman was referring to his lecture tour on the tenth anniversary of the Hungarian Revolution of 1956. Robert A. Hill arranged his Toronto talk on the subject.

58   In a letter to Robert A. Hill and Martin Glaberman, James described the analysis in Walter Kaufmann's *Hegel: Reinterpretation, Texts, and Commentary* (1965) as "far and away the best I know." James seemed to be especially impressed with Kaufmann's analysis of Hegel's Preface to *Phenomenology of Mind* and he asked that a copy of his *Notes on Dialectics* be sent to Kaufmann and that a "bourgeois press" be pursued for the book. C.L.R. James to Robert A. Hill and Martin Glaberman, 29 October 1966 [Glaberman, WSU Box 8–6].

59   Roberts is referring to Facing Reality's annual conference in Detroit in mid-September, 1966.

60   *Flambeau* magazine was published in St. Vincent (1965–1968) and covered a range of political, artistic, and philosophical questions related to St. Vincent and the Caribbean as a whole. Martin Glaberman's speech, "C.L.R. James: The Man and His Work," appeared in the November 1966 issue of the magazine and was recently published in a collection of *Flambeau*'s articles in Kenneth John, Baldwin King and Cheryl L.A. King, (eds,) *Quest for Caribbean Unity: Beyond Colonialism* (Madison, NJ: Kings-SVG, 2006), 167–170.

61   See C.L.R. James, "Lenin and the Problem," in C.L.R. James, *Nkrumah and the Ghana Revolution* (Westport, CT: Lawrence Hill & Co., 1977), 189–213.

62   During his North American lecture tour between December 1966 and March 1967 James entered the United States for the first time since having been expelled in 1953.

63   C.L.R. James, *Education, Agitation and Propaganda* (mimeographed, 1943); Detroit: Facing Reality, 1968.

64   Franklyn Harvey.

65   Andy Anderson, *Hungary '56* (London, UK: Solidarity, 1964).

66   "The Americanization of Bolshevisim" forms part of a section of *Education, Agitation and Propaganda*.

67 V.I. Lenin, *Selected Works,* Vols. VII & VIII (1937; New York: International Publishers, n.d.).

68 Cheddi Jagan (1918–1997), co-founder of the People's Progressive Party (PPP), former chief minister of British Guiana. Historically, the PPP had strong ties with the former Soviet Union and from 1964 to 1992 it sat in opposition to PPP co-founder and president of Guyana, Forbes Burnham of the People's National Congress.

69 A Reference to James's pamphlet, *Every Cook Can Govern: A Study of Democracy in Ancient Greece* (Detroit: Correspondence Publishing Co., 1956).

70 The first and only edition of the journal was published in October 1968 under the title *Caribbean International Opinion: Dynamics of Liberation.* The issue included two essays by James: "A Brief Outline of Political Economy" and "State Capitalism and the French Revolutionary Tradition".

71 Roberts is referring to the manuscript that was eventually published under the title *Nkrumah and the Ghana Revolution* (Westport, CT.: Lawrence Hill and Company, 1977) and the "article" he is referring to is perhaps the chapter in the book entitled "Lenin and the Problem."

72 Foreign Language Publishing House.

73 Che Guevara, *Venceremos! The Speeches and Writings of Ernesto Che Guevara,* ed. John Gerassi (New York: Macmillan, 1968).

CLR JAMES: THE MAN AND HIS WORK

1 Boris Sourvarine, *Stalin: A Critical Survey of Bolshevism* (New York: Alliance Book Corp, 1939).

2 C.L.R. James, *Modern Politics* (1960; Detroit: bewick/ed, 1973).

CLR JAMES: BEYOND THE MOURNFUL SILENCE

1 James in referring to a vision of a two-party system in the Caribbean. The first consists of "a united body of the great mass of the local population;" the second, a "party representing the great industrial, commercial and financial interests and those whose status depends of these." C.L.R. James, "Tomorrow and Today: A Vision," in George Lamming and Martin Carter (eds.), *New World: Guyana Independence Issue,* 2(3), 1966, 86.

2 Ibid.

3 C.L.R. James, "Marxism for the Sixties," *Speak Out,* no. 2, May 1965, 2.

4 This book was never produced.

ON THE BANNING OF WALTER RODNEY FROM JAMAICA

1 At the time of James's talk, Rodney had published scholarly articles such as "Portuguese Attempts at Monopoly on the Upper Guinea Coast, 1580–1650," *The Journal of African History,* 6(3), 1965; "African Slavery and Other Forms of Social Oppression on the Upper Guinea Coast in the Context of the Atlantic Slave-Trade," *The Journal of African History,* 7(3), 1966; and "A Reconstruction of the Mane Invasions of Sierre Leone," *The Journal of African History,* 8(2), 1967. In 1970, he published *A History of the Upper Guinea Coast, 1545–1800* (Oxford: Clarendon Press, 1970).

2 Referring to the protests in Jamaica in response to his expulsion, Walter Rodney stated: "Those blacks in Jamaica did not go out in the streets to get killed because of me or any individual— they did it for themselves. I have only been in Kingston for nine months, so the extent of their reaction indicates the depth of the problem." Rodney also made the point that "The myth says that Jamaicans are a happy people in the sun, and that the Jamaican government is democratic—this just

isn't true." According to *The Montreal Gazette*, Rodney suggested that armed revolution was the only way to change the situation in Jamaica (Anon., *The Montreal Gazette*, October 18, 1968, pp 1, 3).

3   C.L.R. James, *Party Politics in the West Indies* (San Juan, Trinidad: Vedic Enterprises, Ltd., 1962), 125.

4   Three people were killed by Jamaican police during the protests in Jamaica following Rodney's expulsion.

5   Ibid., 135.

6   Frank Walcott (1919–1999) was a central figure in the trade union movement and a politician who served the Barbados Workers' Union for more than forty years.

SUPPORT AK PRESS!

AK Press is a worker-run collective that publishes and distributes radical books, visual/audio media, and other material. We're small: a dozen people who work long hours for short money, because we believe in what we do. We're anarchists, which is reflected both in the books we publish and the way we organize our business: without bosses.

Currently, we publish about twenty new titles per year. We'd like to publish even more. Whenever our collective meets to discuss future publishing plans, we find ourselves wrestling with a list of hundreds of projects. Unfortunately, money is tight, while the need for our books is greater than ever.

The Friends of AK Press is a direct way you can help. Friends pay a minimum of $25 per month (of course we have no objections to larger sums), for a minimum three month period. The money goes directly into our publishing funds. In return, Friends automatically receive (for the duration of their memberships) one free copy of every new AK Press title as they appear. Friends also get a 20% discount on everything featured in the AK Press Distribution catalog and on our web site—thousands of titles from the hundreds of publishers we work with. We also have a program where groups or individuals can sponsor a whole book. Please contact us for details.

To become a Friend, go to www.akpress.org.

Printed in the USA
CPSIA information can be obtained
at www.ICGtesting.com
JSHW022207140824
68134JS00018B/904